First published in the USA by

SULBY HALL PUBLISHERS

PO Box 6867

Malibu CA 90264

www.sulbyhall.com

Canada: 28 Duncannon Drive,

Toronto ON M5P 2M1

www.sulbyhall.com

SULBY HALL
PUBLISHERS

Artwork and book design by Neel Muller.

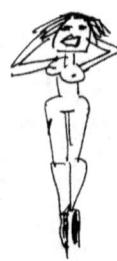

Drawings of Women

by Neel Muller

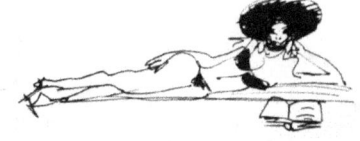

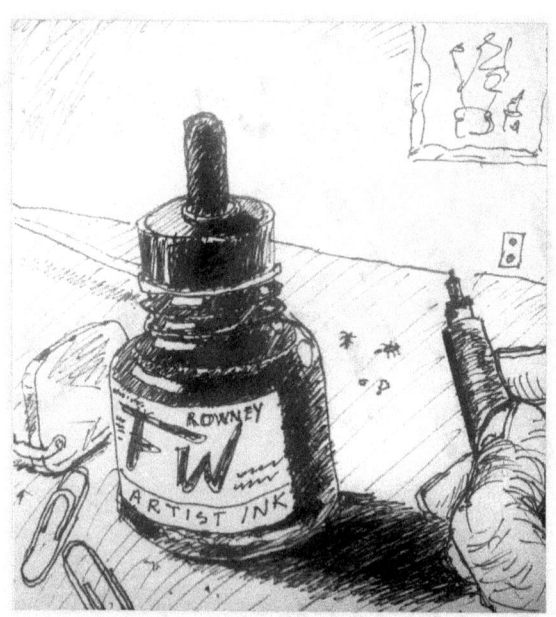

From the top of my head all the way down to the tip of my pen.

Acknowledgments

Thanks to all my friends who have pushed me to publish this
book of my drawings. I probably would never have pulled it off
without their constant nagging.

Preface and warning.

I started to draw when I was a little boy. In High School I was constantly in trouble because I was always being caught drawing instead of studying. That would often lead to serious physical punishment at my school in Pretoria, South Africa. I did have a great, and I must say, beautiful dark haired art teacher who I was in love with. (She did not know it, of course)

Eventually, I became an art director in the advertising business working at many ad agencies in South Africa, England and here in Los Angeles. My drawing skills came in very handy at work especially before the days of the computer. I was able to quickly sketch out storyboards and ad ideas for presentations etc. So, my drawing was a tool I used at work every day. Often, I would pretend I couldn't draw because I would end up having to do everyone else's drawings.

A few years ago started drawing just for the joy of it. Sort of like when I was at school but thankfully without the punishment. I always loved drawing women and realized that if I ever put a little book together I would have enough women drawings to make it worthwhile. So here it is.

WARNING: Some images are a bit naughty and not exactly politically correct. Many of my nudes are nude. If you find yourself offended, step outside, have a good sneeze and enjoy the rest of your day.

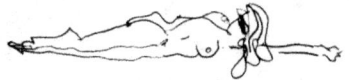

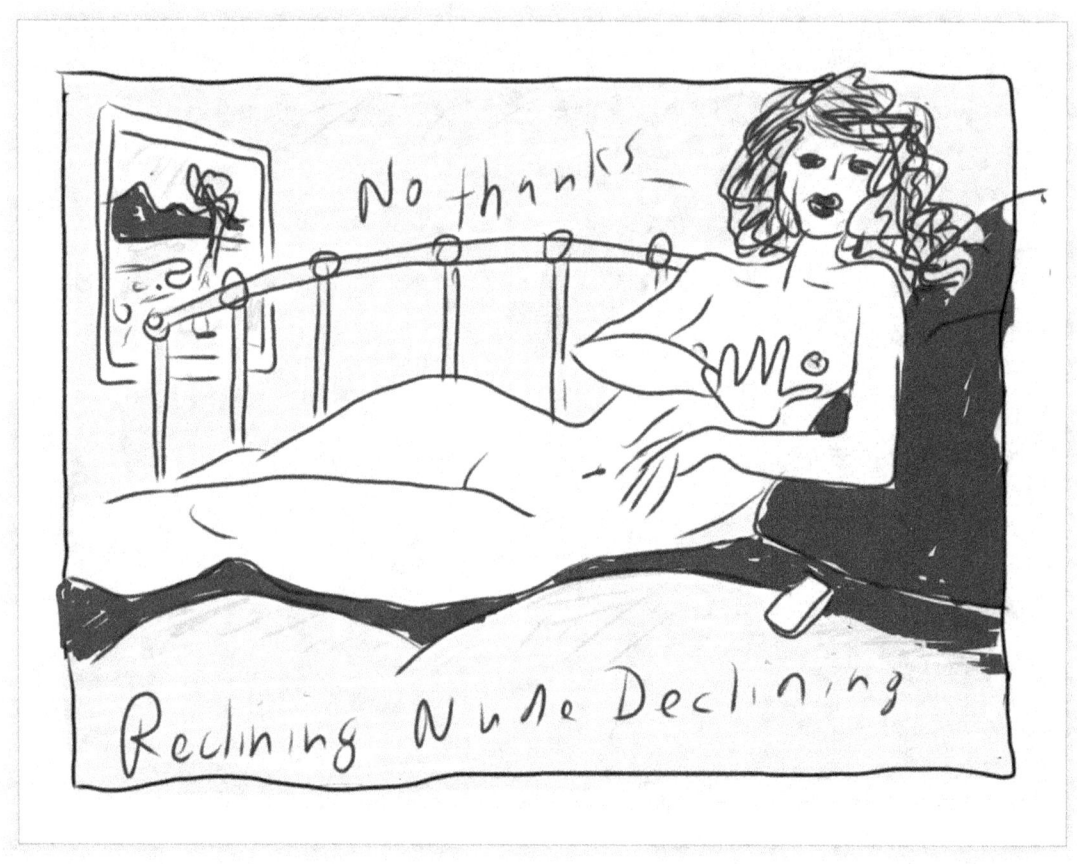

Reclining nude declining.

I offered her a cup of tea and she graciously declined. Strange. I make such good tea.

Women can be such a mystery.

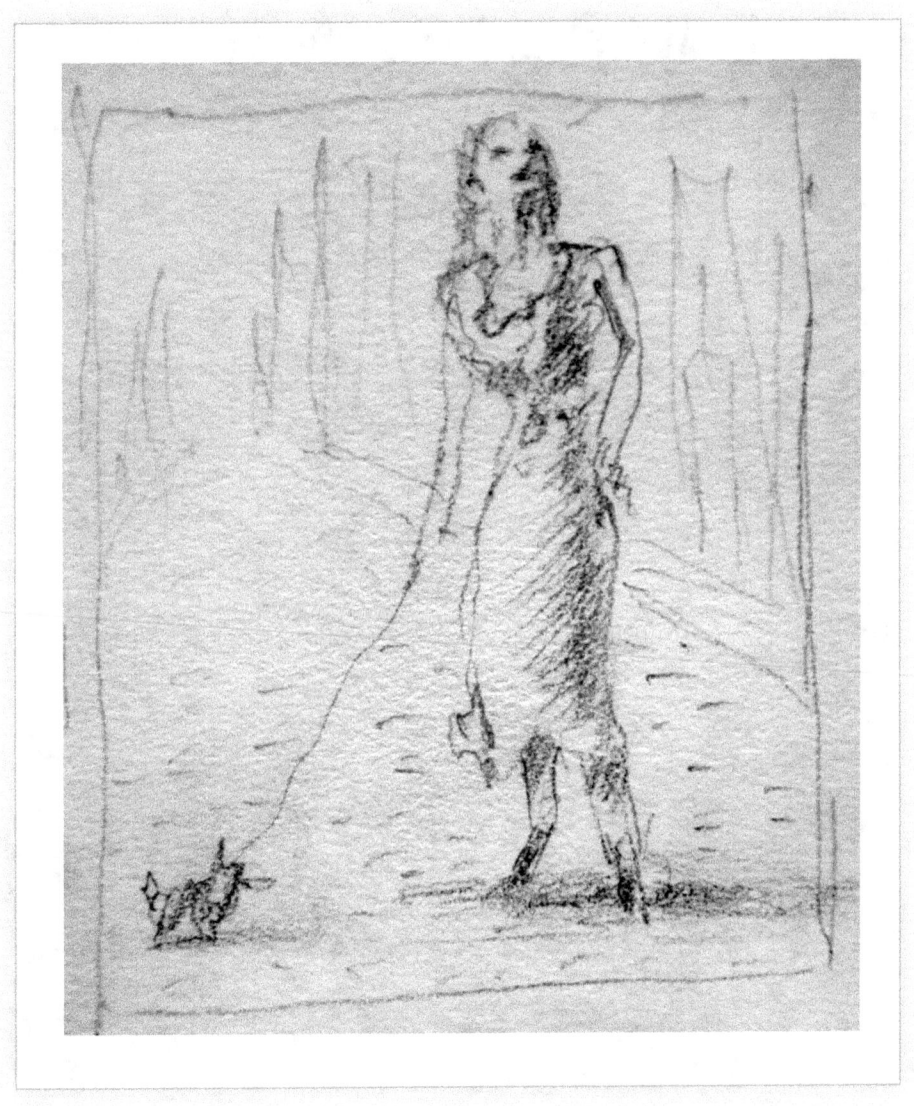

Girl with small dog.

Drawn in France, where everyone has a doggie.

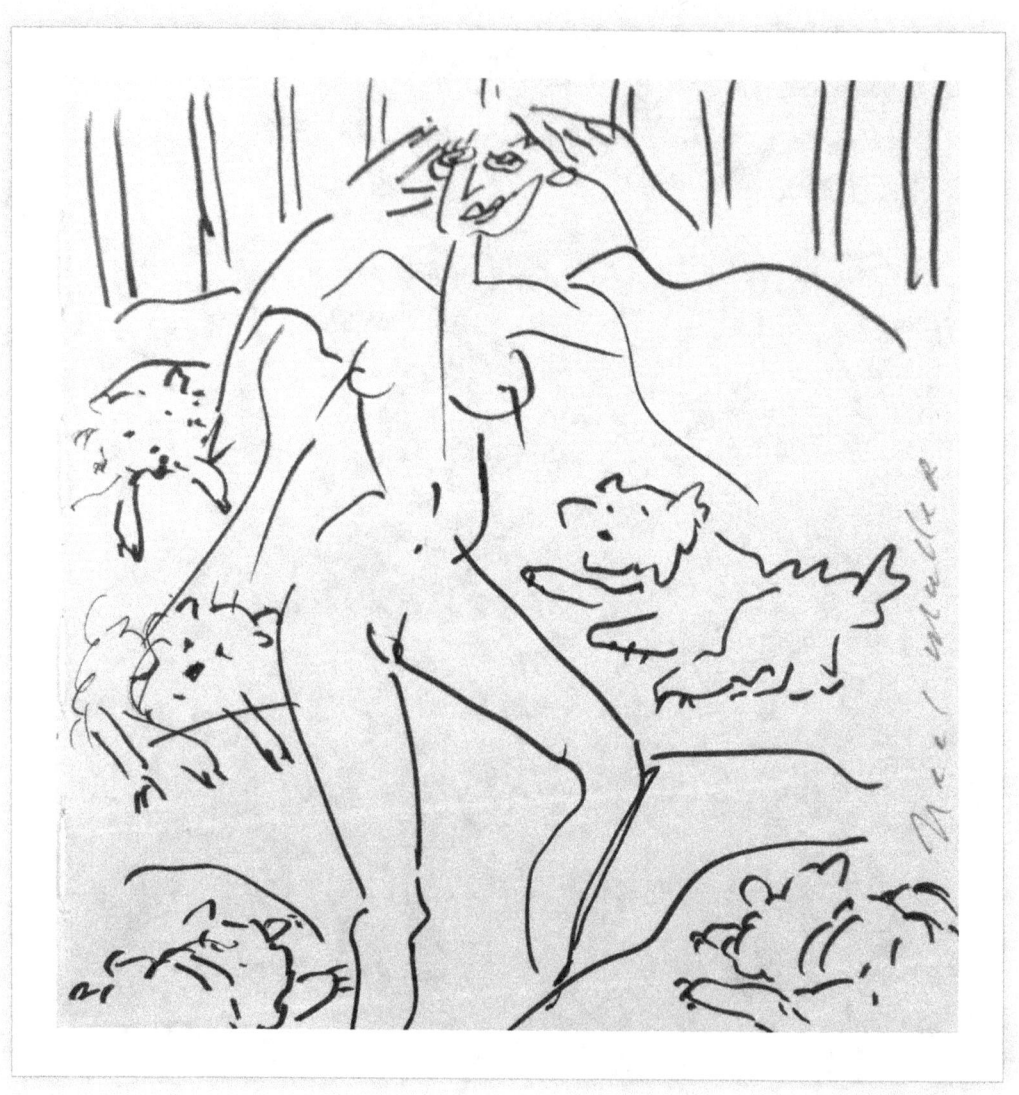

Five dogs.

I counted them just to make sure.

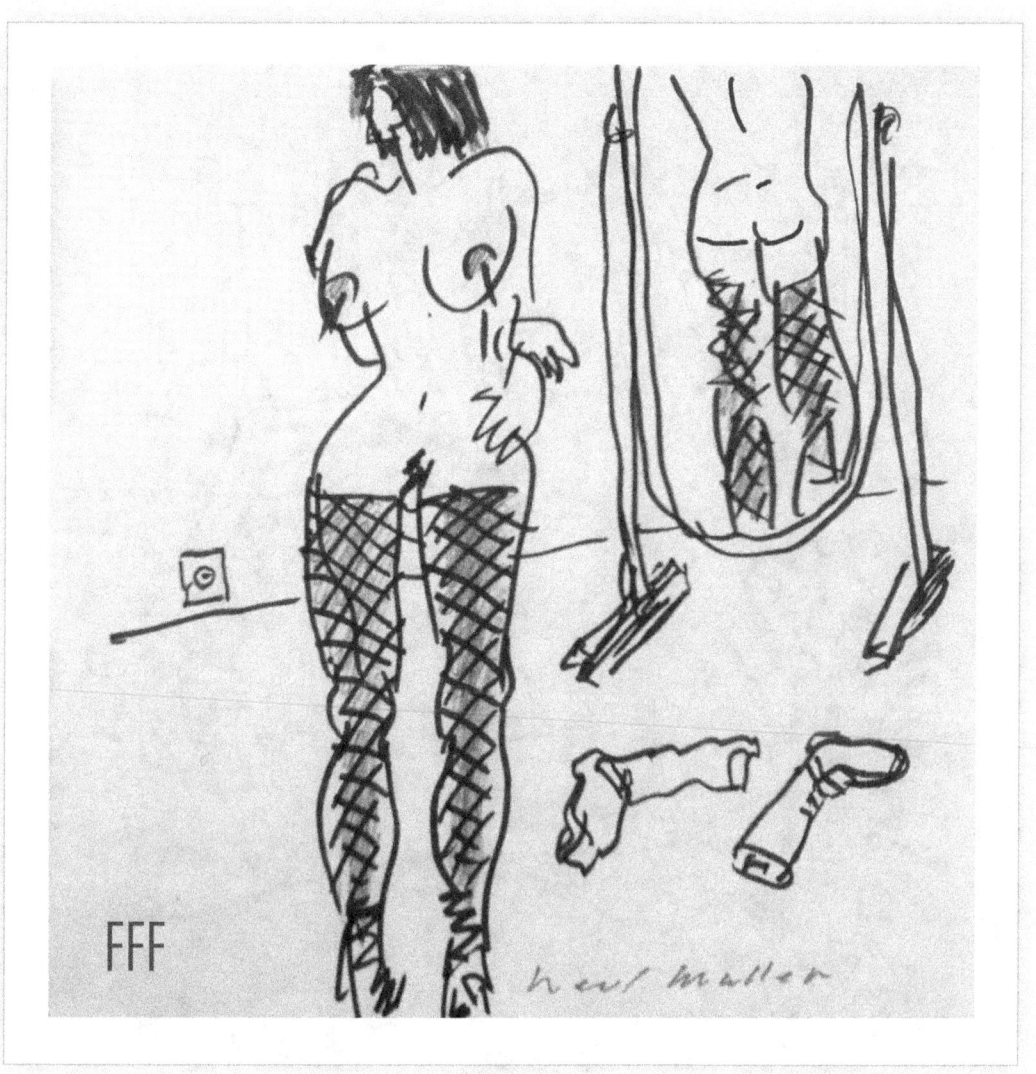

Full frontal and French.

Hence the stockings.

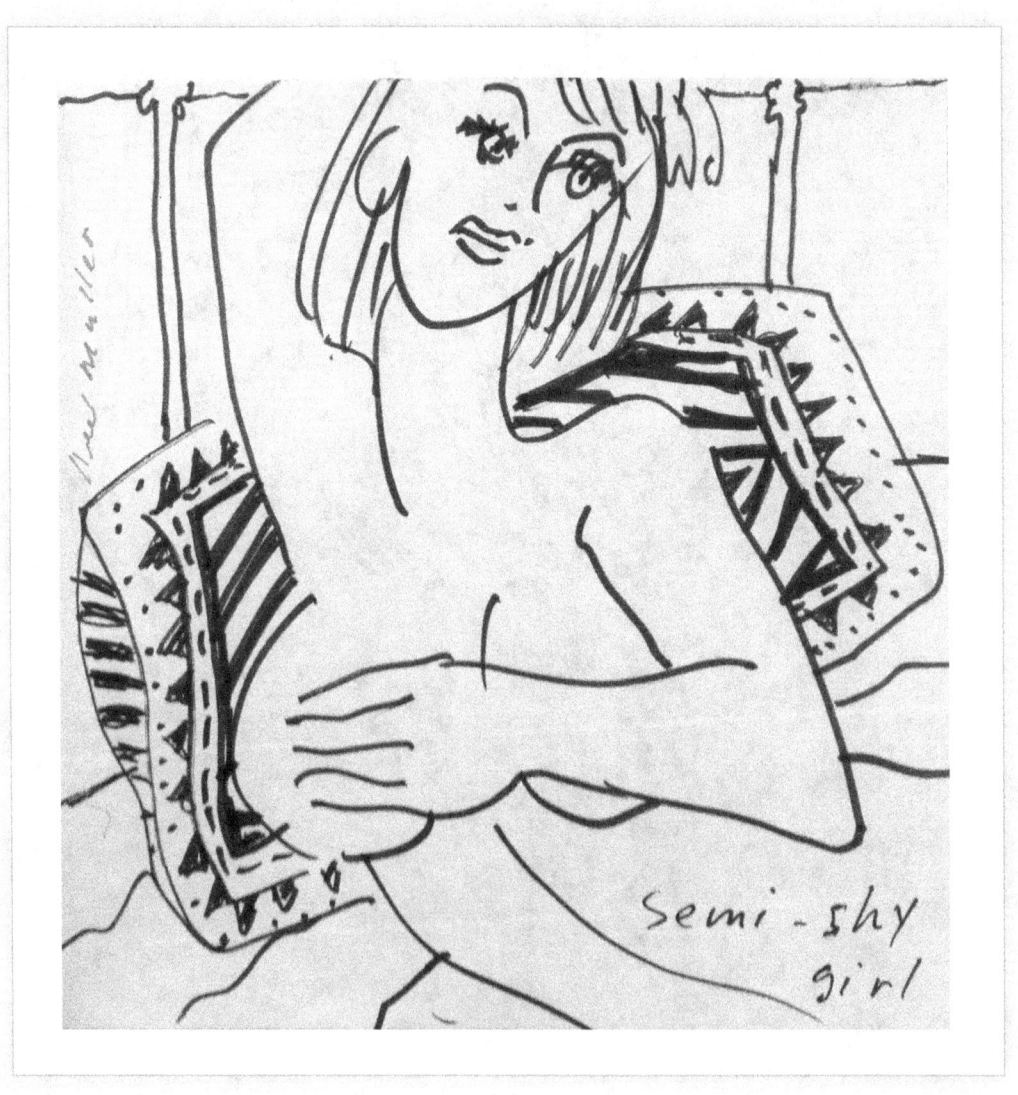

Semi-shy girl.

Yes she was.

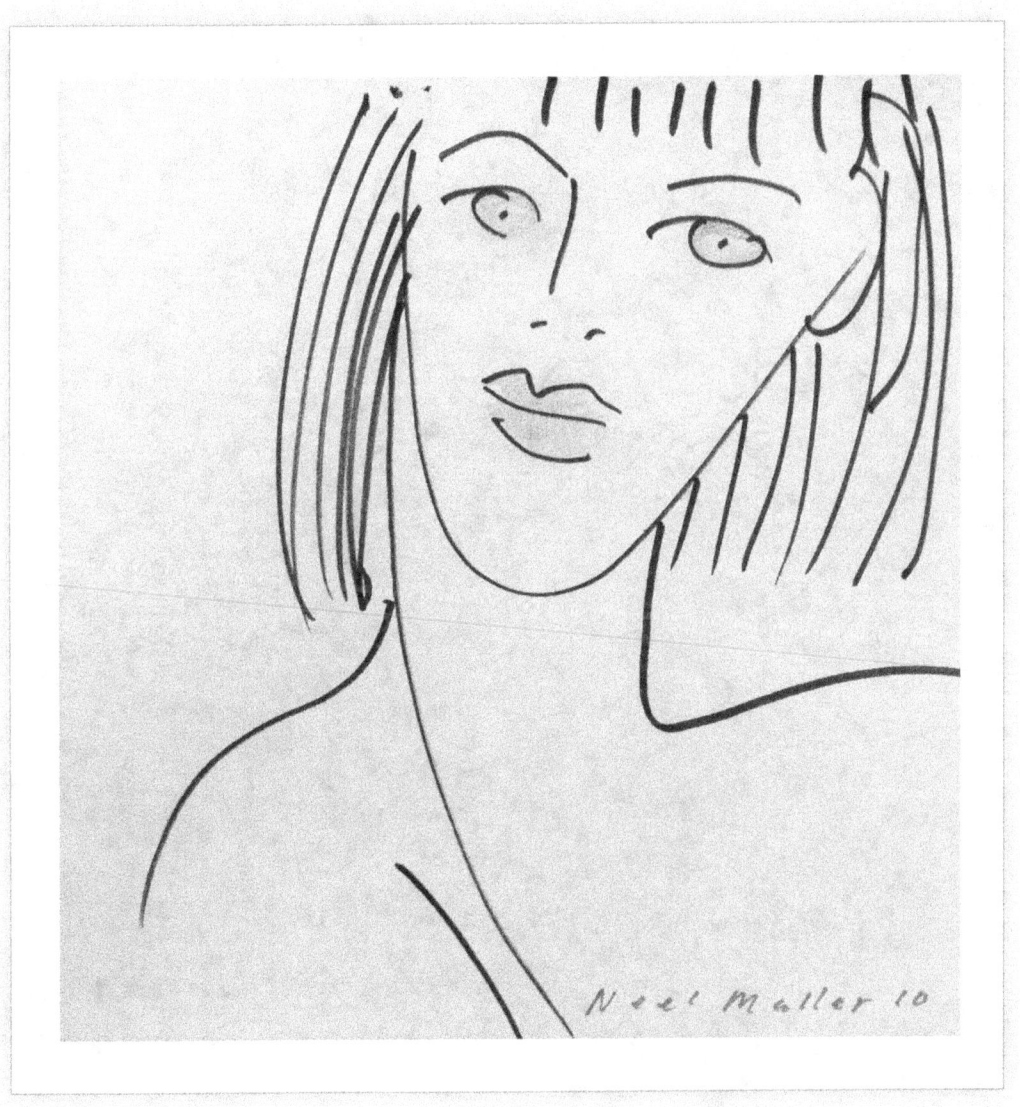

Girl.

Yes she is.

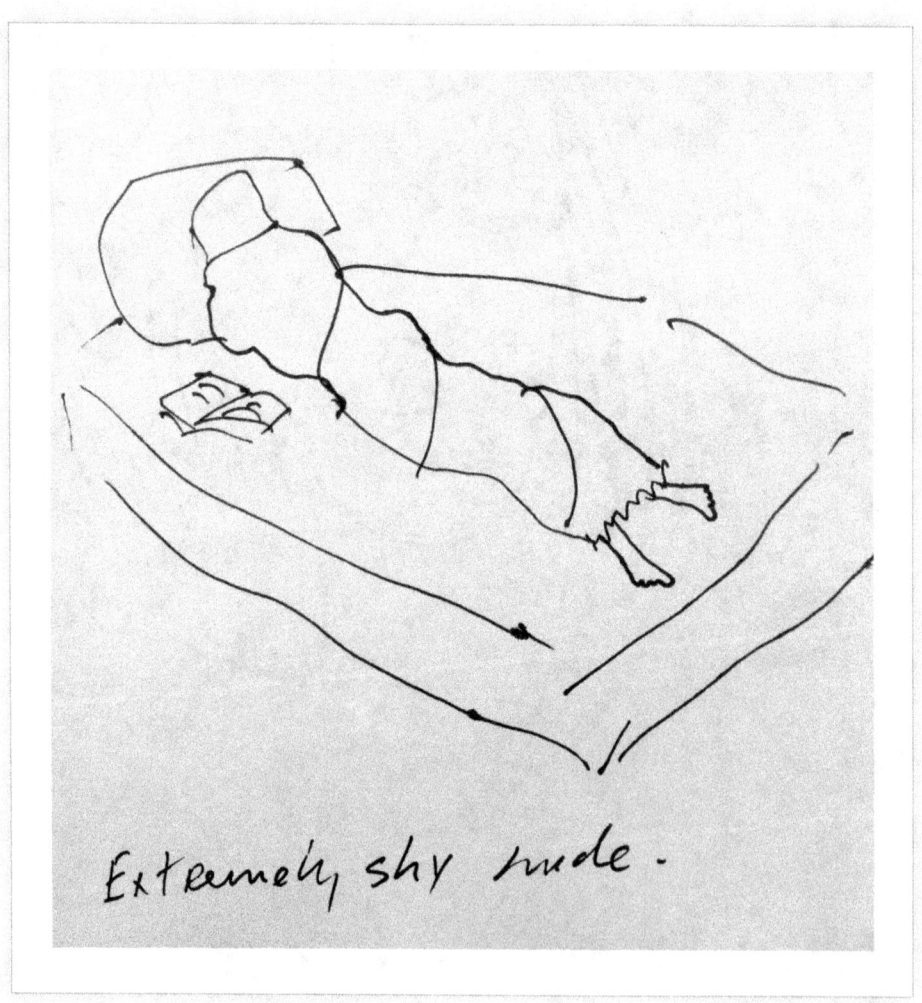

Extremely shy nude.

She did show her feet.

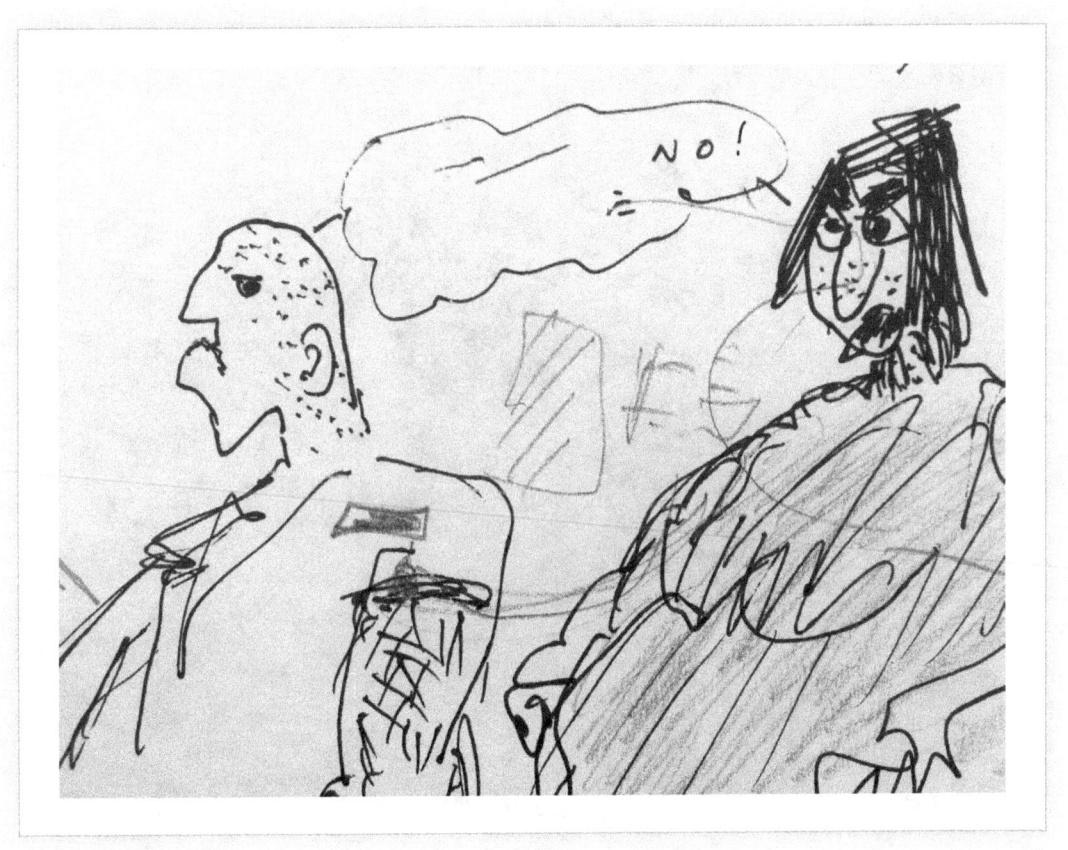

Wife says NO!

Women are the civilizers of society. So they often have to say no.

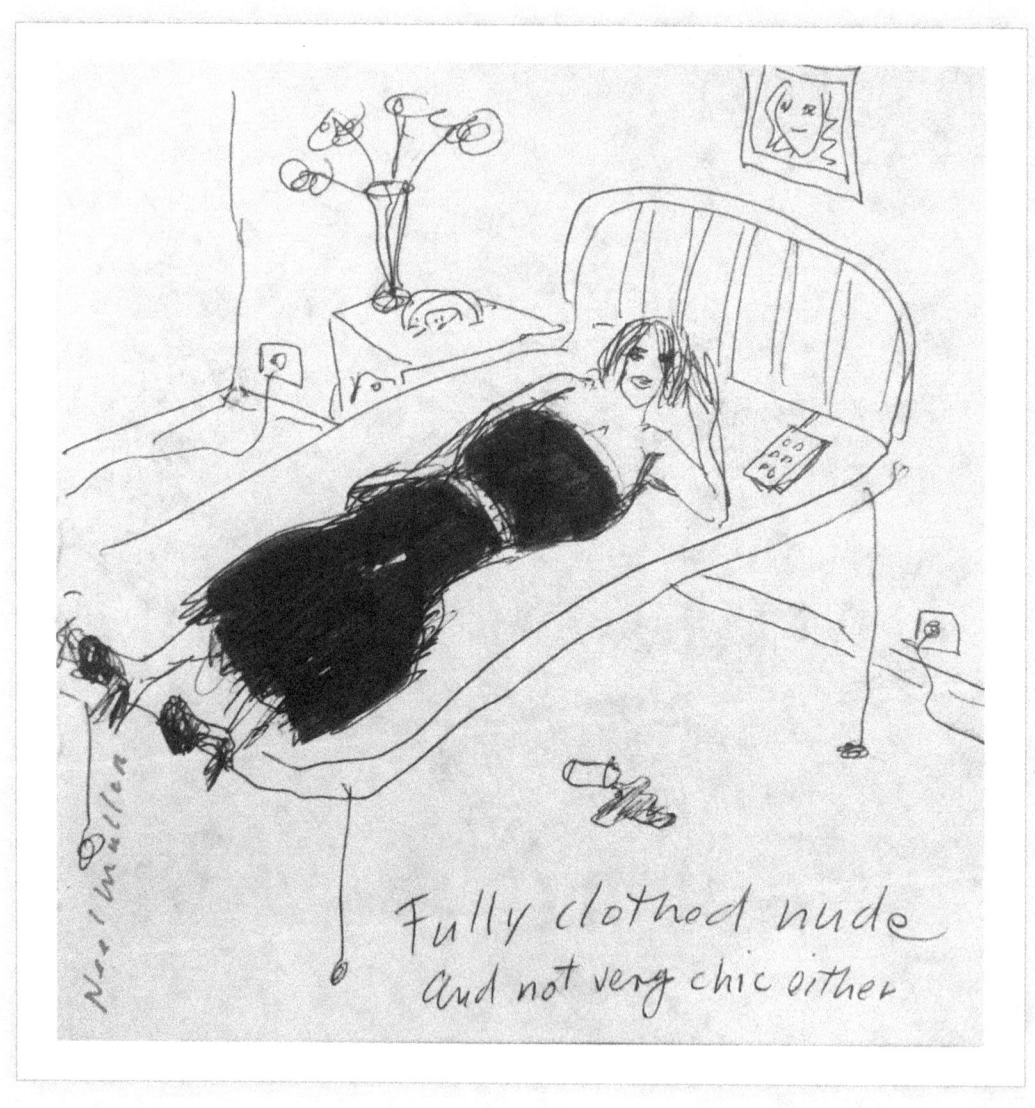

Fully clothed nude and not very chic either.

Actually, she's quite a likable person, irrespective of her complete lack of style.

You cannot hate her.

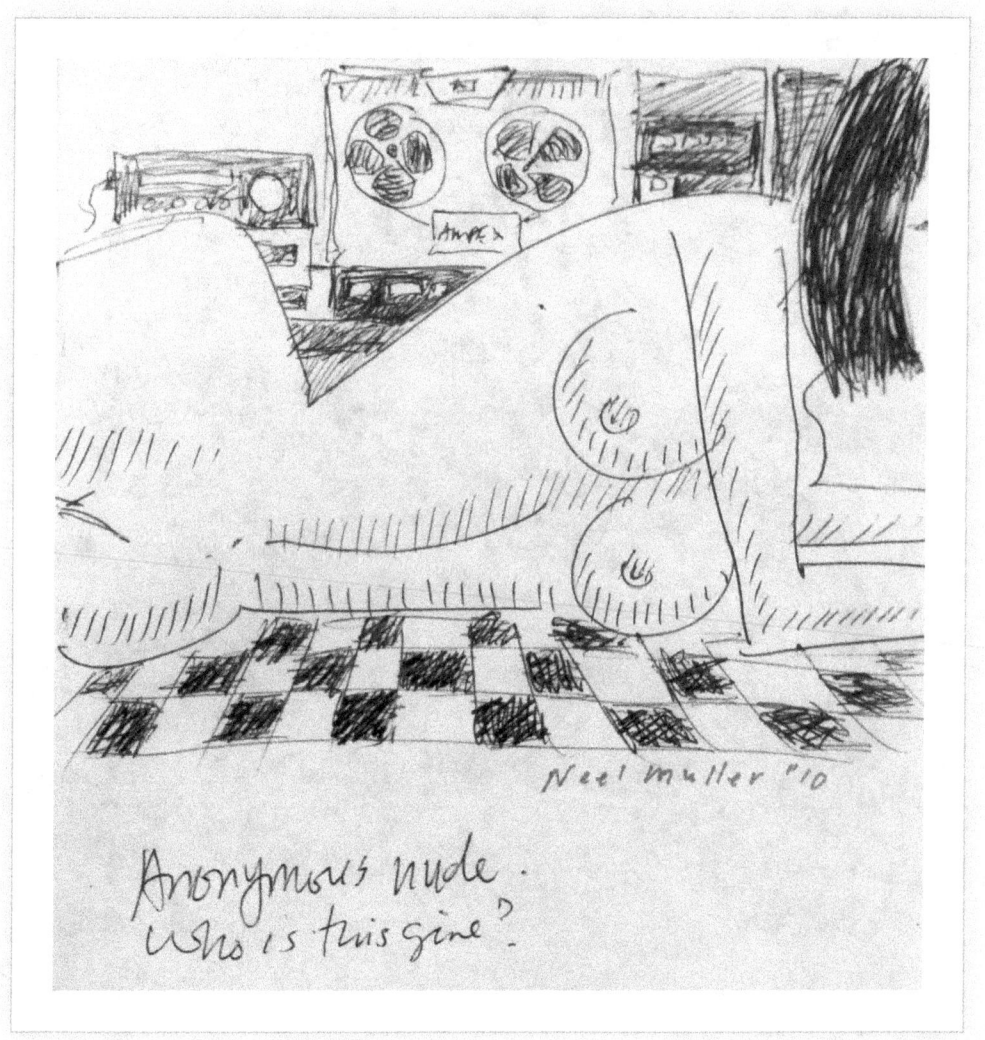

Anonymous nude.

Who is this girl? Why does she own a reel-to-reel tape recorder?

Does she sing the blues? We will never know.

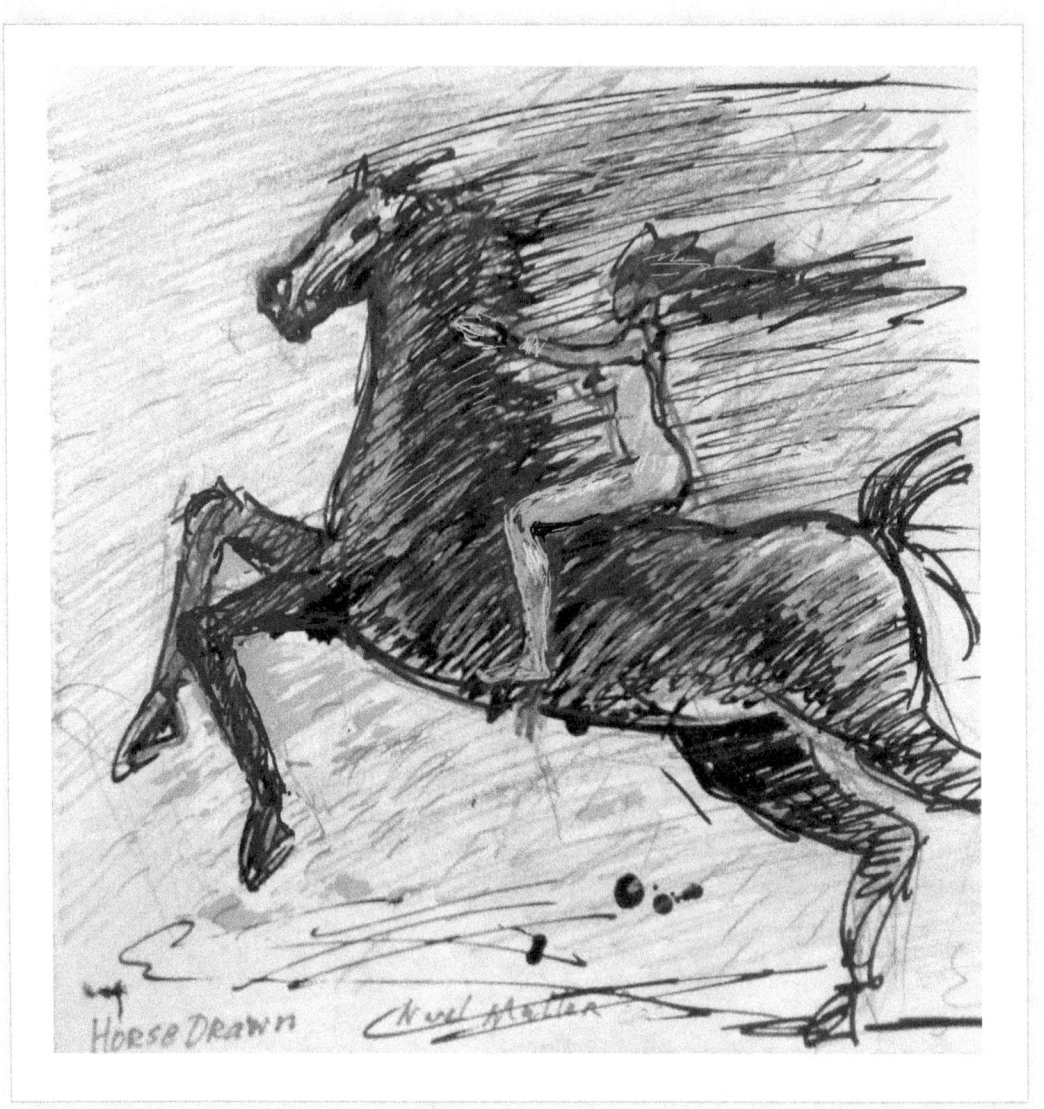

Horse drawn.

This is NOT Lady Godiva as many people have thought.

And, by the way, it's a terrible drawing.

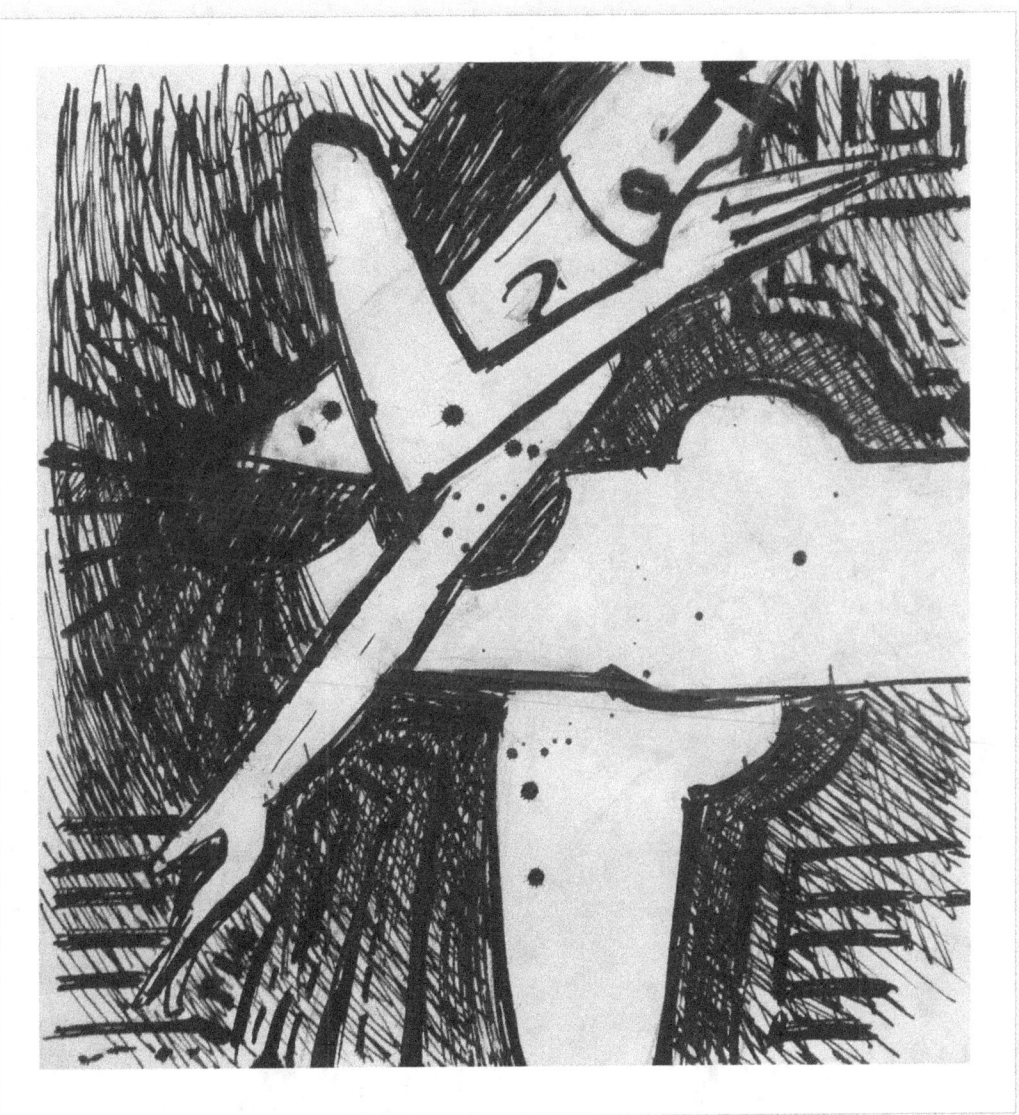

Woman bent out of shape.

For some or other reason.

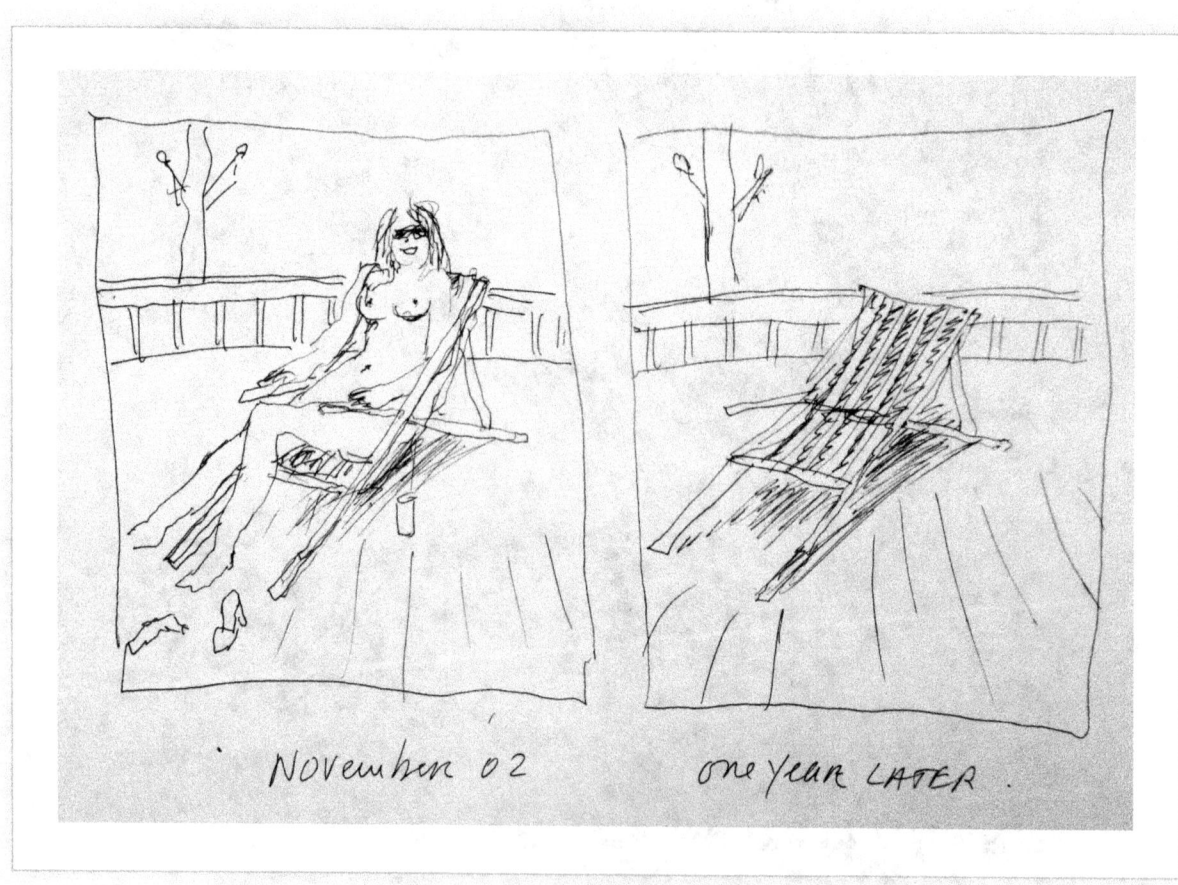

One year later.

Times marches on. And so did she.

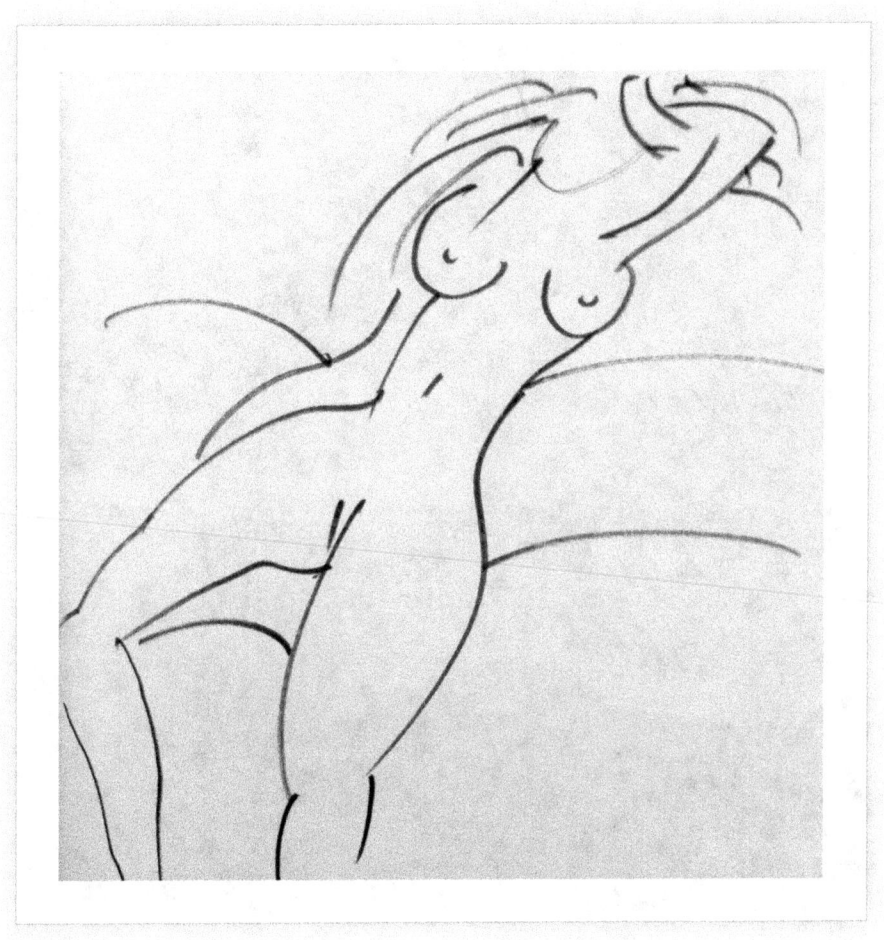

Non-shy girl.

Comfortable in her own skin.

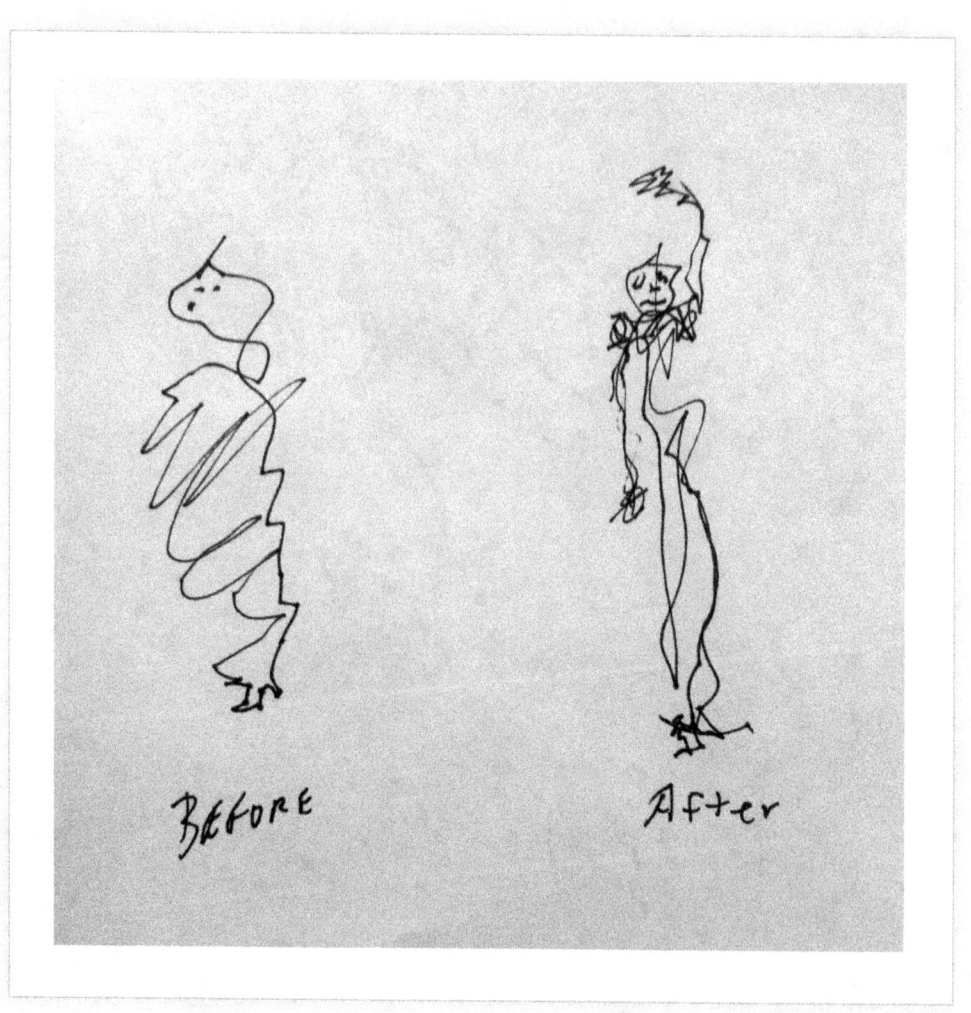

Before. After.

Modern medicine at its best.

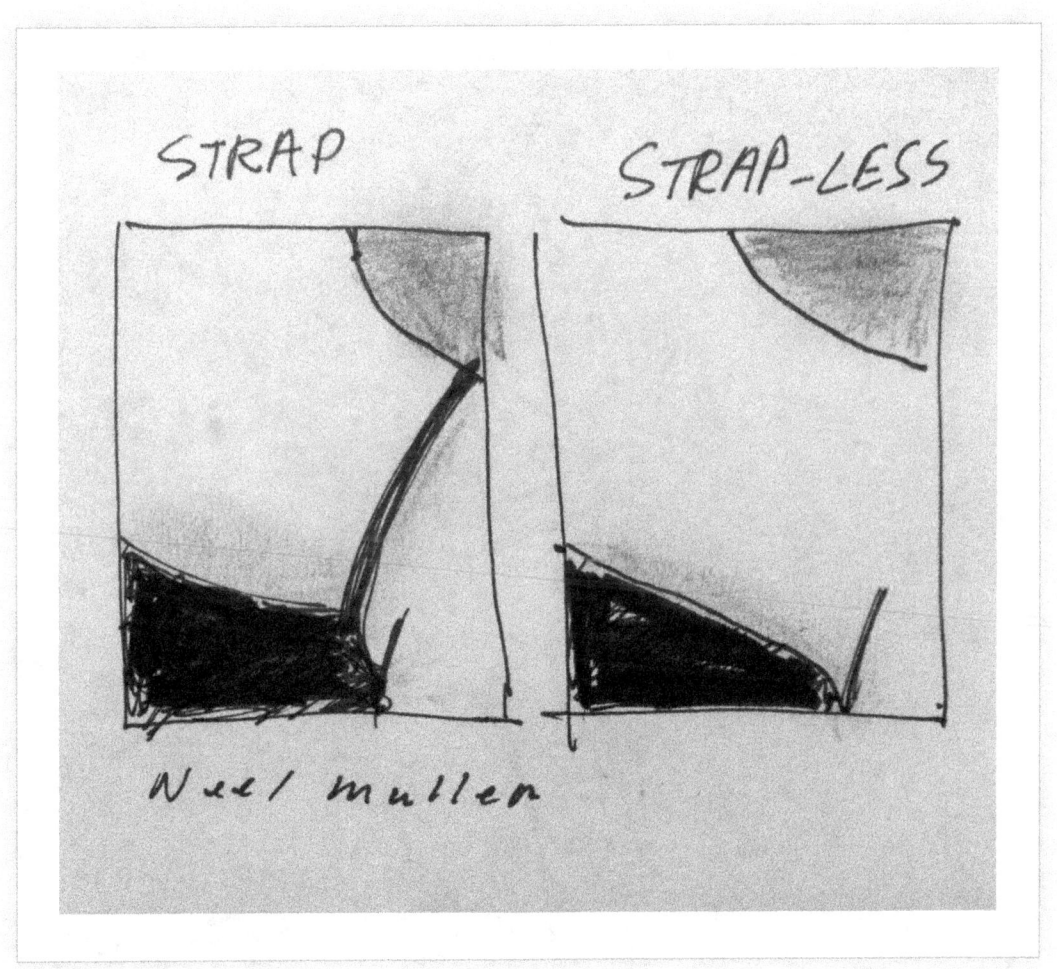

Strap. Strapless.

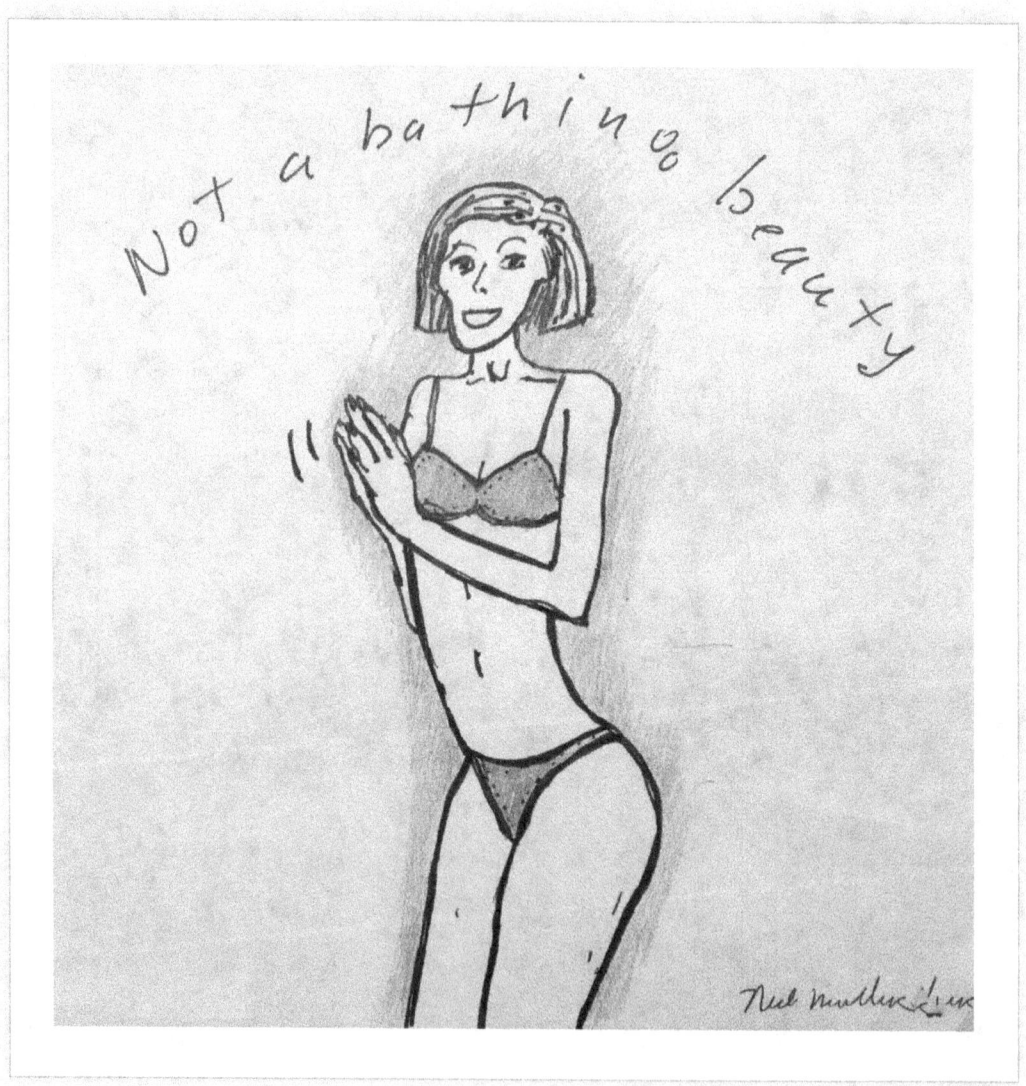

Not a bathing beauty.

She was a slightly nervous girl, who talked a mile a minute

with a squeaky voice, but she grew on me.

Then I forgot all about her. Don't even remember her name. Kinda sad.

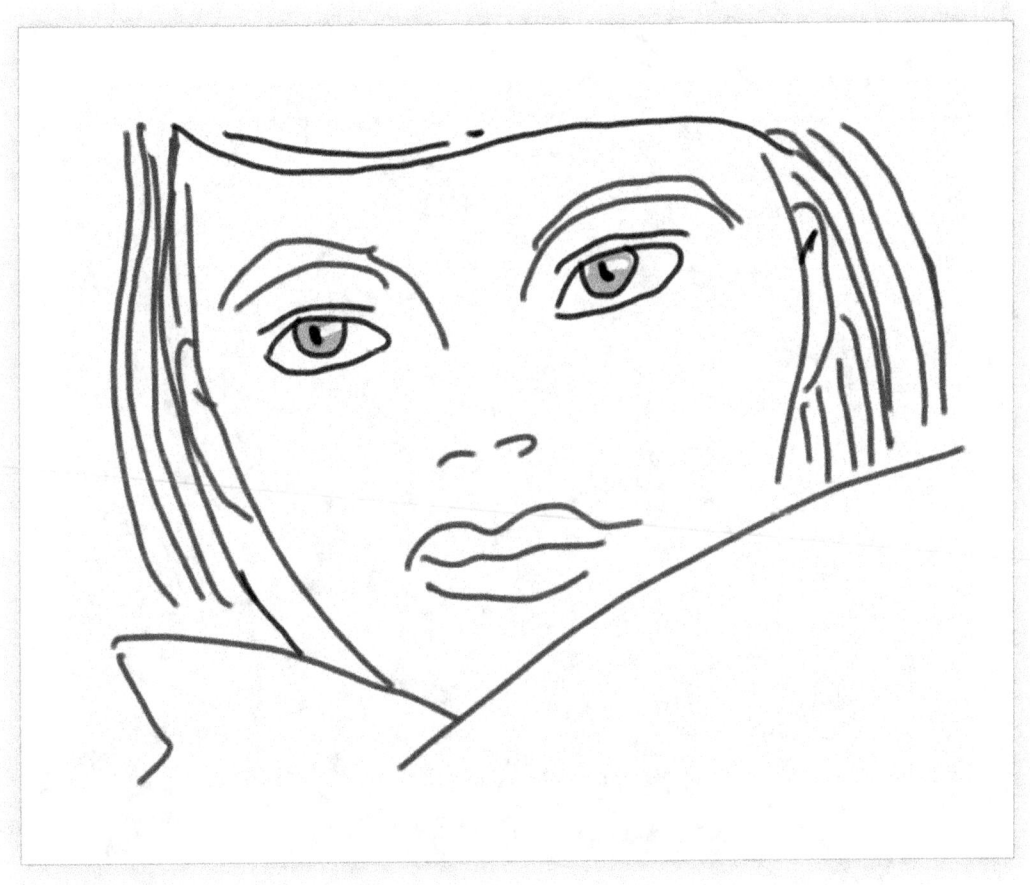

Easy on the eyes.

Drawn from memory on my iPad one early morning. (But not too early)

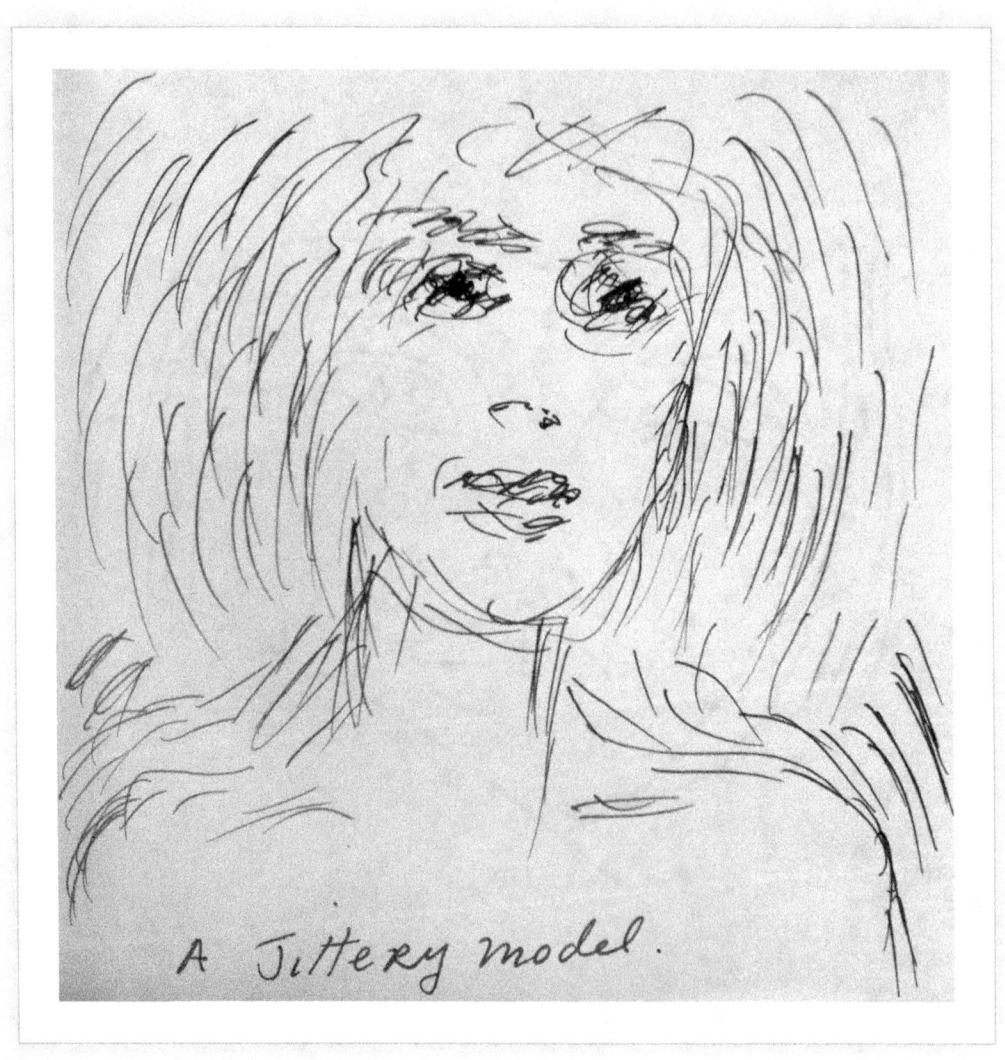

A jittery model.

Or was the artist jittery? Damn good question.

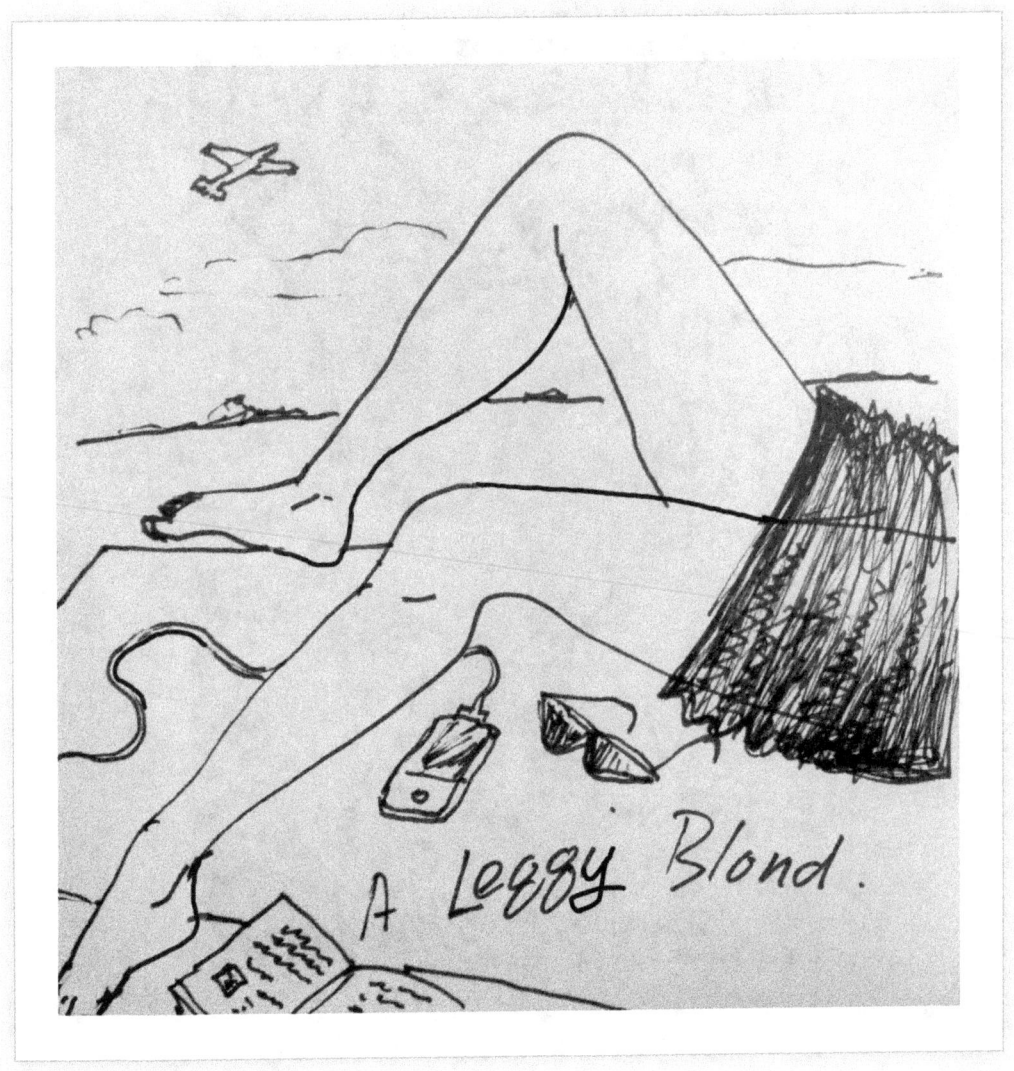

Leggy blond #1.

She started charging her smart phone and stopped reading her self-help book.

There was a lot going on.

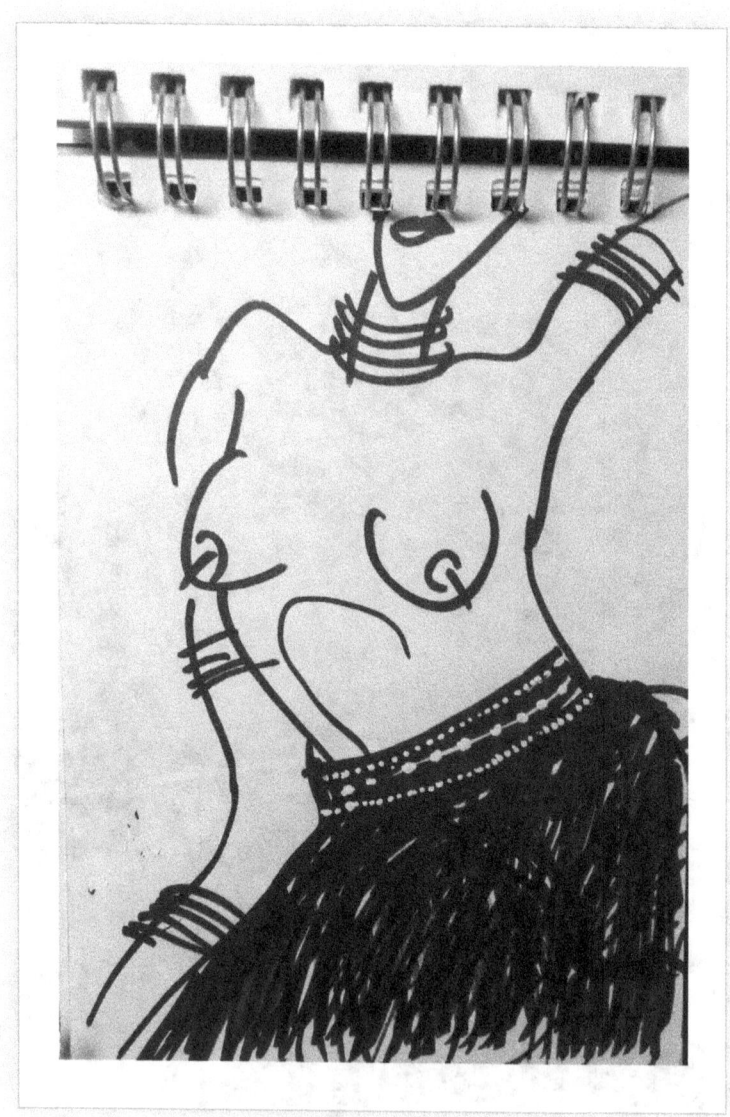

Tribal woman with rings.

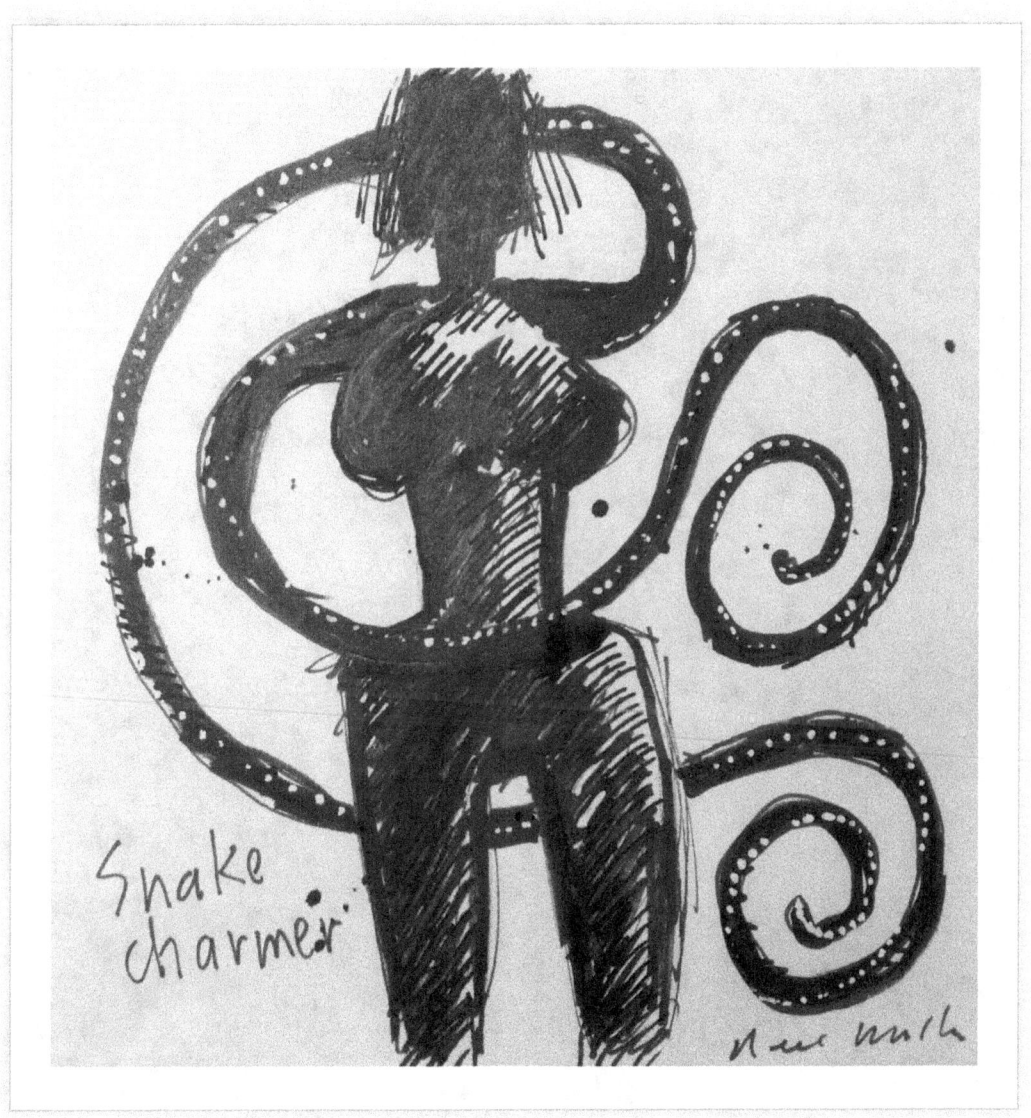

Snake charmer.

Danger.

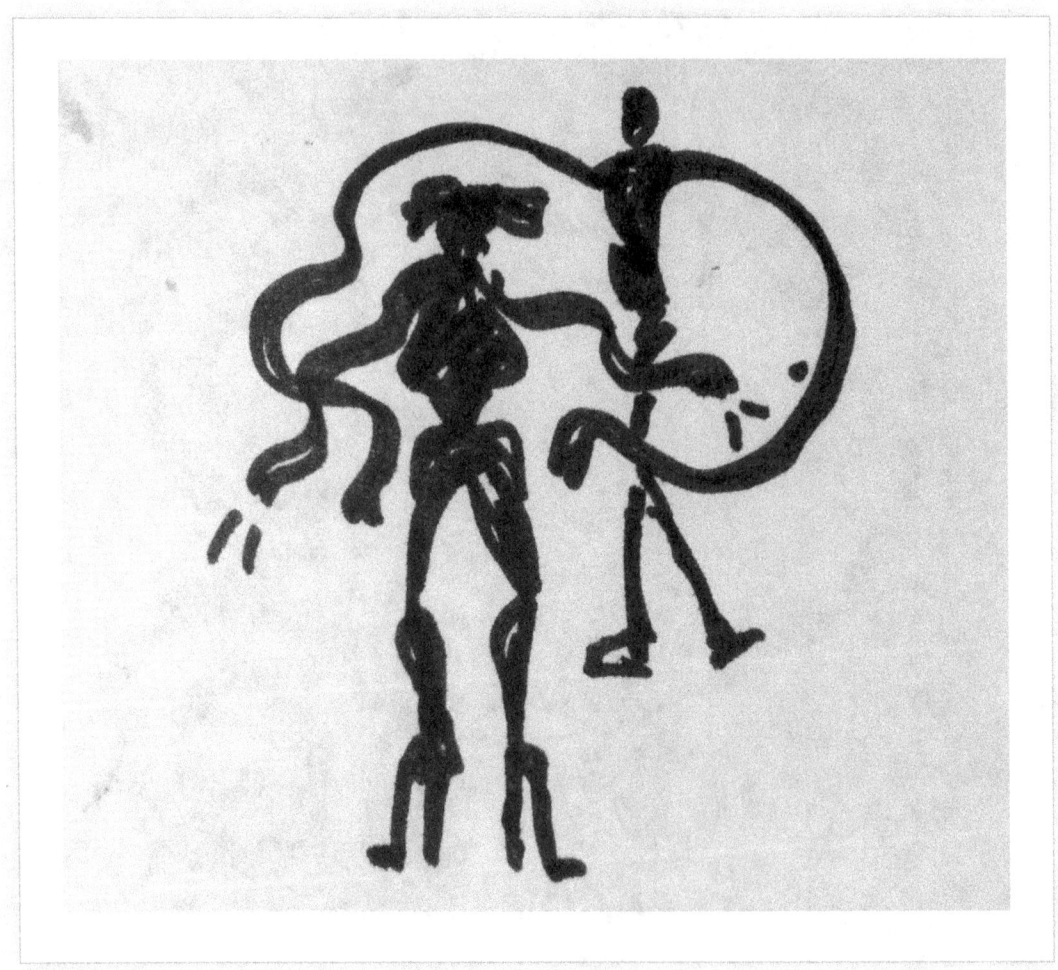

Dancing for no reason.

Life is too short not to dress up and dance around.

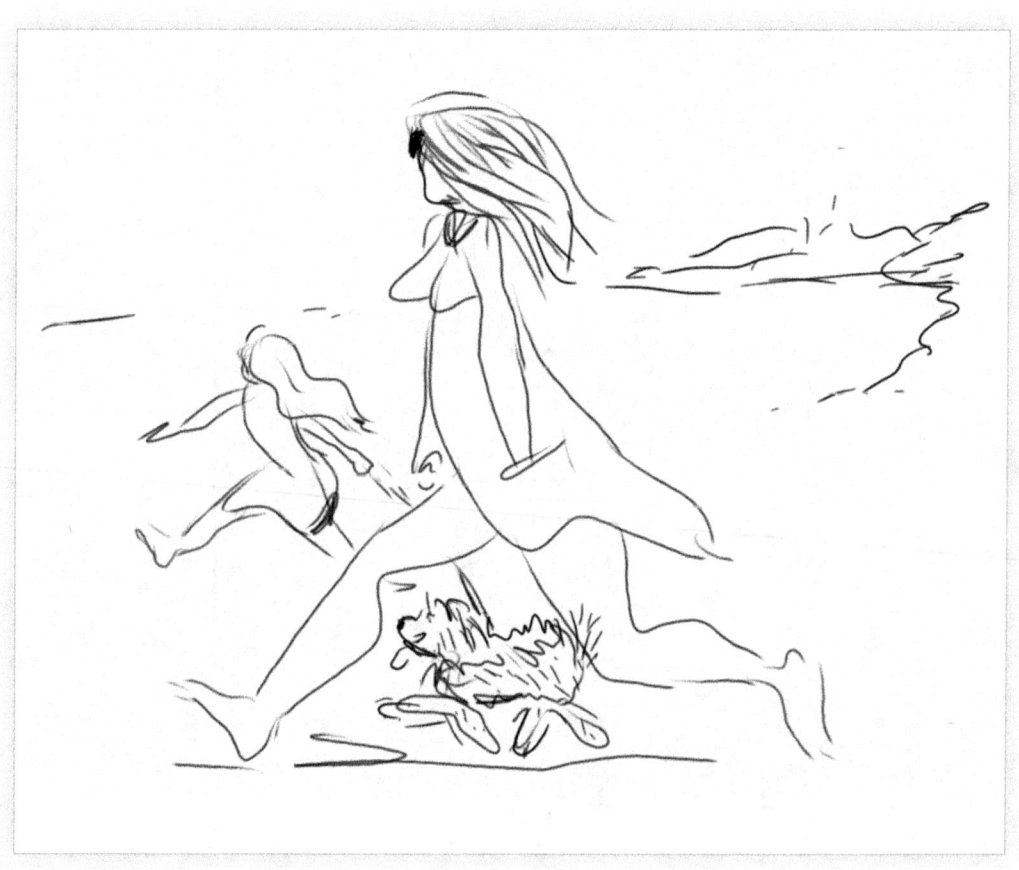

3 Malibeauties in Malibu.

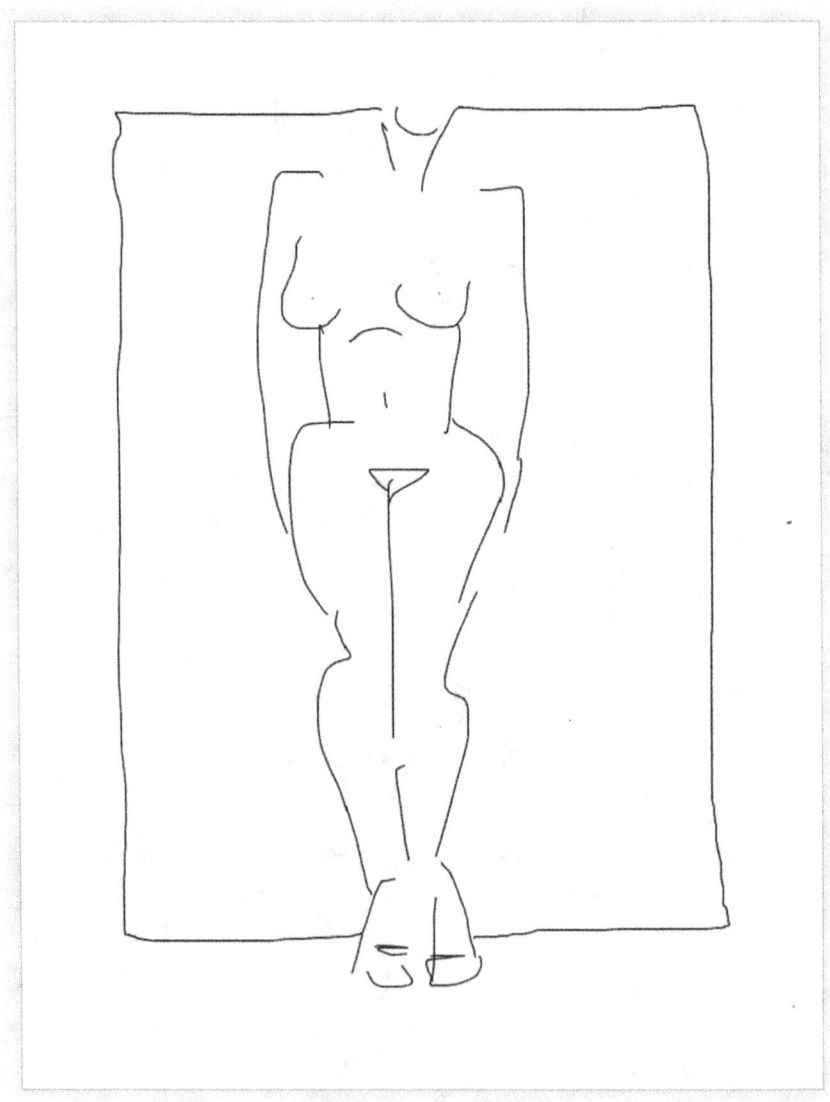

Quick nude.

10.3 seconds to be precise.

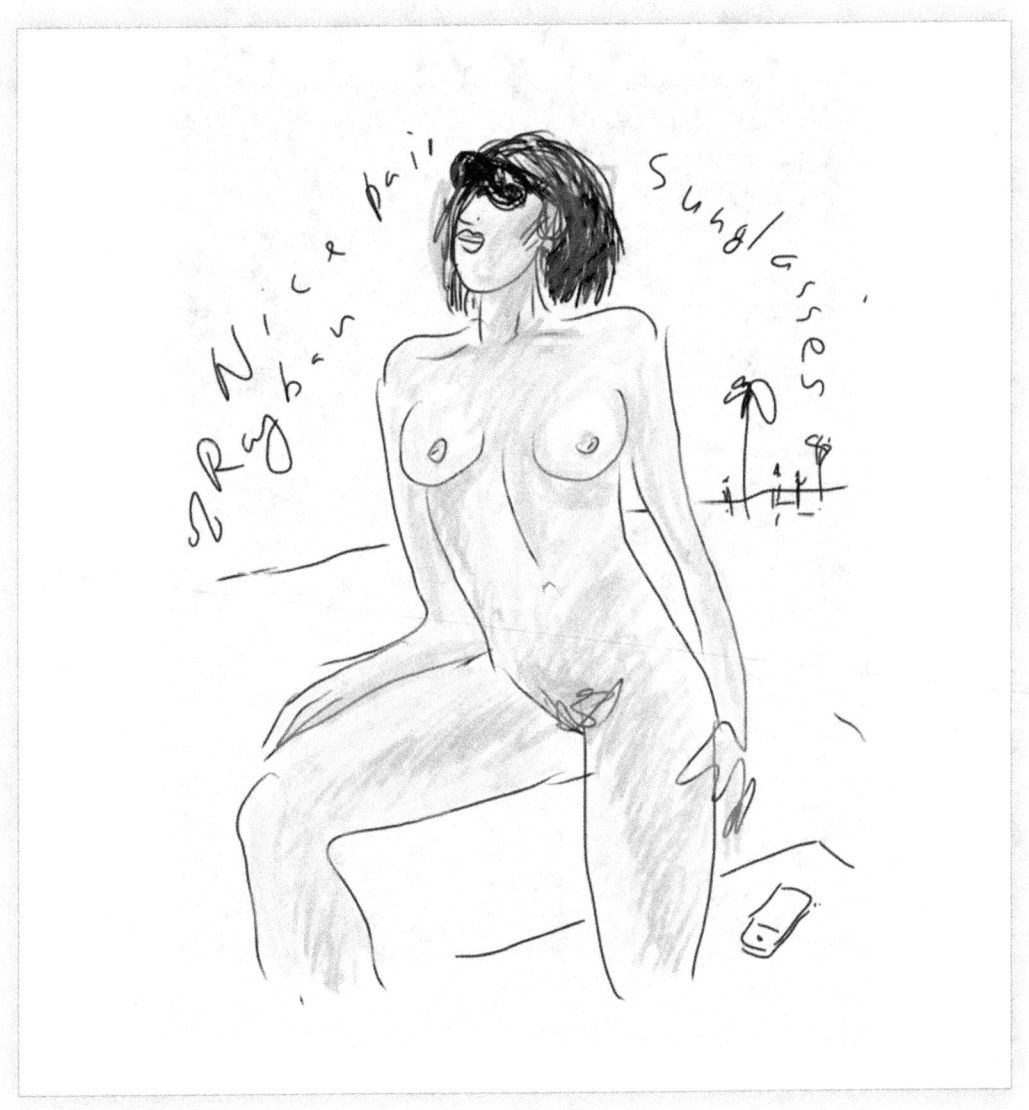

Nice pair of Ray-Ban sunglasses.

When you live in Los Angeles, sunglasses are your most valuable possession.

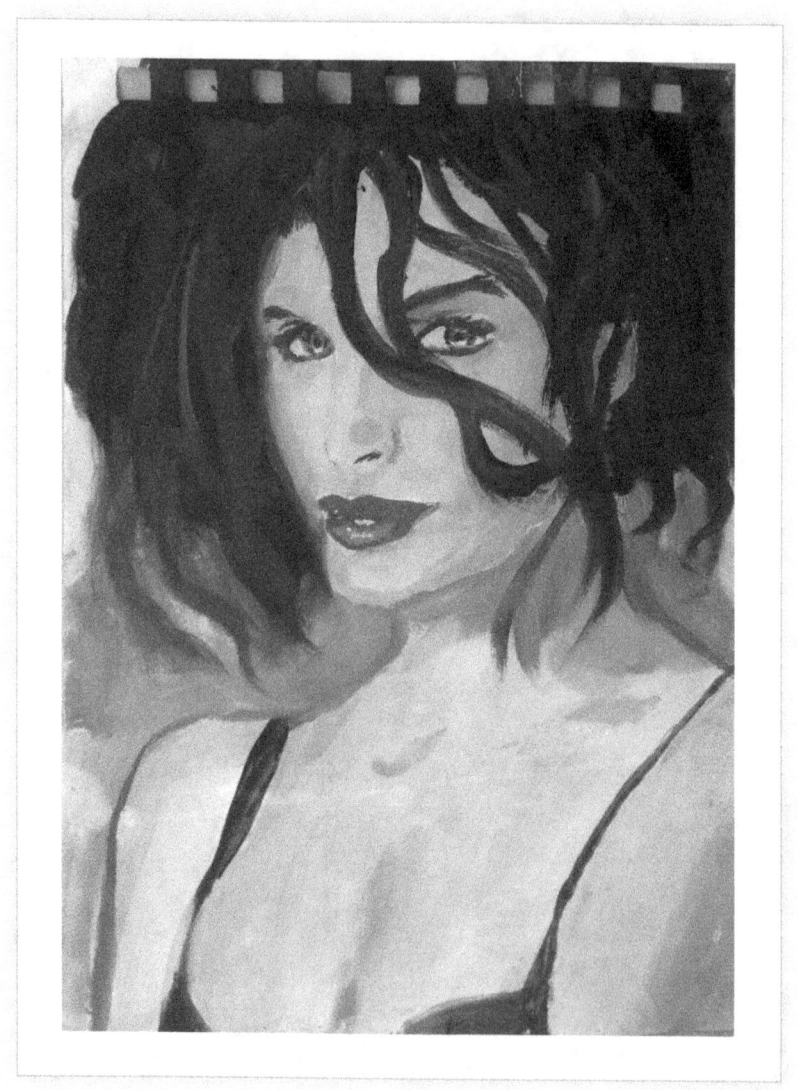

Face in oil.

She seems to be a popular one.

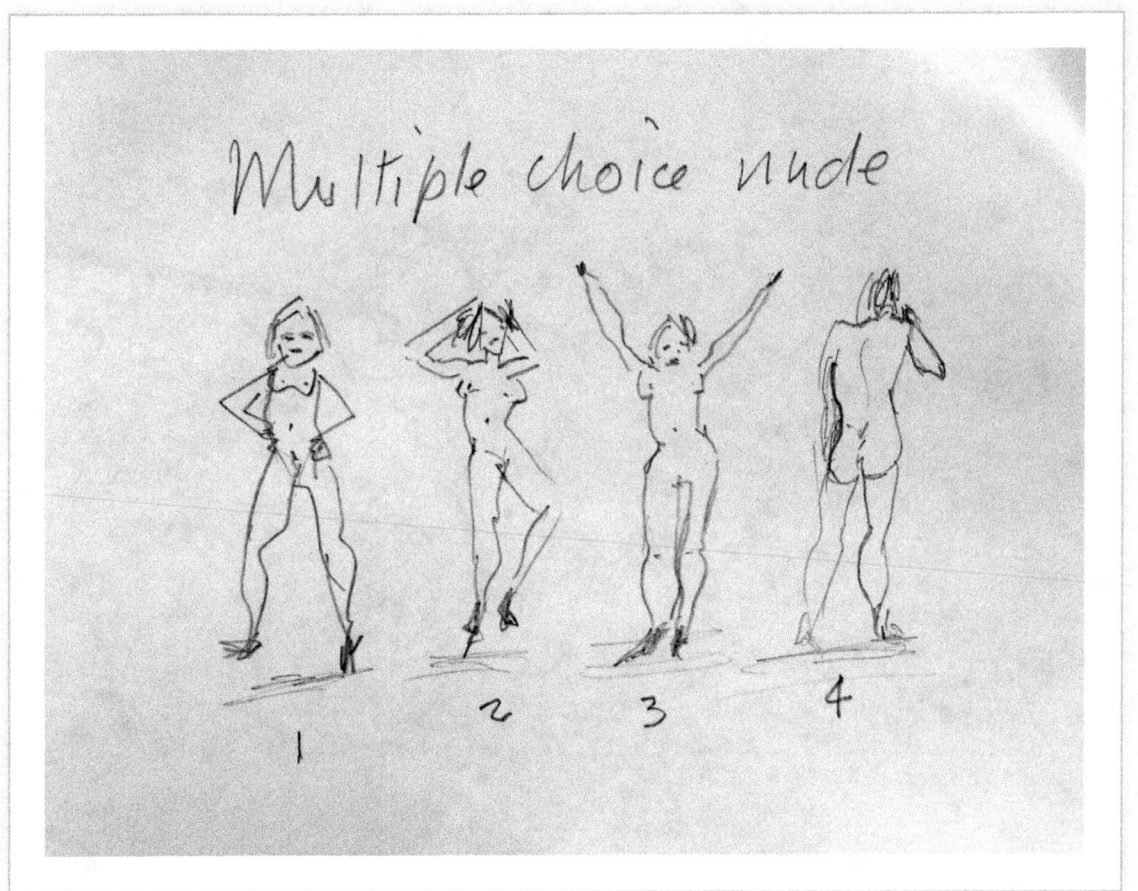

Multiple choice nude.

Which one do you lean towards?

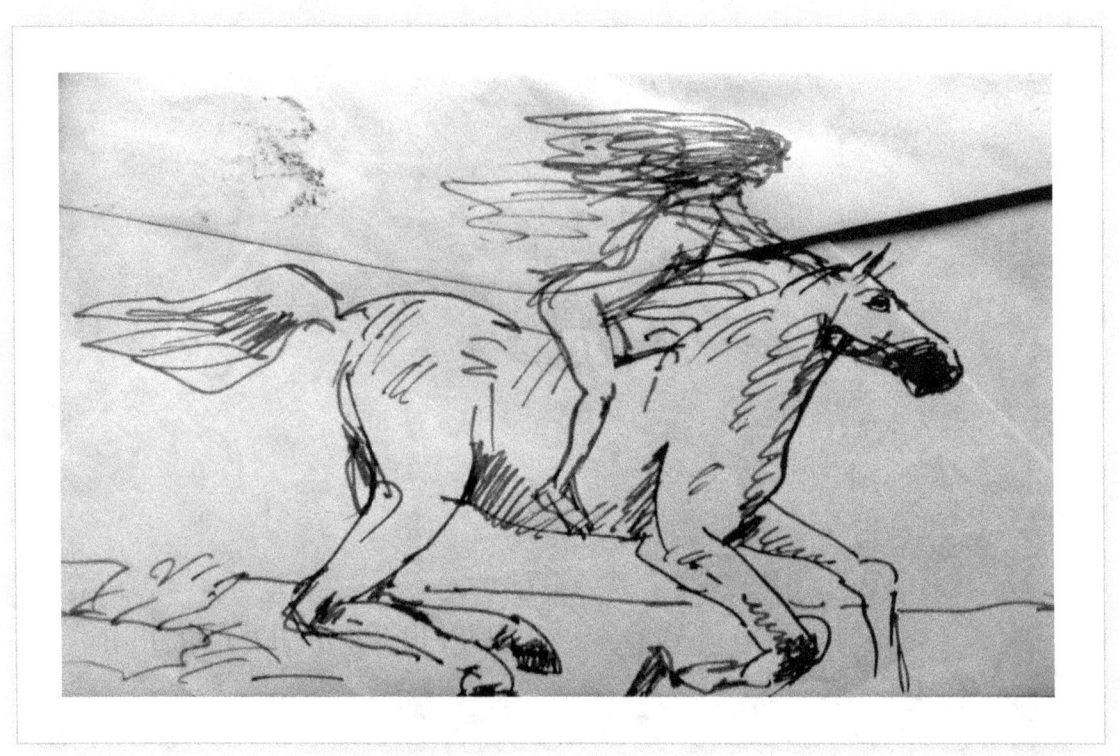

Lady Godiva on an envelope.

Pen and ink on the back of a Verizon bill. Or was it the gas bill? Did I ever pay it?

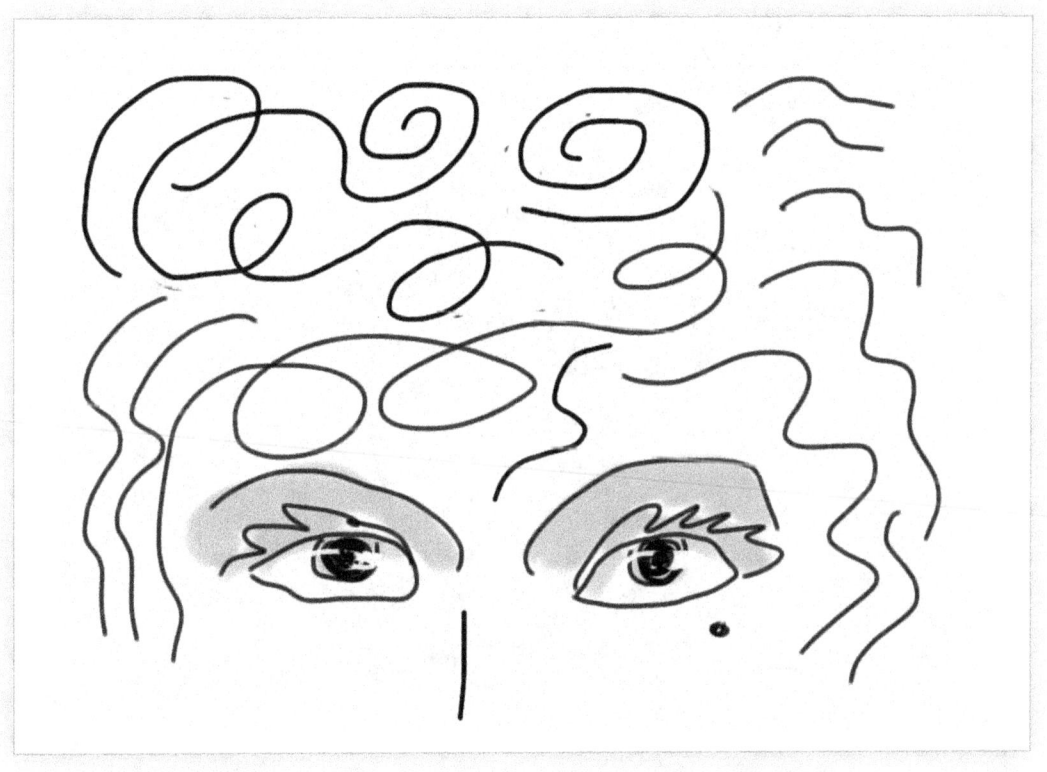

Bedroom eyes.

It's good to have a set of eyes around the bedroom.

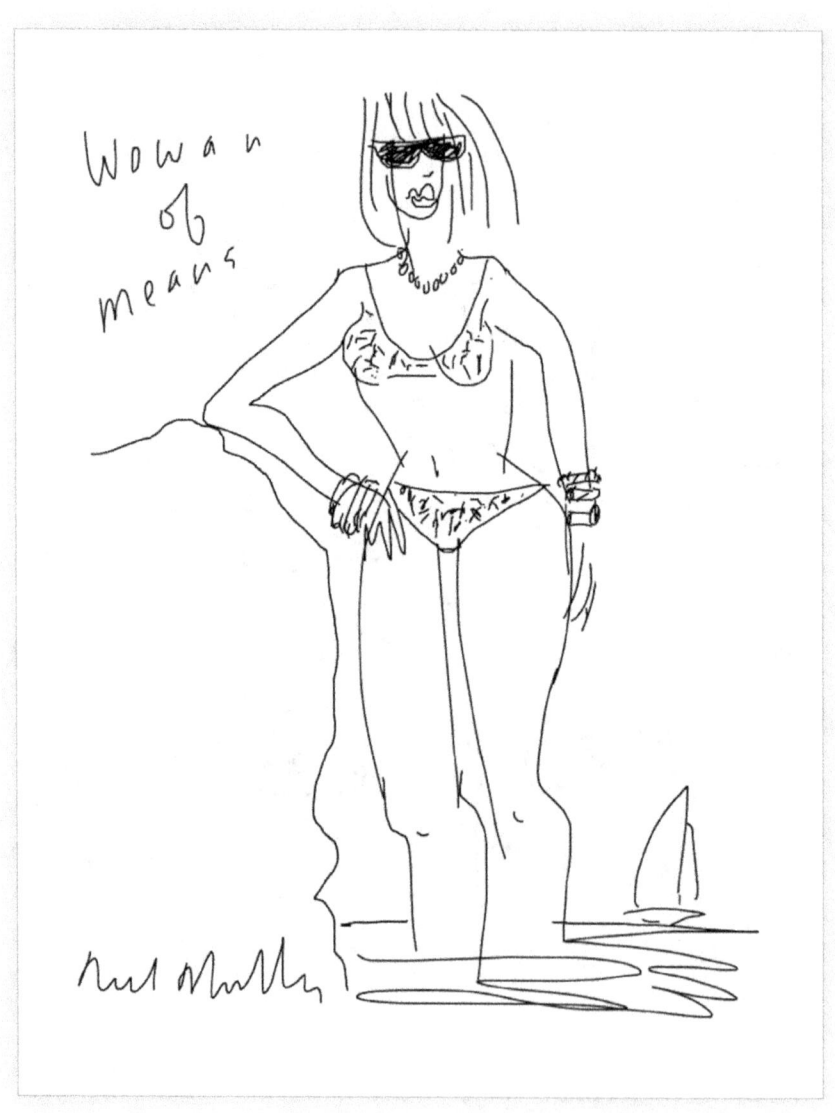

Woman of means.

She was a glowing success.

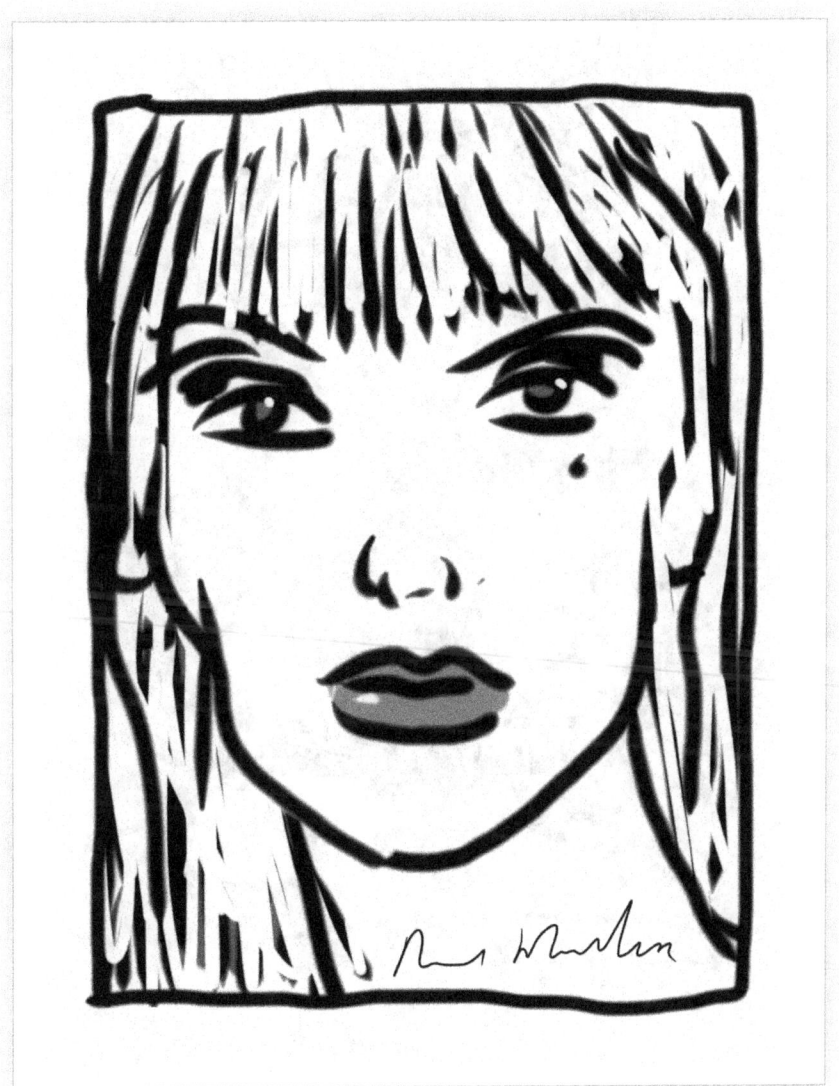

A looker.

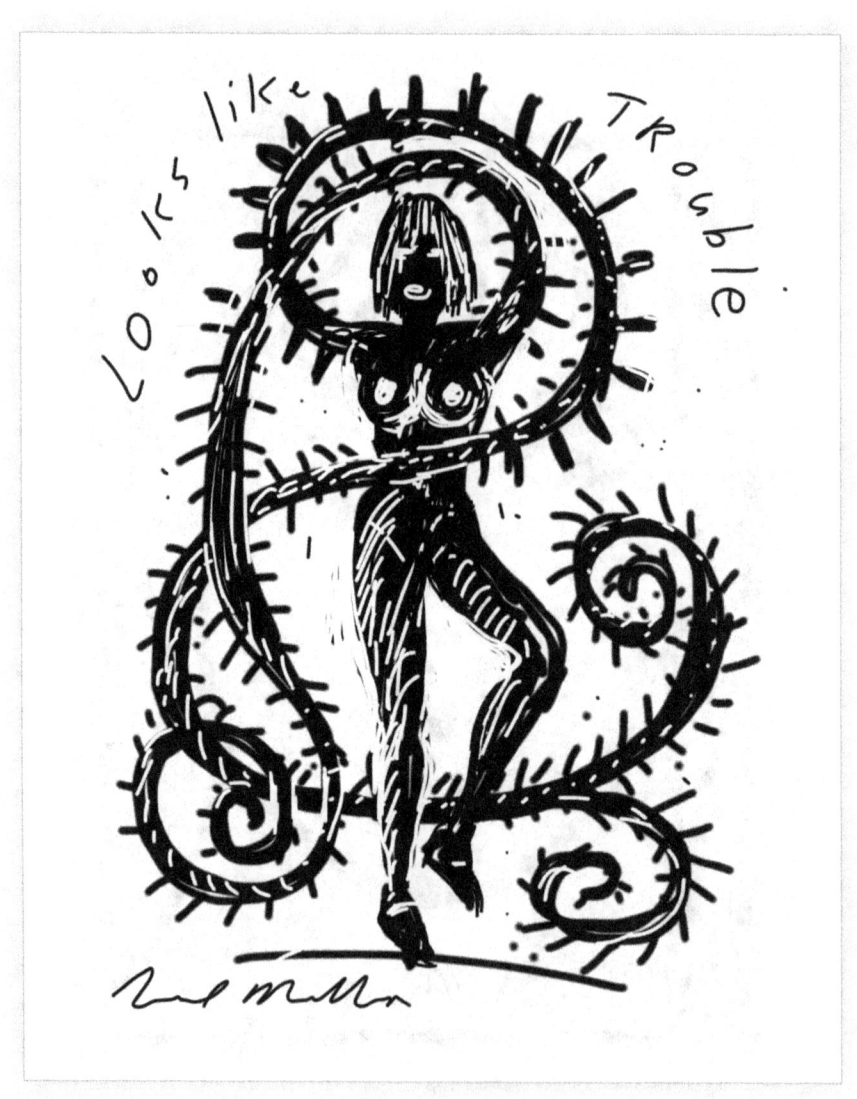

Looks like trouble.

At this stage in my life I can spot trouble from very far away.

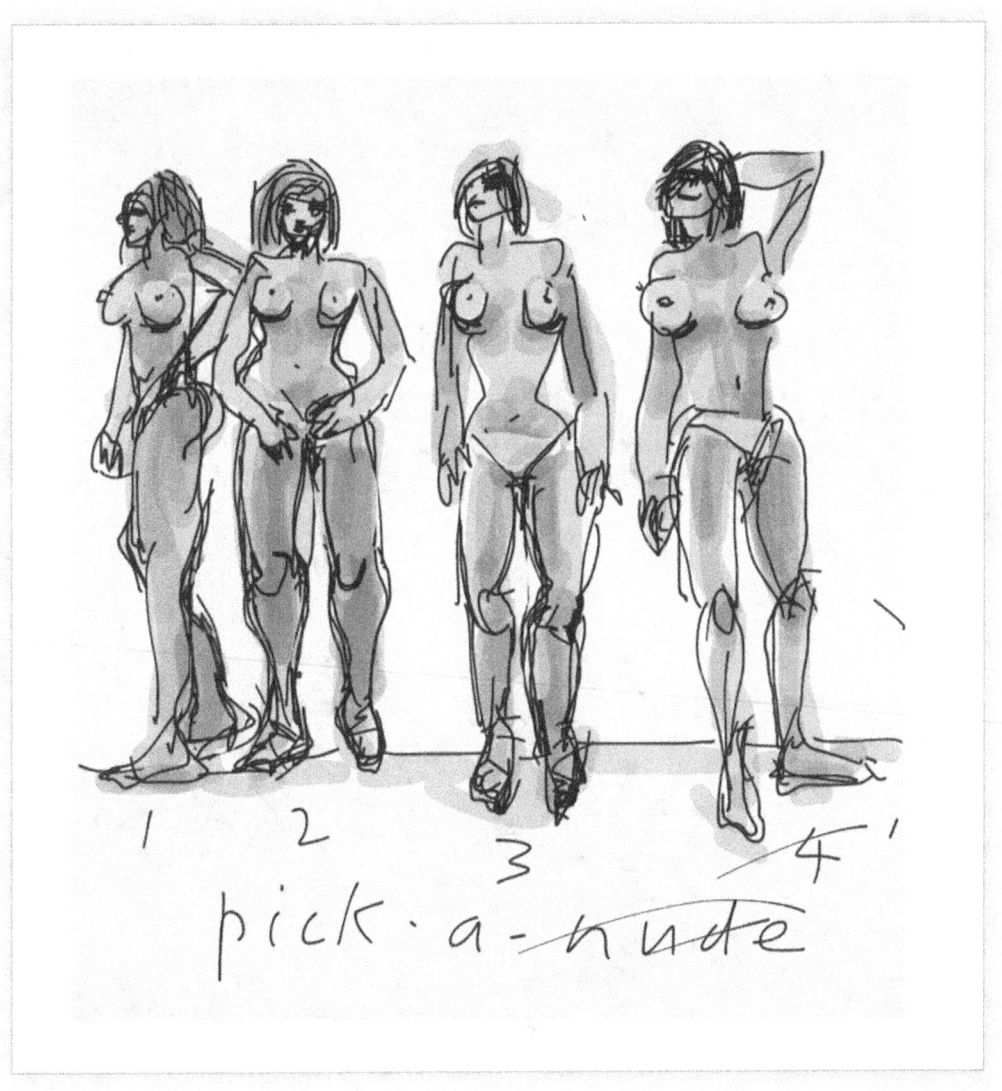

Pick a nude.

It's between 2 and 3 for me.

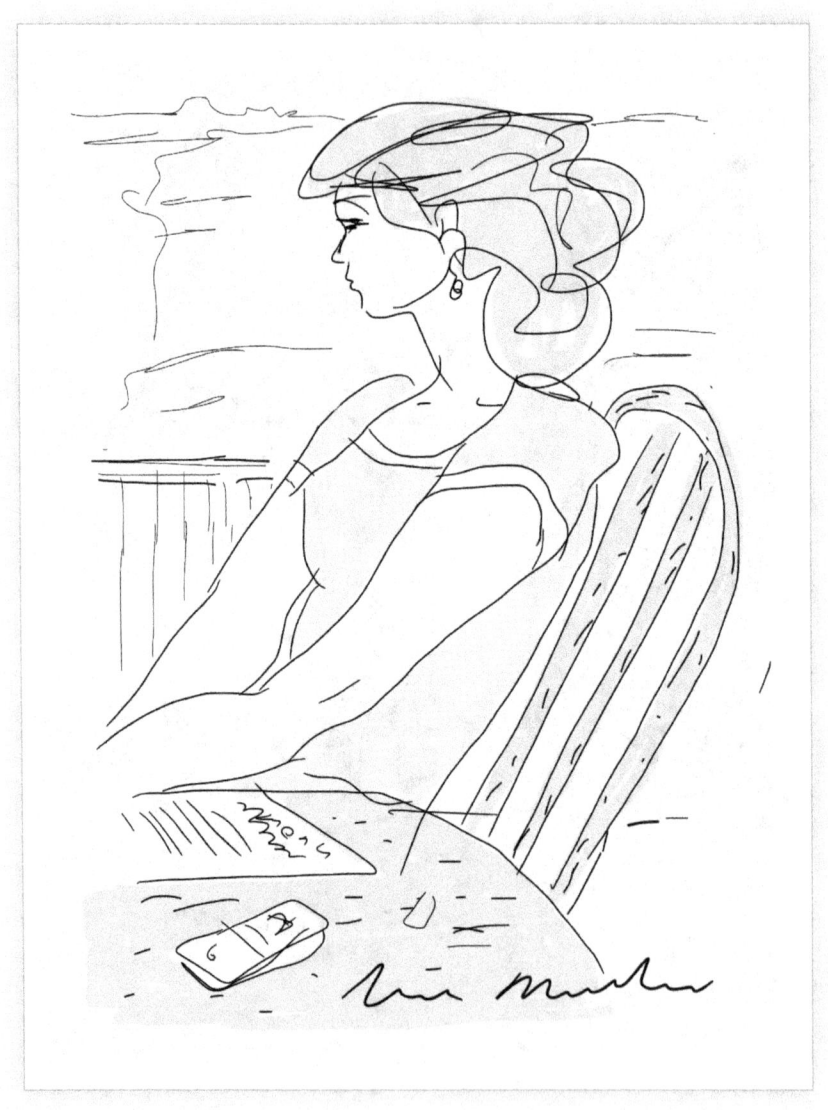

Girl with menu.

She's waiting to order because her lunch date has not arrived.

She's wondering if she should call or not.

I thinks she's going to order a small salad. Not sure.

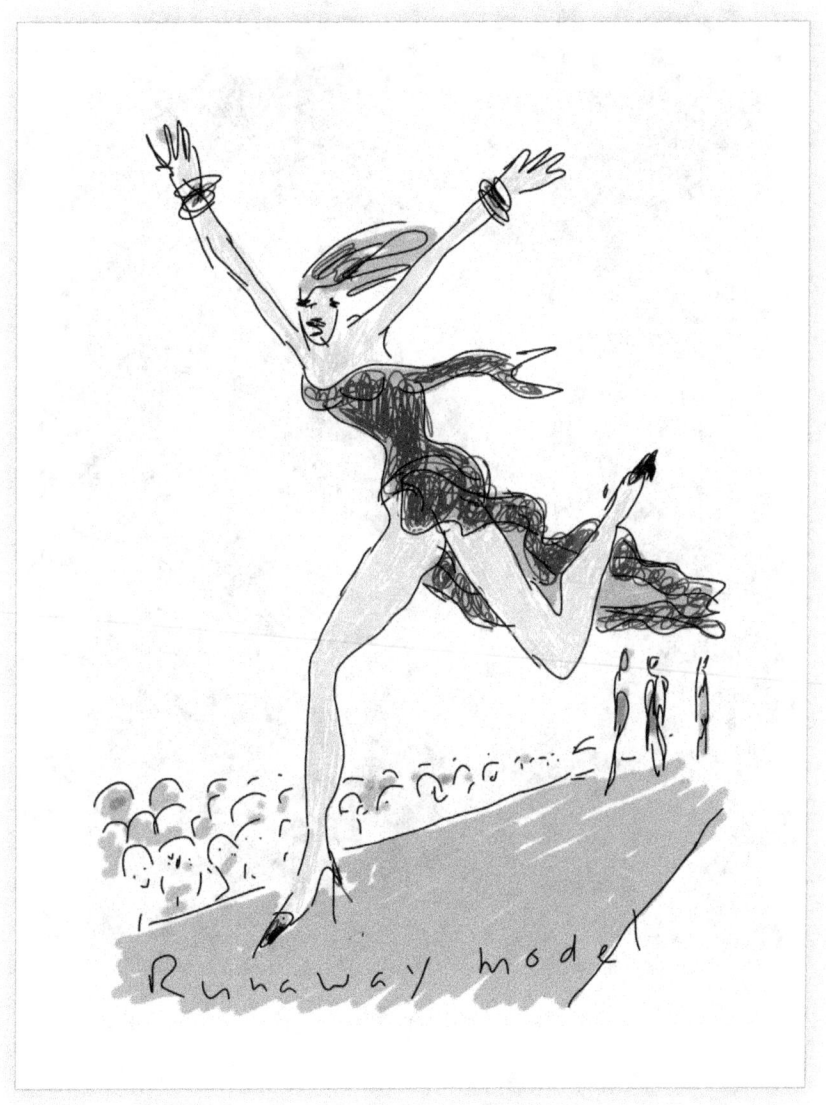

Runaway model.

Some models are hard to keep.

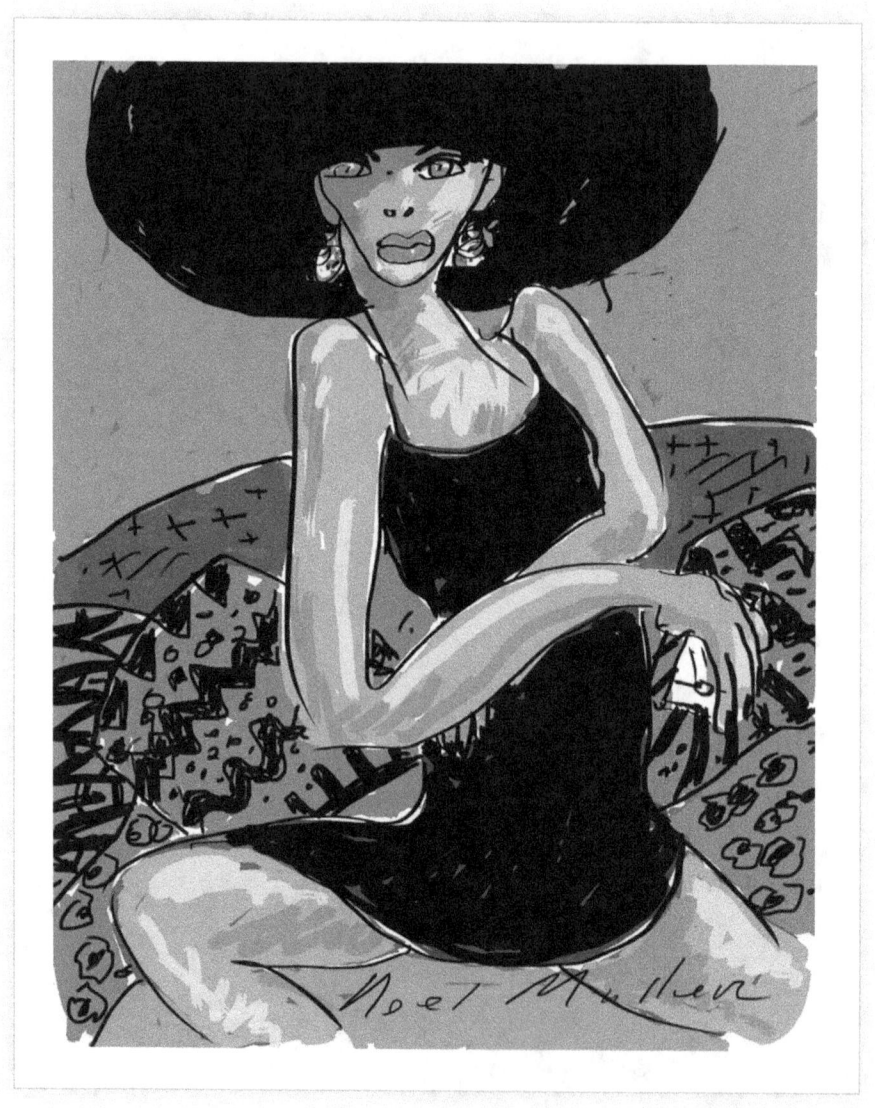

Fancy hatter.

Here is someone I like and appreciate. Full of intensity. With her own unique style.

With tons of humor and brain power ready to flare up at a moment's notice.

A true participator in the world. A free spirit bar none.

An original cut. I kiss you big.

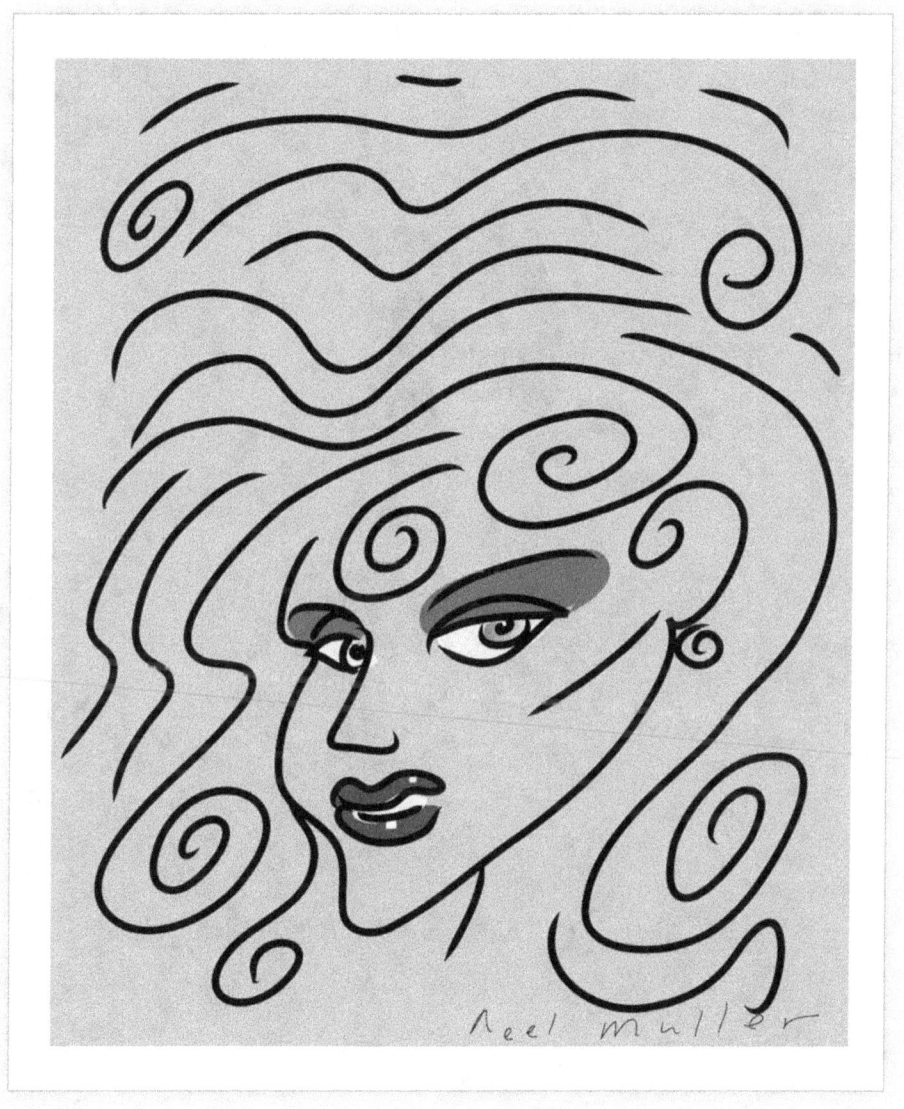

The heiress's hair.

Only a heiress can afford such an elaborate hairdo.

The question is whether she is really happy with her life?

My guess is that she has as many good days as bad days just like all of us,

but at least she can enjoy a first class plane ticket.

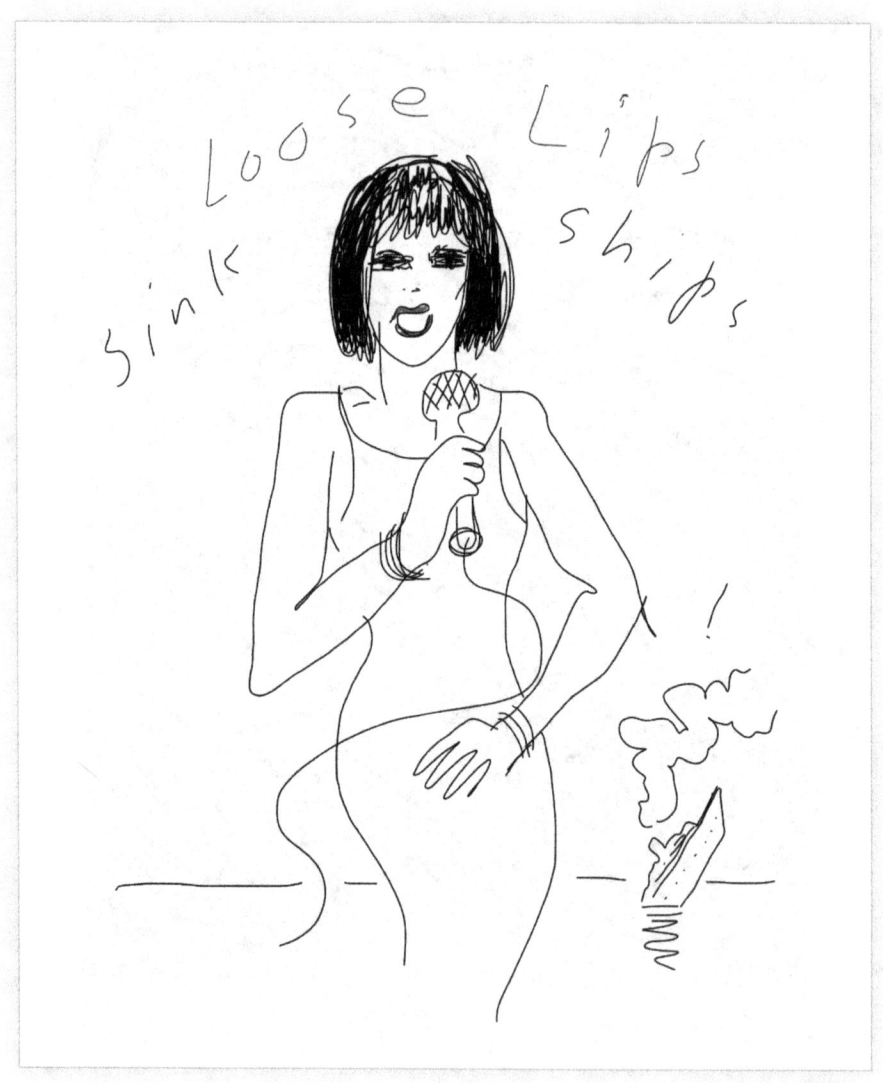

Loose lips sink ships.

She jumped out of my brain onto the page one morning.

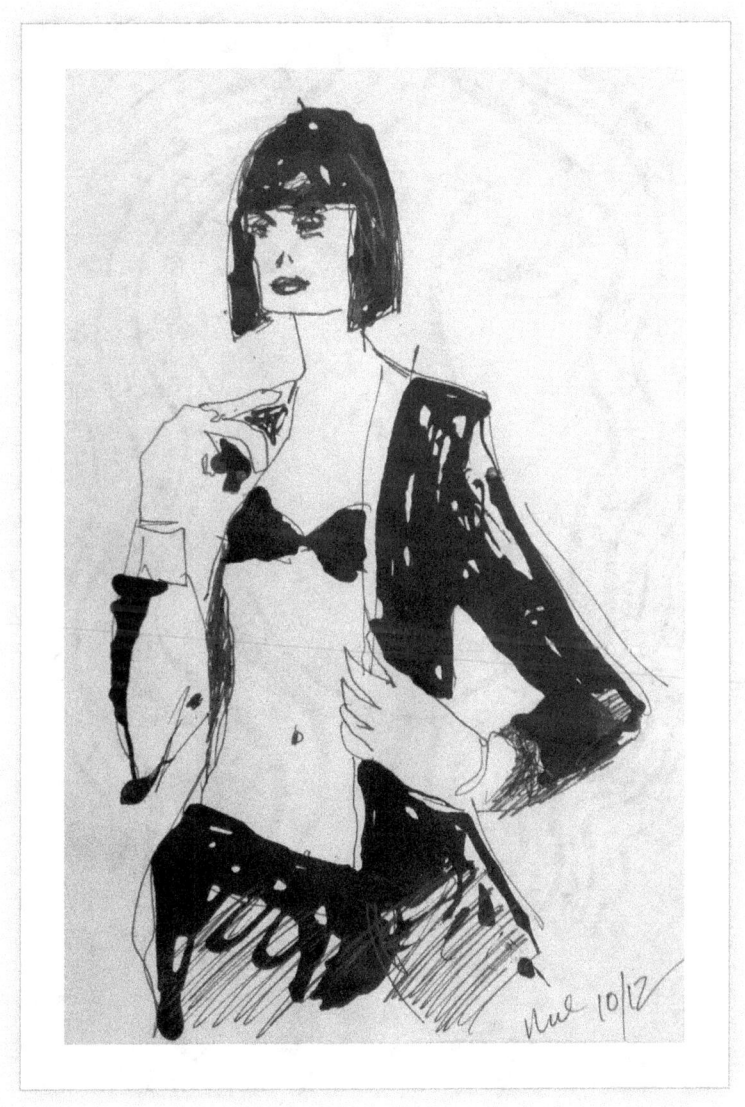

Lanky girl.

Not much to say about this drawing other than that I drew her

from a photo in a magazine whose name I can't remember.

I usually draw from memory.

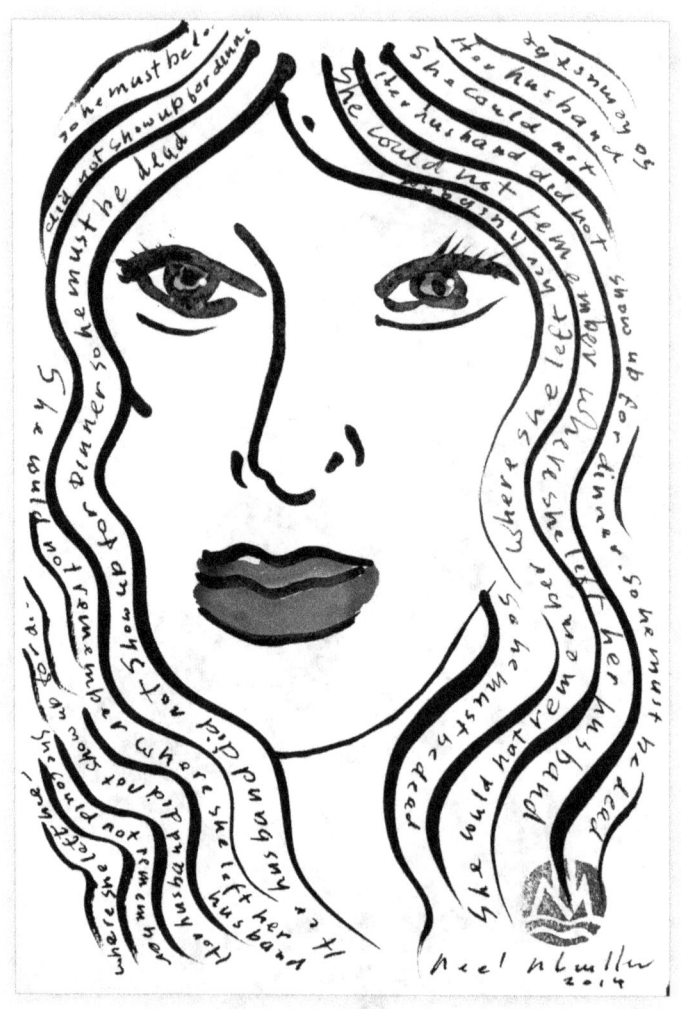

Forgetful woman.

She lost track of everything; her keyes, her glasses, her husnabd etc.

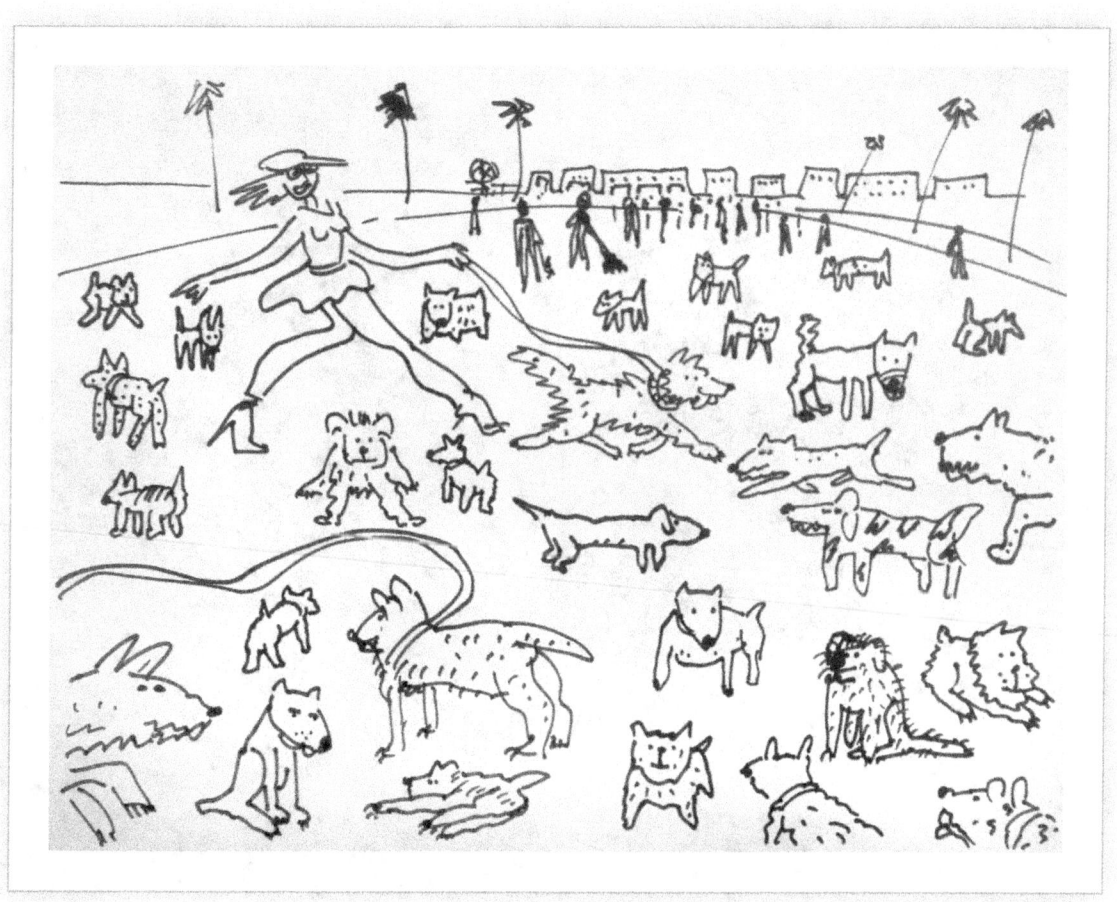

She waltzed through the dog park in Venice, California.

To the beat of rap music. Or was it yap music?

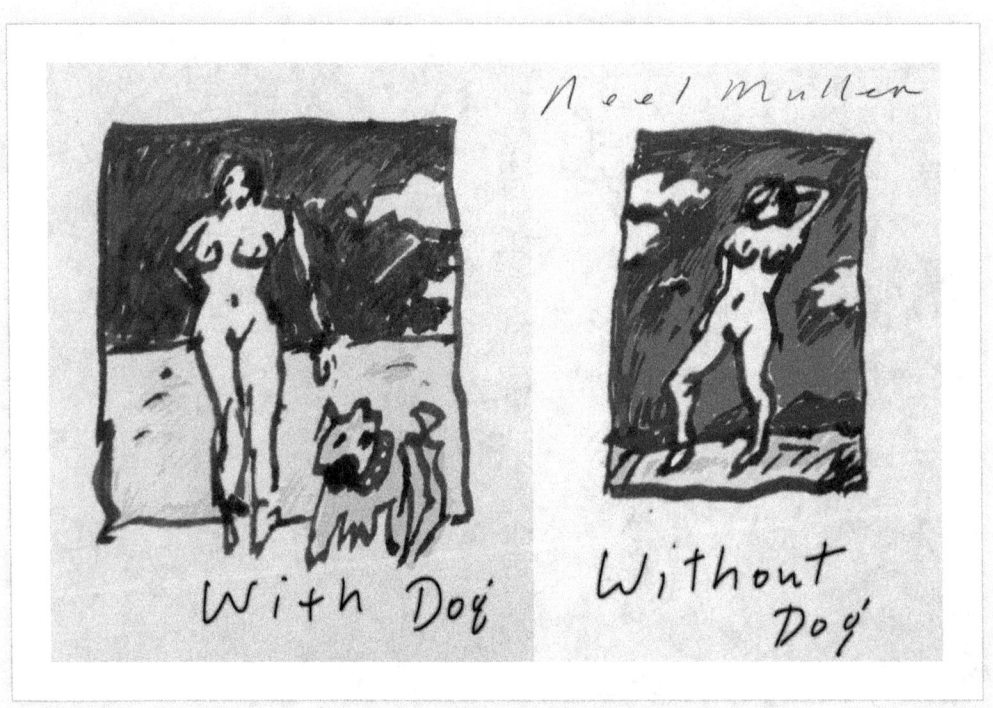

With dog. Without dog.

Either one is fine with me.

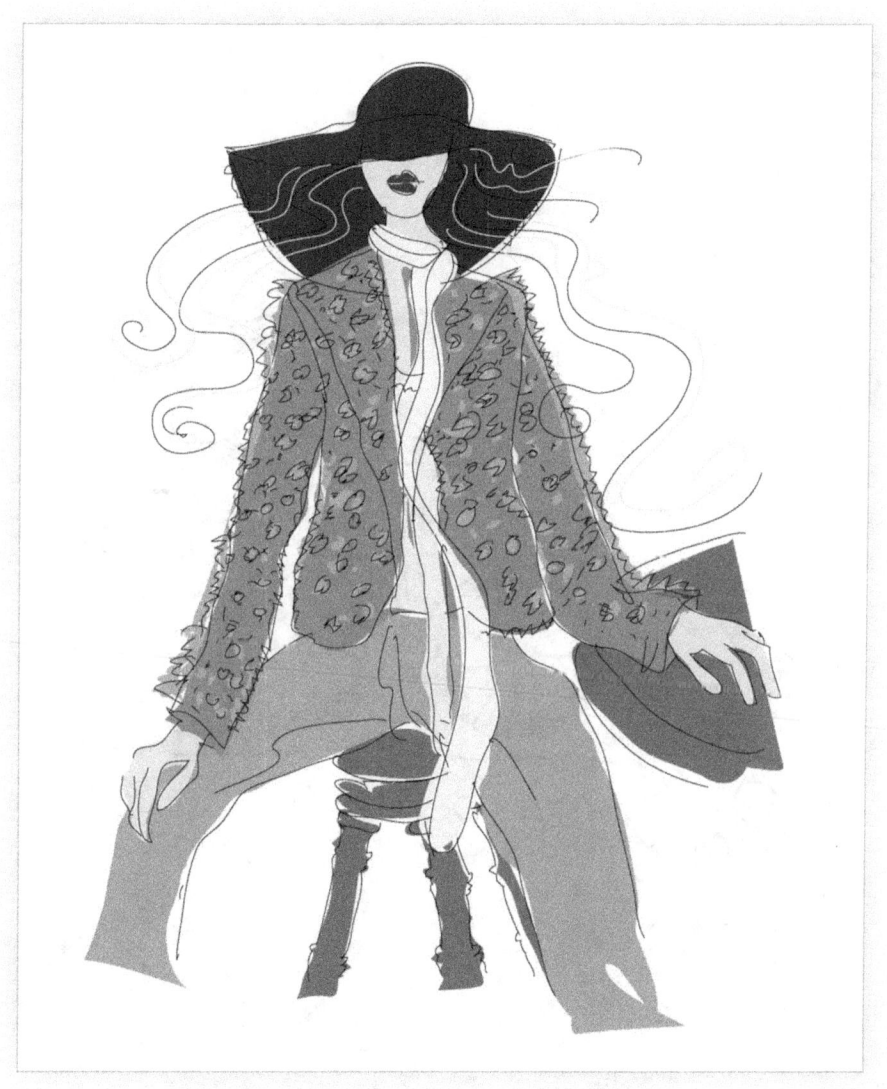

Woman of color.

Trust me, she's colorful.

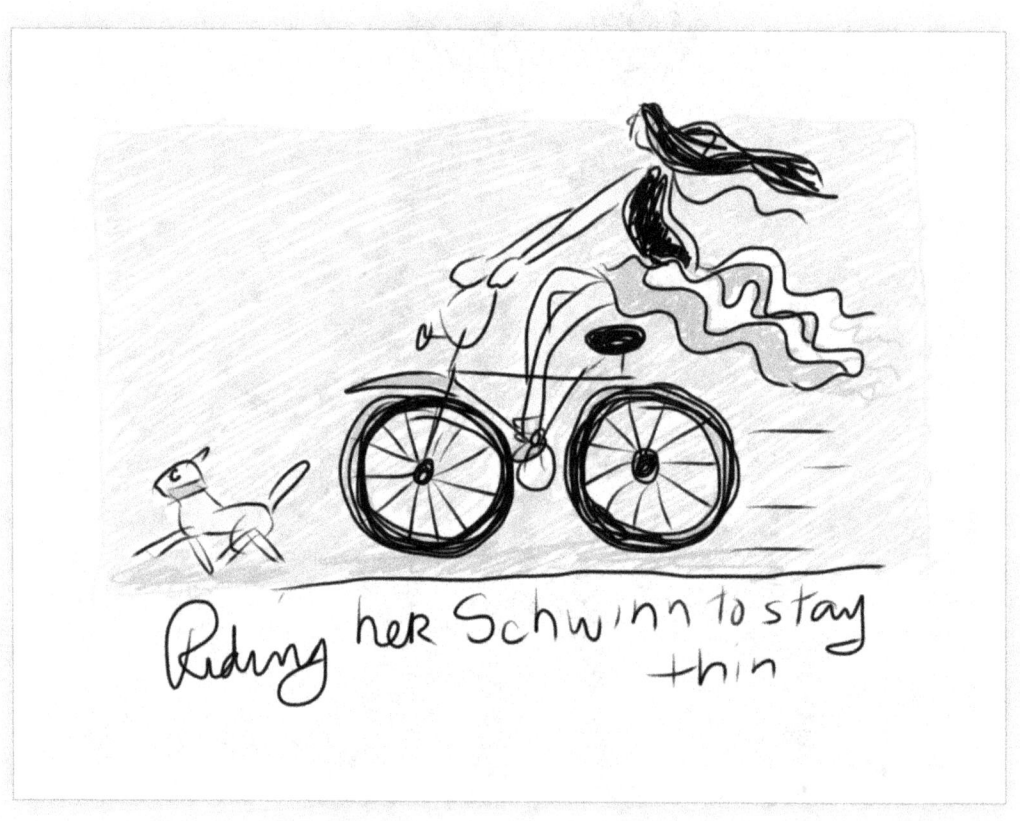

Riding her Schwinn to stay thin.

No helmet.

No ugly riding gear with logos all over it.

No leash on dog.

No regard for local laws.

Perfect.

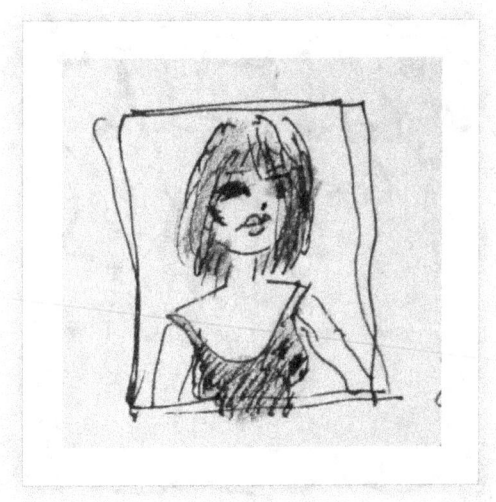

Petite woman.

Micro sketch.

Macro attitude.

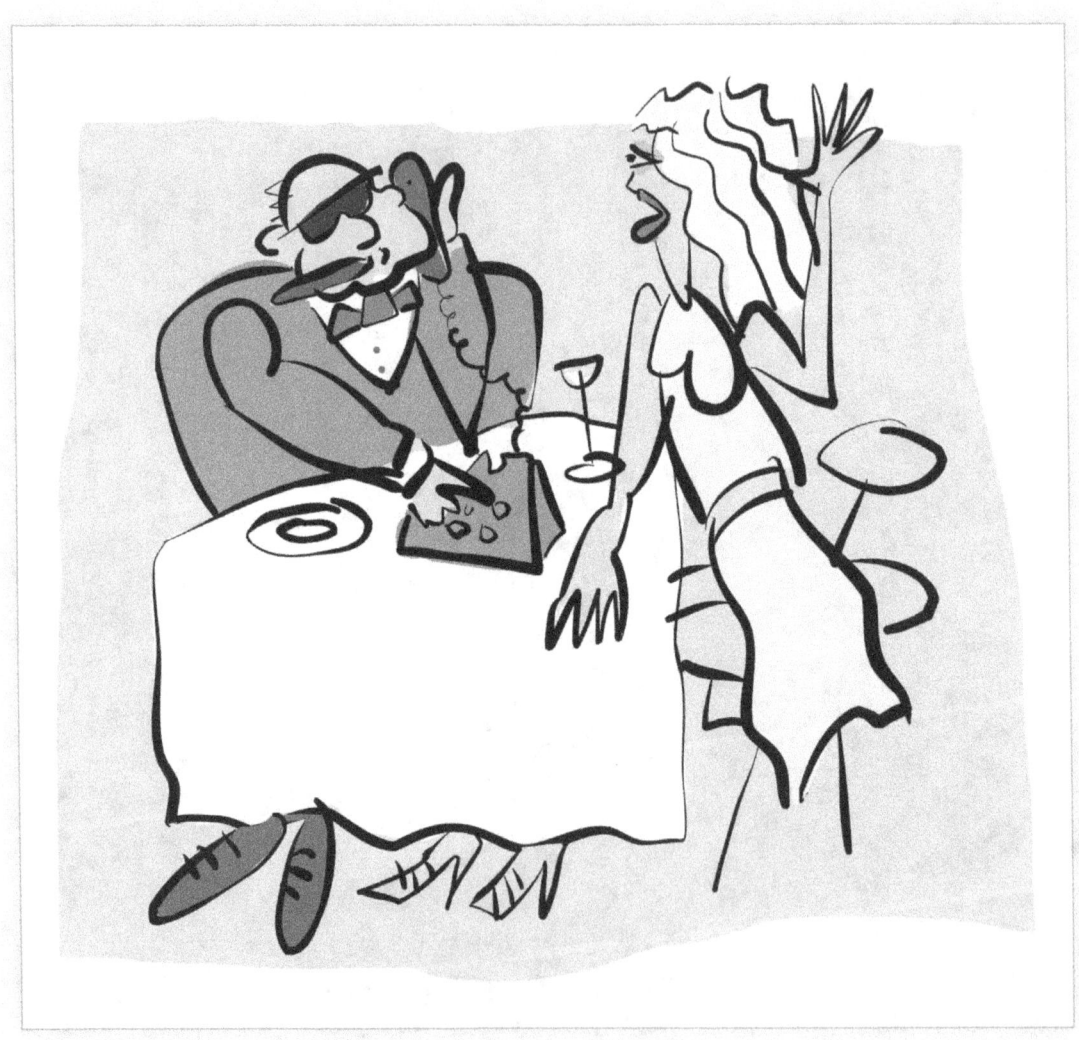

Trophy wife lunch.

With loud table manners.

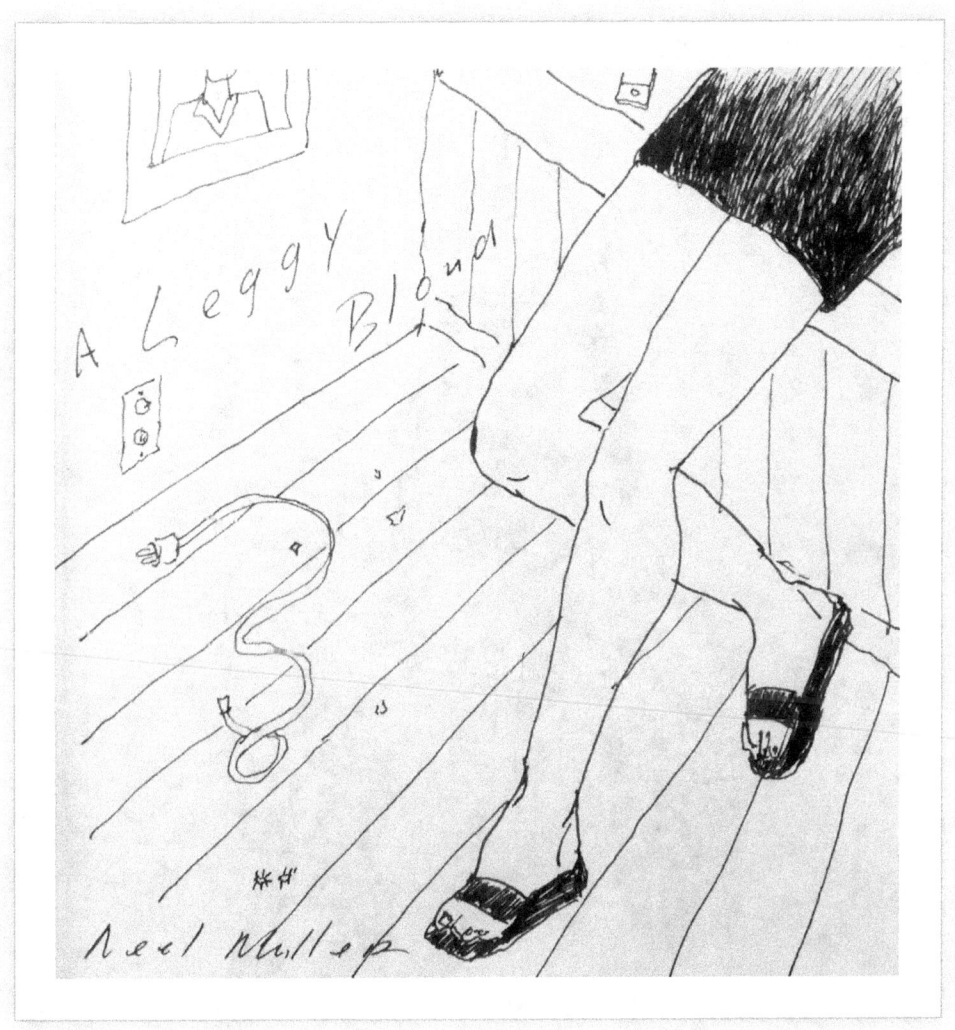

Leggy blond #2.

Getting ready to charge her iPhone. Or maybe she'll wait and charge it in the car

on the way to meet her friend. That way she won't accidentally forget to bring it along.

Hope nobody steps on her charger while she is away, possibly rendering it useless.

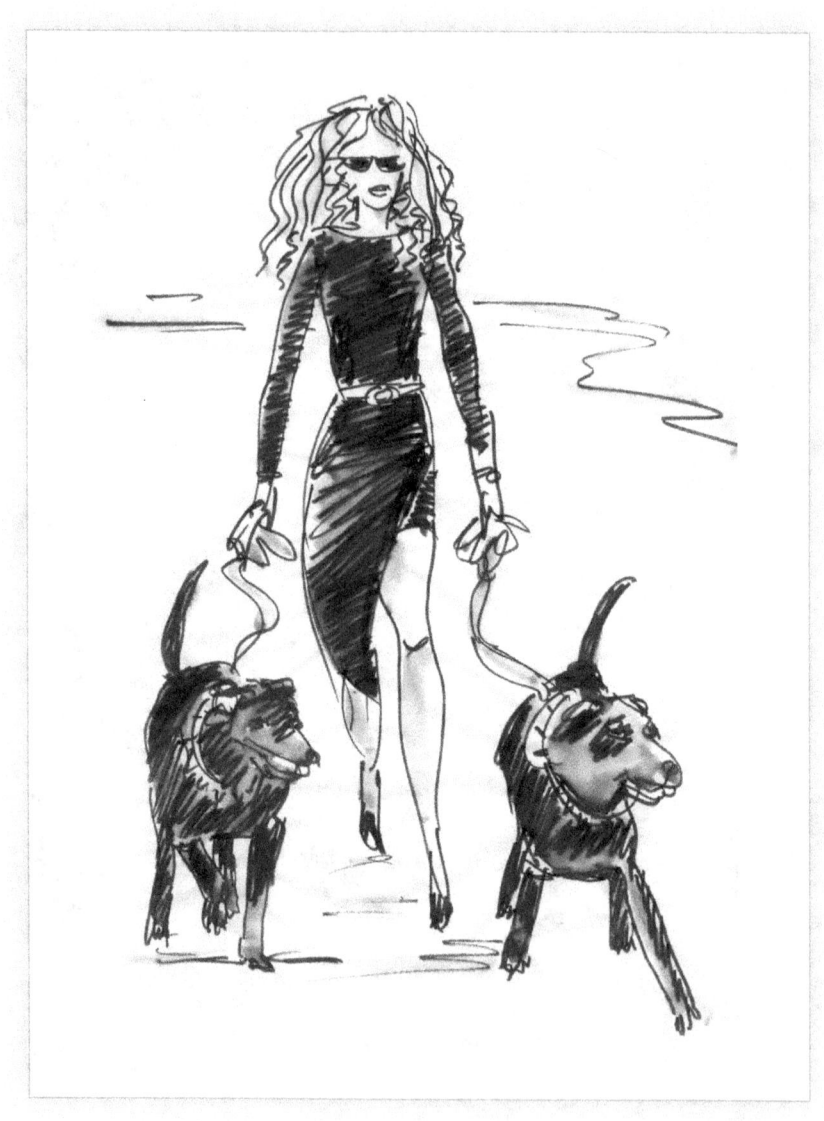

Animal control.

The dogs think they are the pack leaders, but they are wrong.

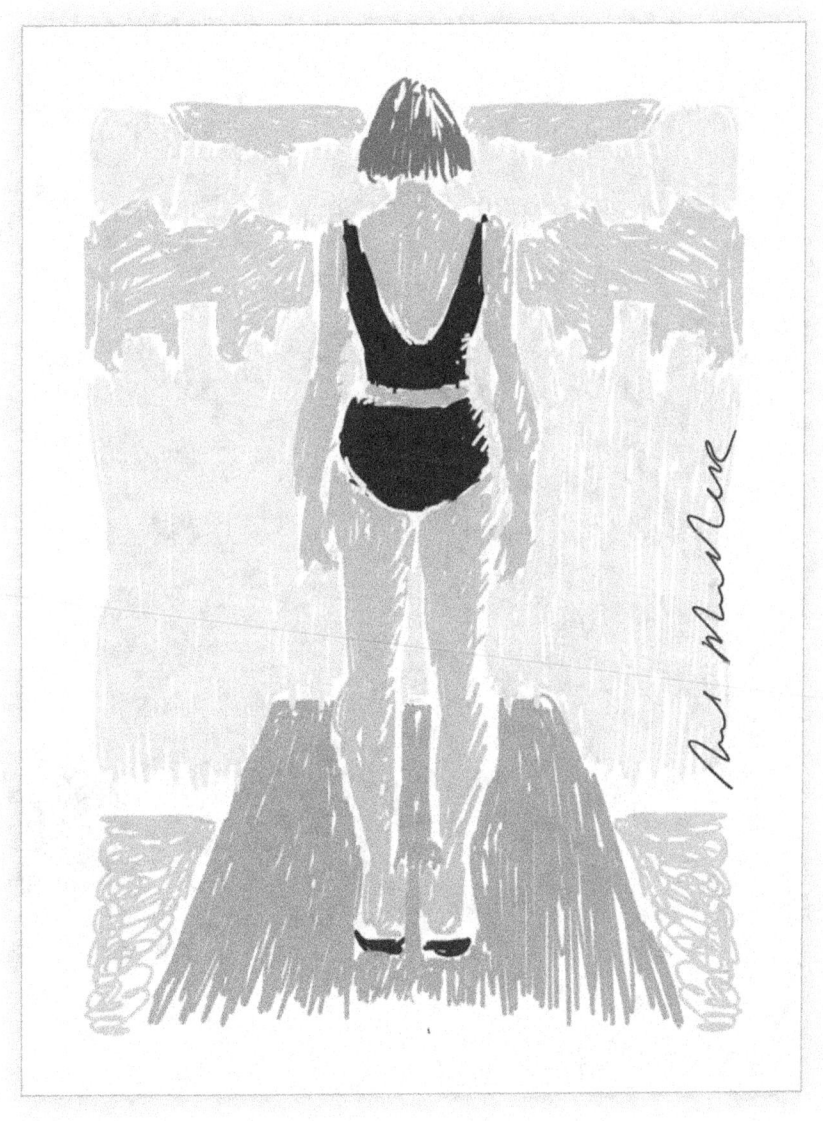

Girl on diving board.

When you dive there's no going back.

That's the beauty of it.

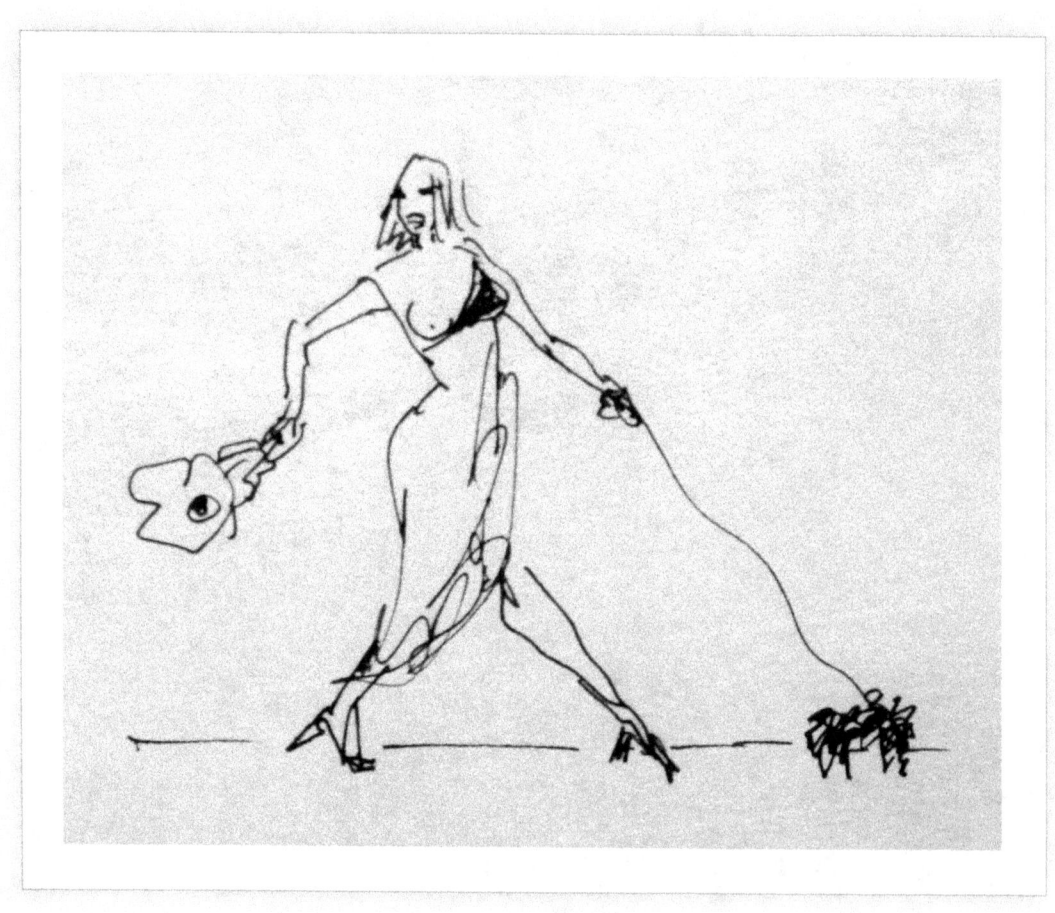

Woman with dog.

Why walk when you can strut?.

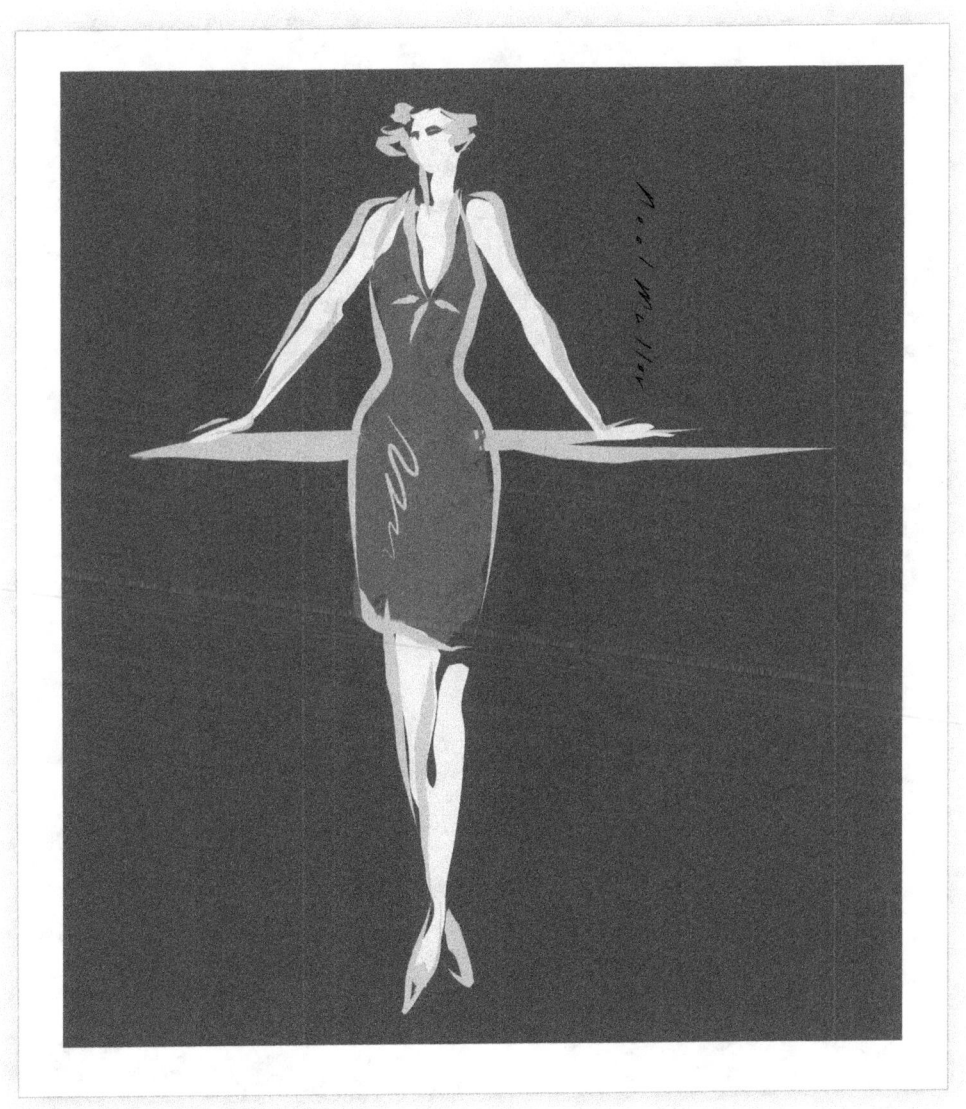

All dressed up and many places to go to.

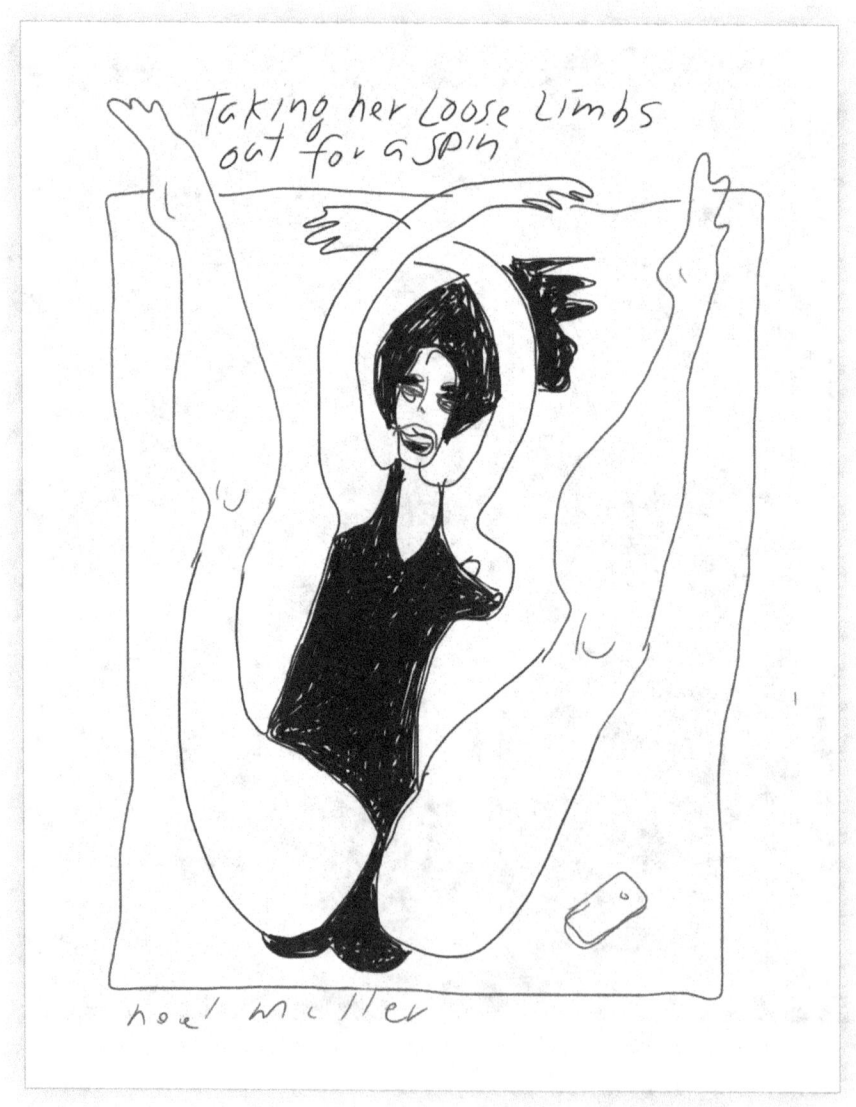

Taking her loose limbs out for a spin.

Her phone was turned off because

she did not want to be disturbed.

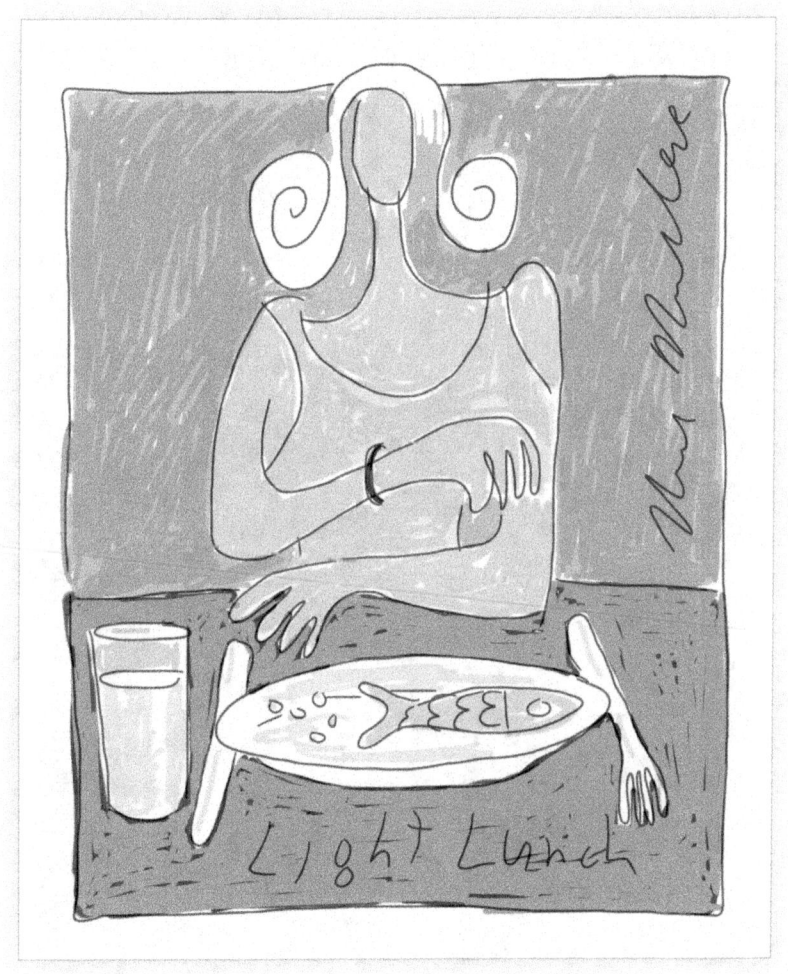

Light lunch.

Portrait of an unknown woman. A fussy eater, no doubt.

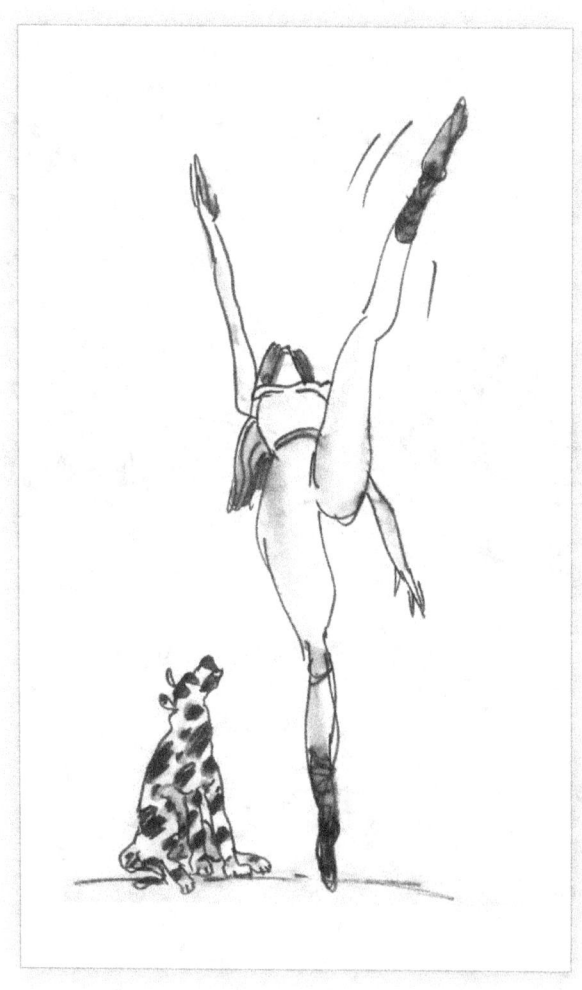

Fancy dancer.

You can tell a lot about a woman by the way she dances.

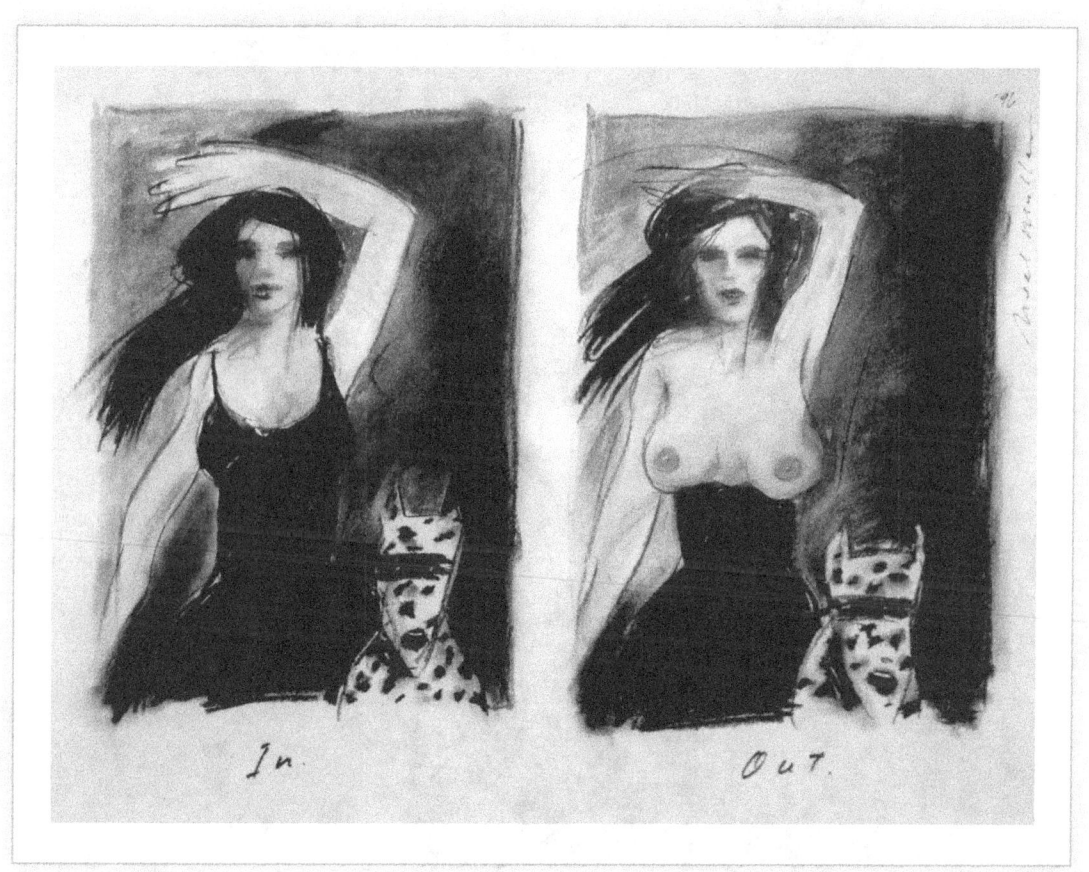

In. Out.

A big difference.

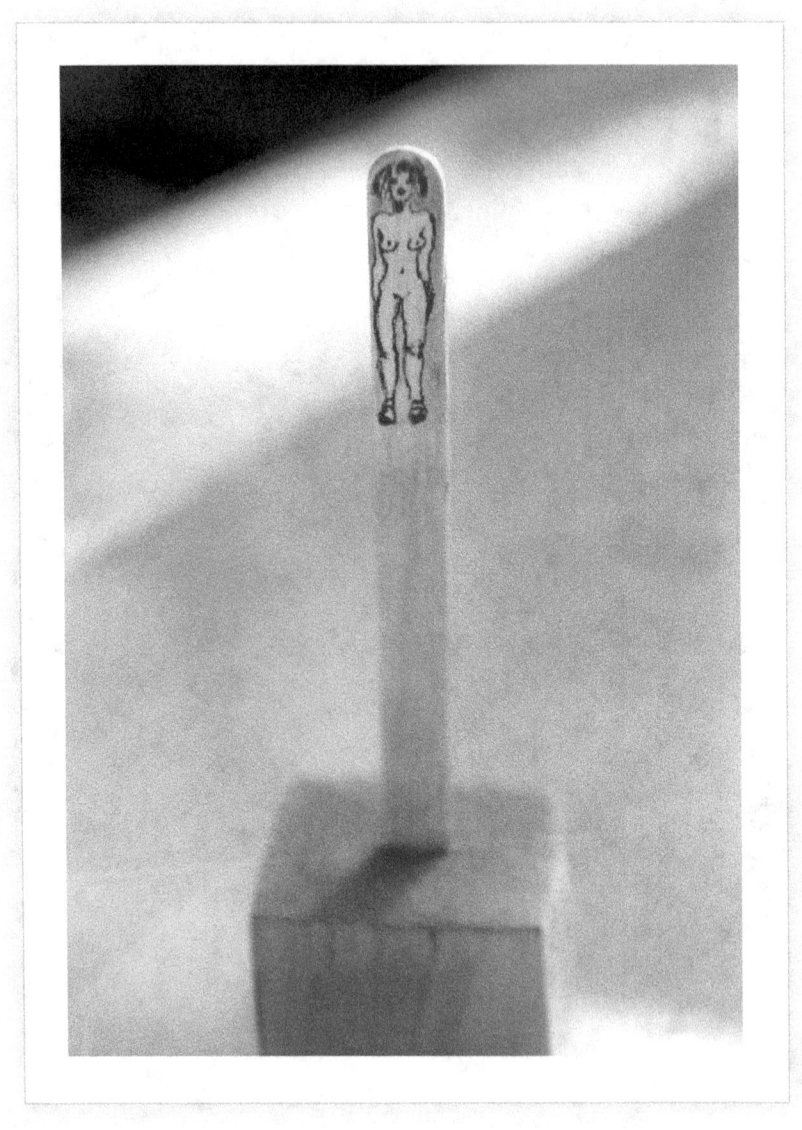

Chick on a stick.

Or if you prefer: Nude on a stick.

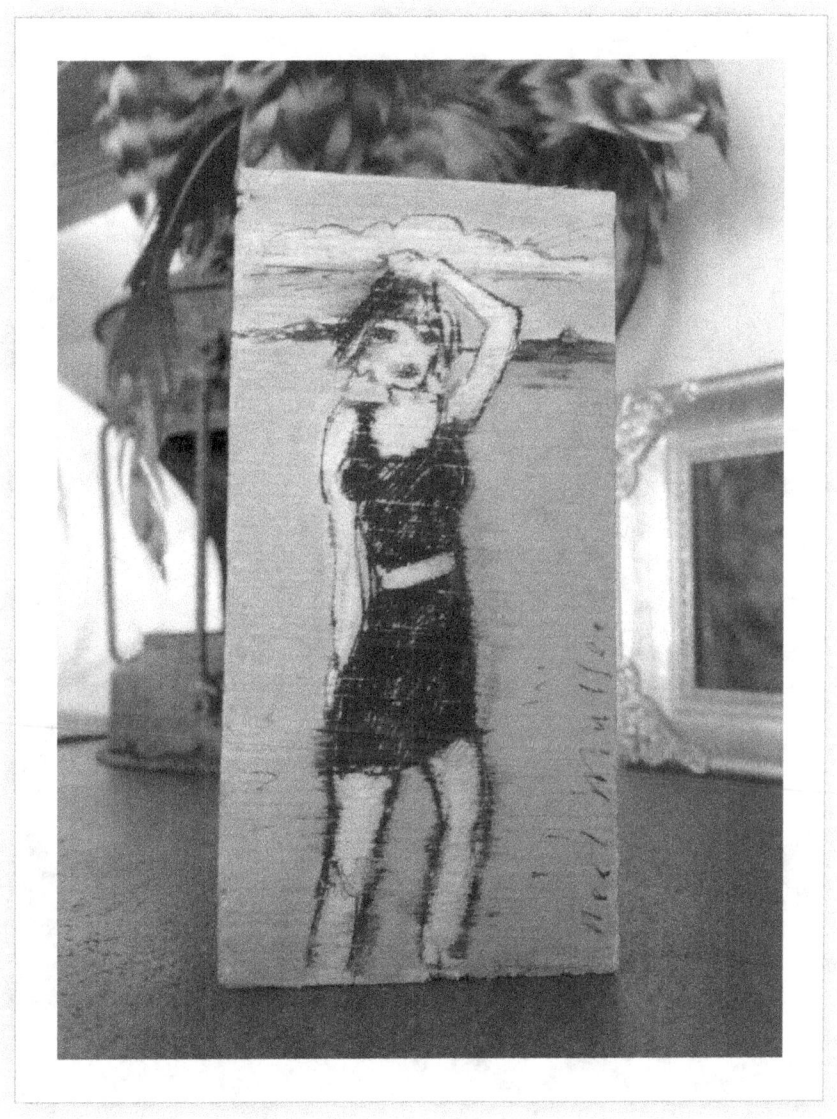

Wife on plywood.

One of many drawings inspired by my lovely wife.

Again, drawn from memory because I can't get her to stay still.

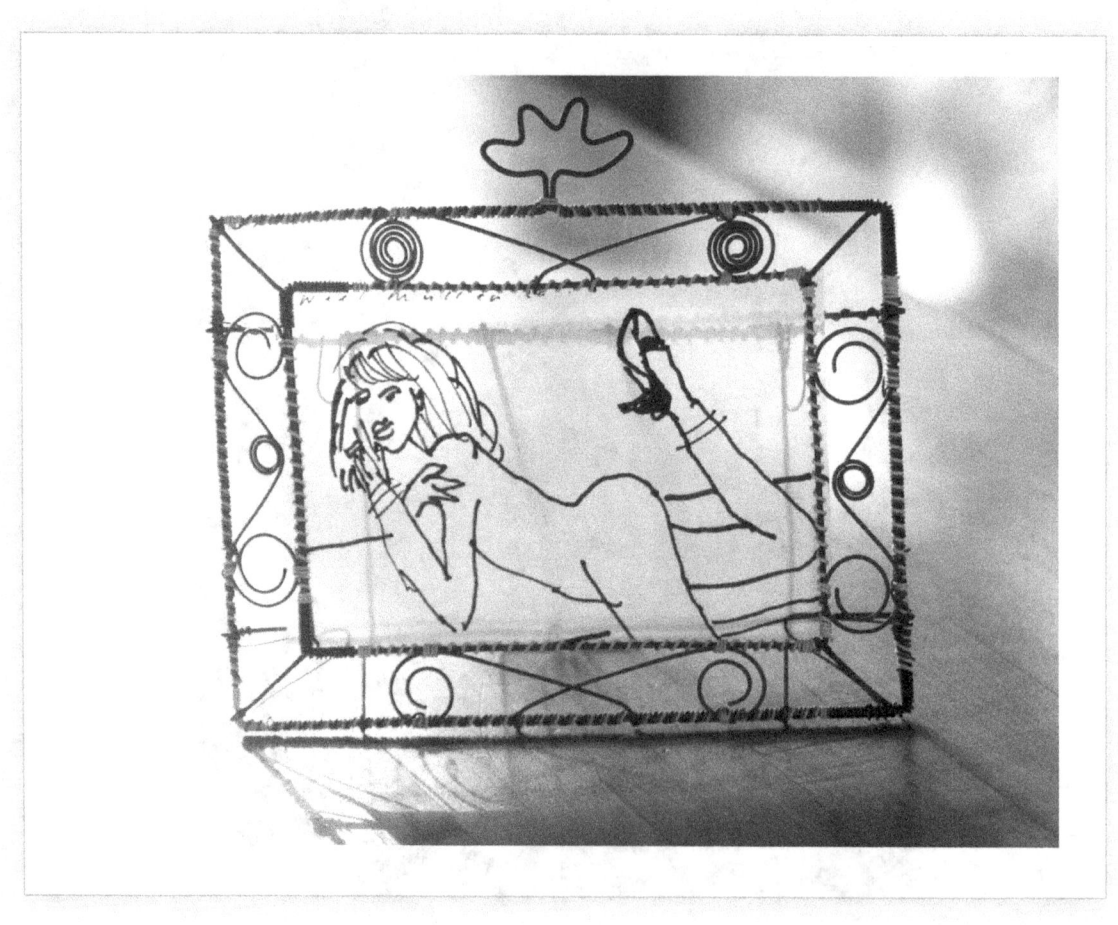

Dame in a frame.

I was wired after I drew this.

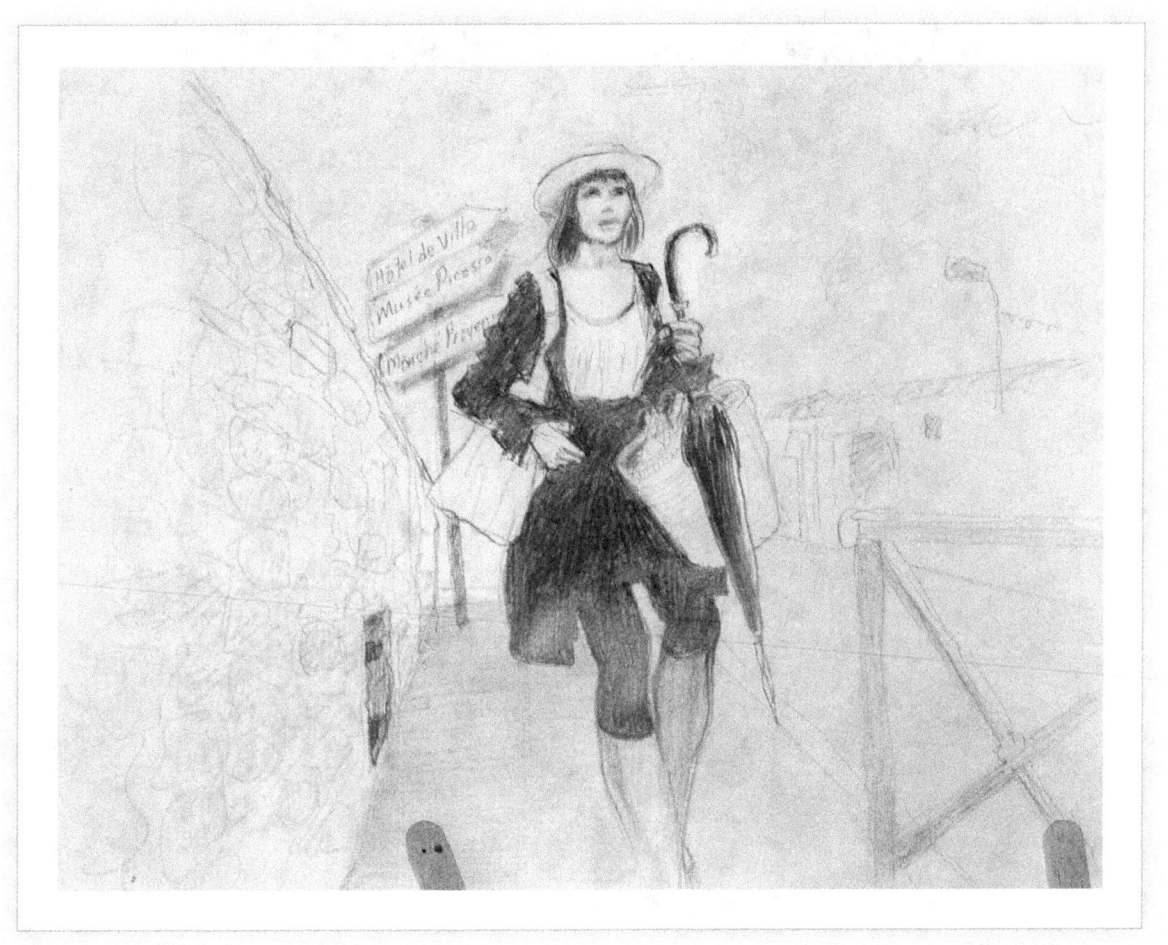

Wife on a shopping assignment.

Off to the shoe stores, expecting rain.

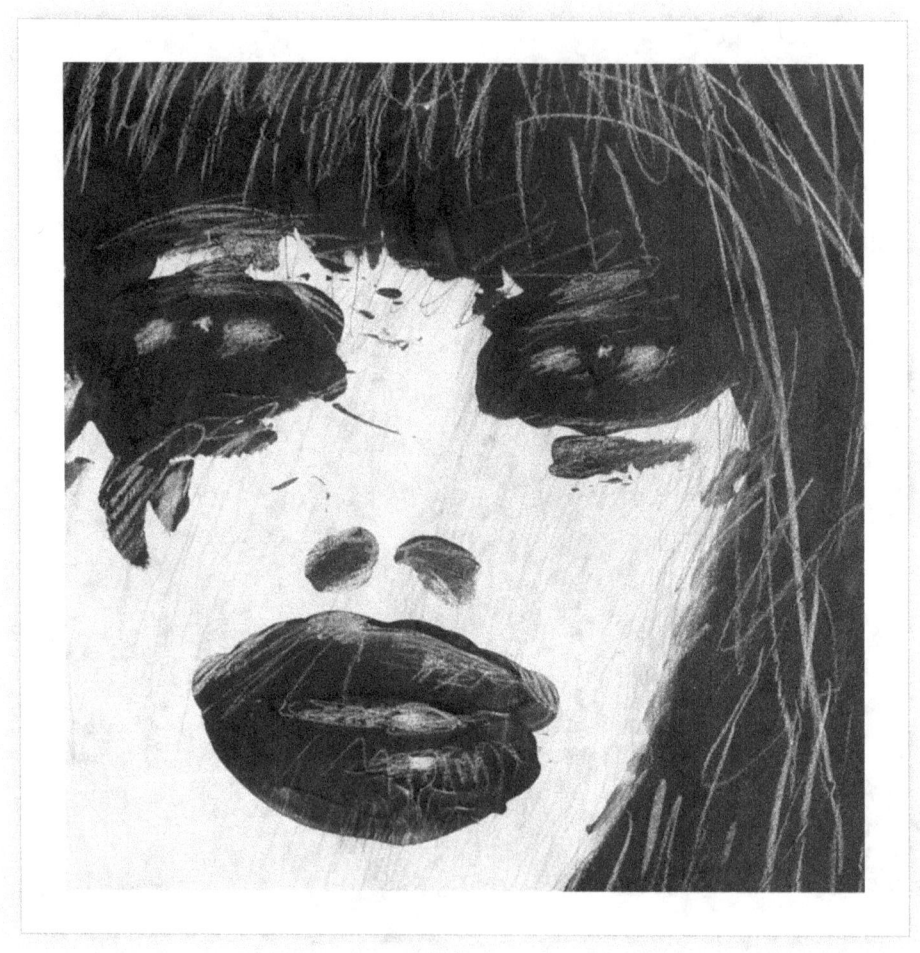

Close-up.

I've gotten weird reactions to this drawing.

It's apparently too close for some people.

I say you can never get close enough.

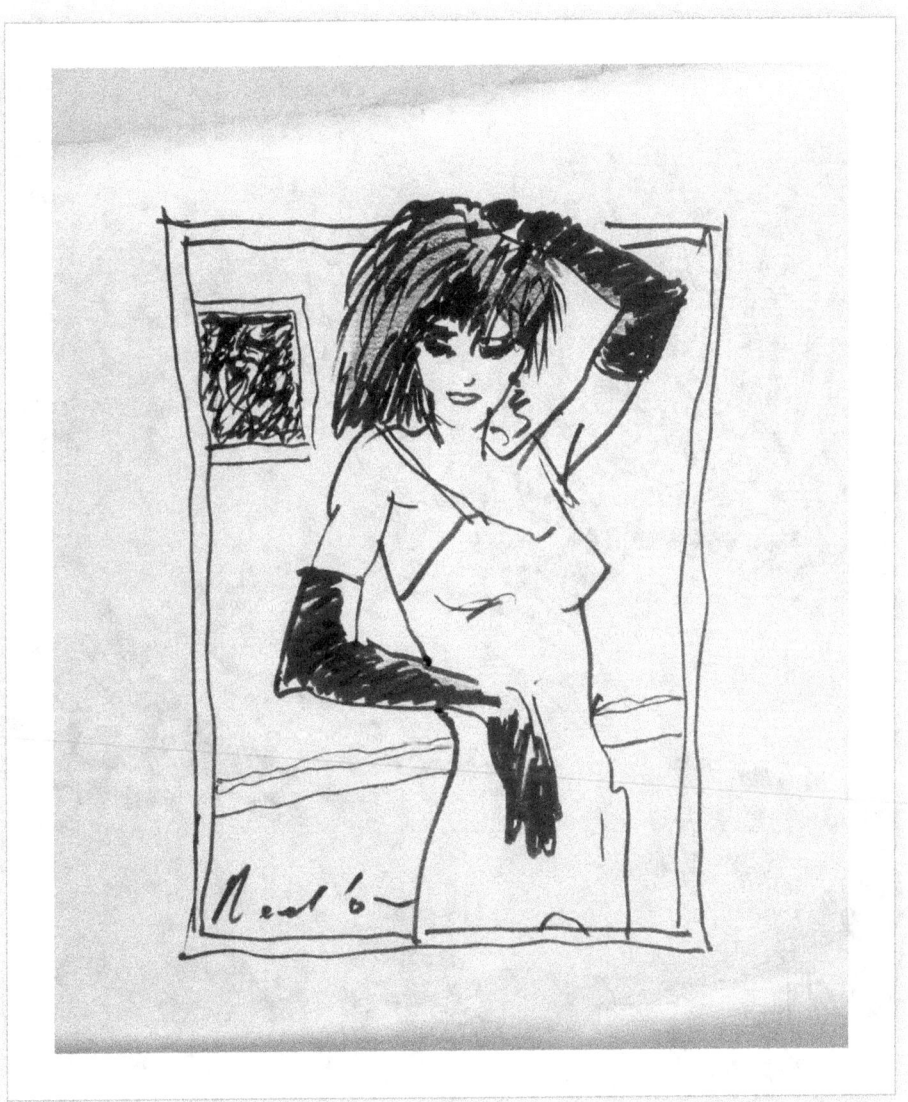

Posing for a better tomorrow.

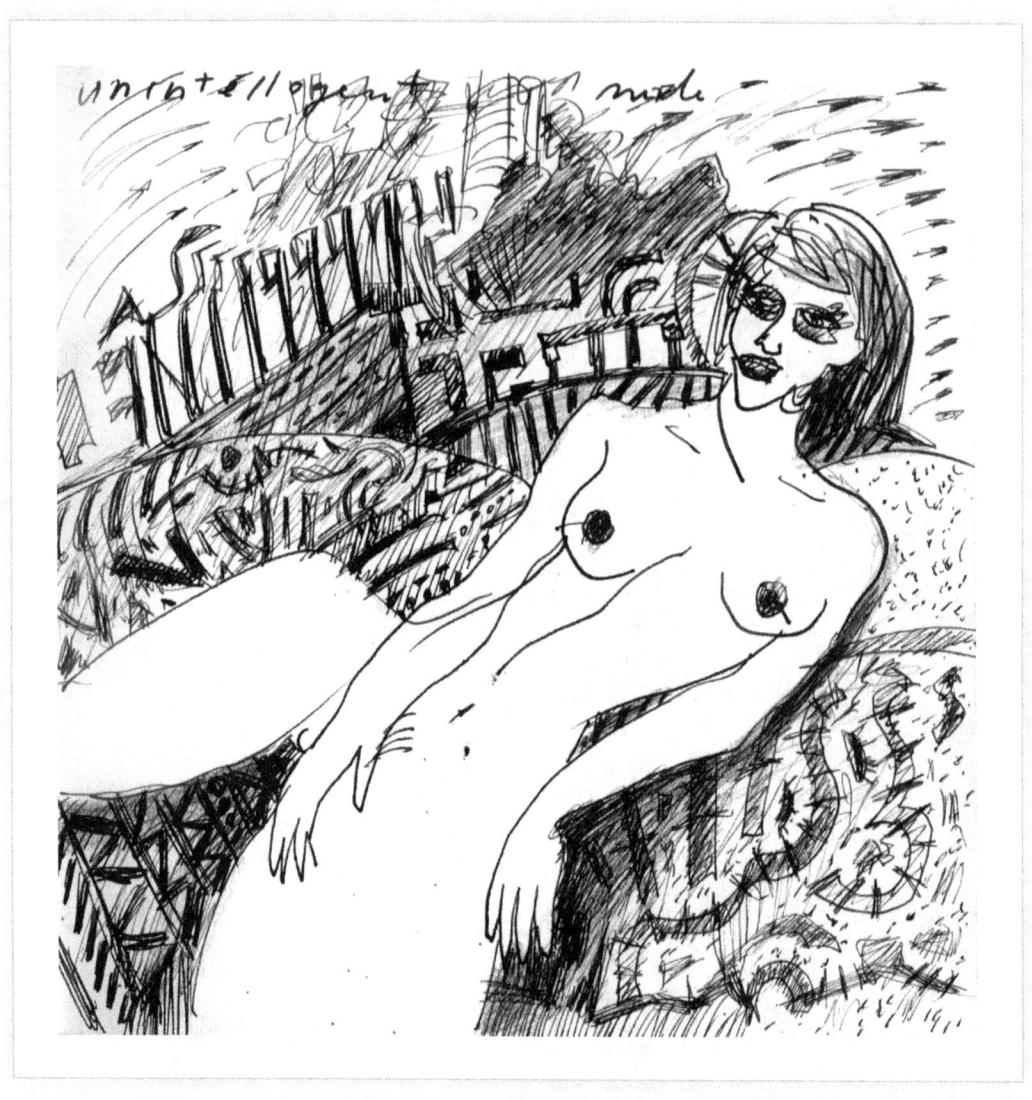

Unintelligent nude.

Not very sharp. Nevertheless, nice.

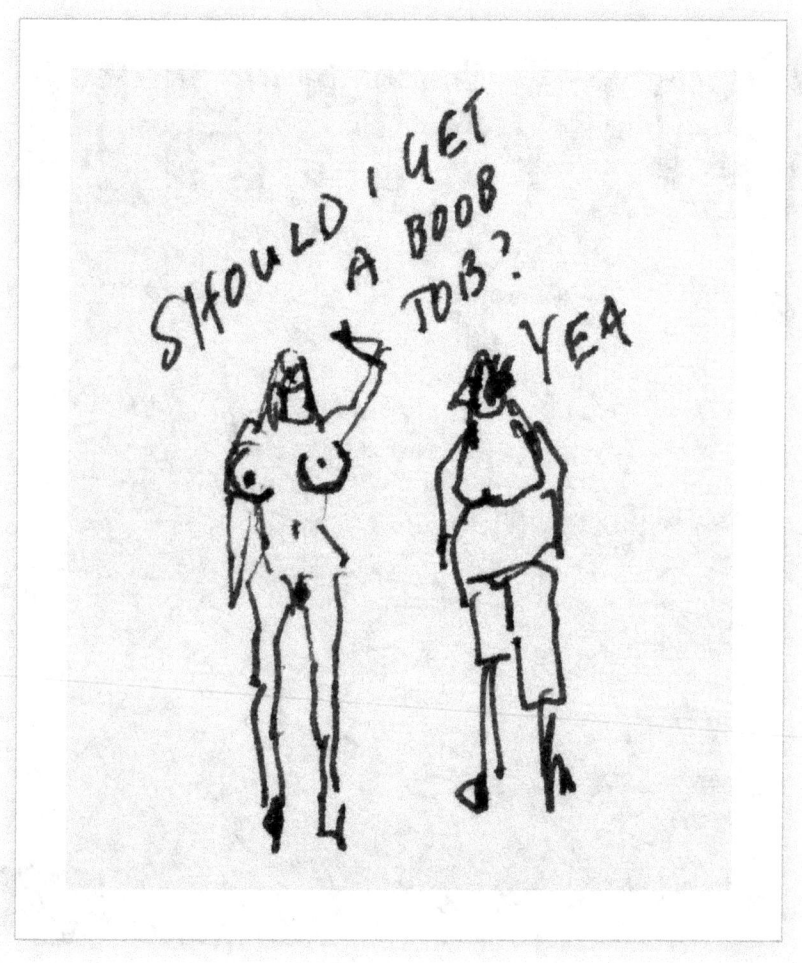

Trick question.

Debatable answer.

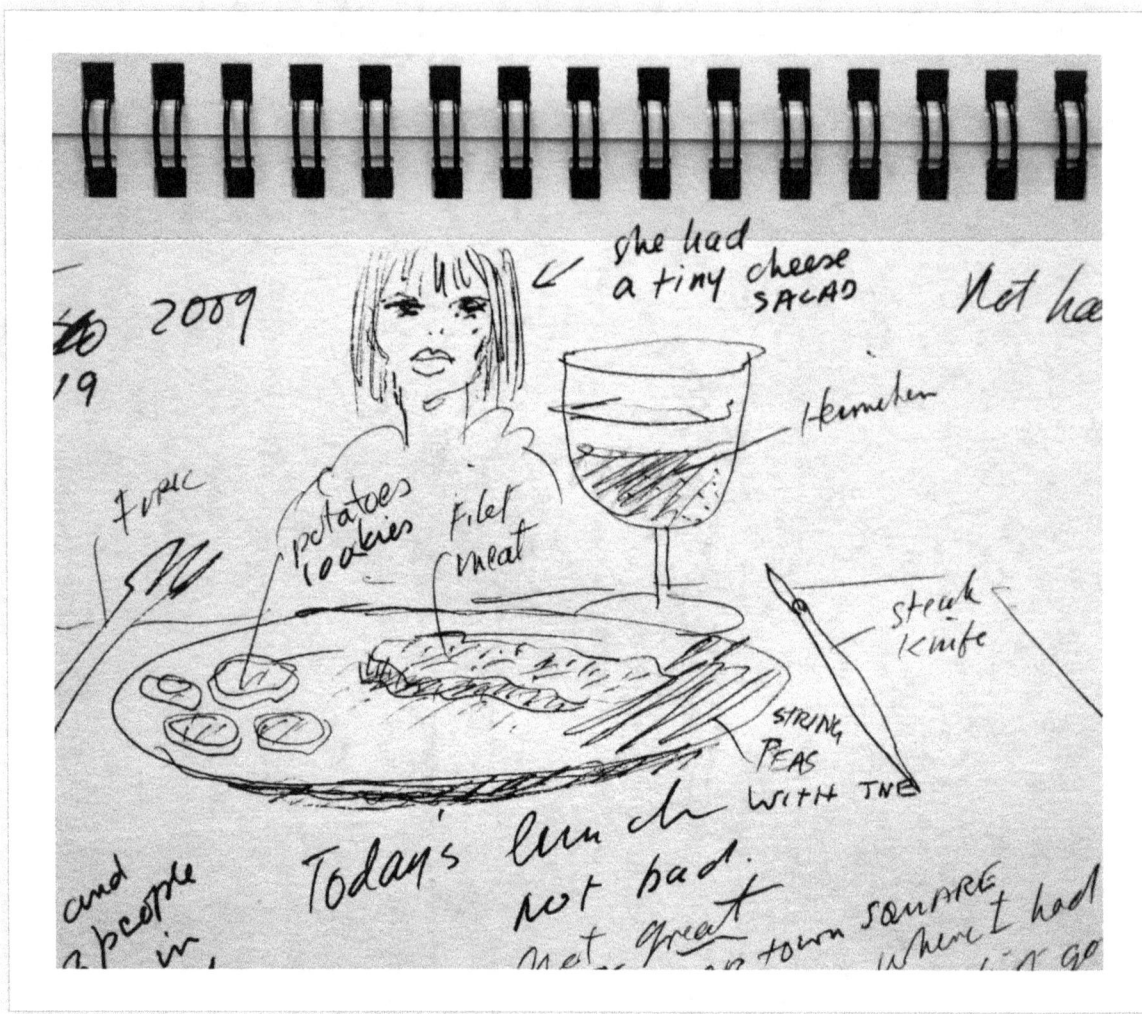

Today's lunch, not bad.

Another fine day in the old town.

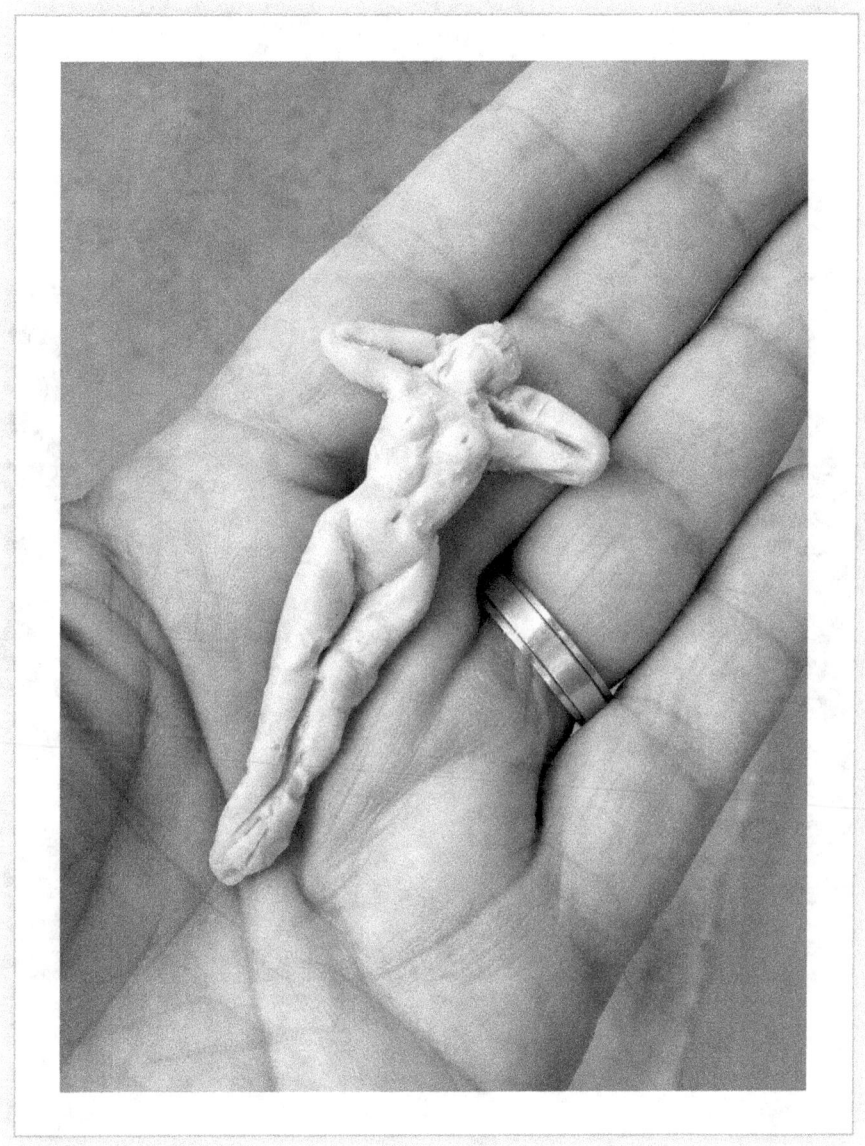

Handy nude.

You never know when you need one.

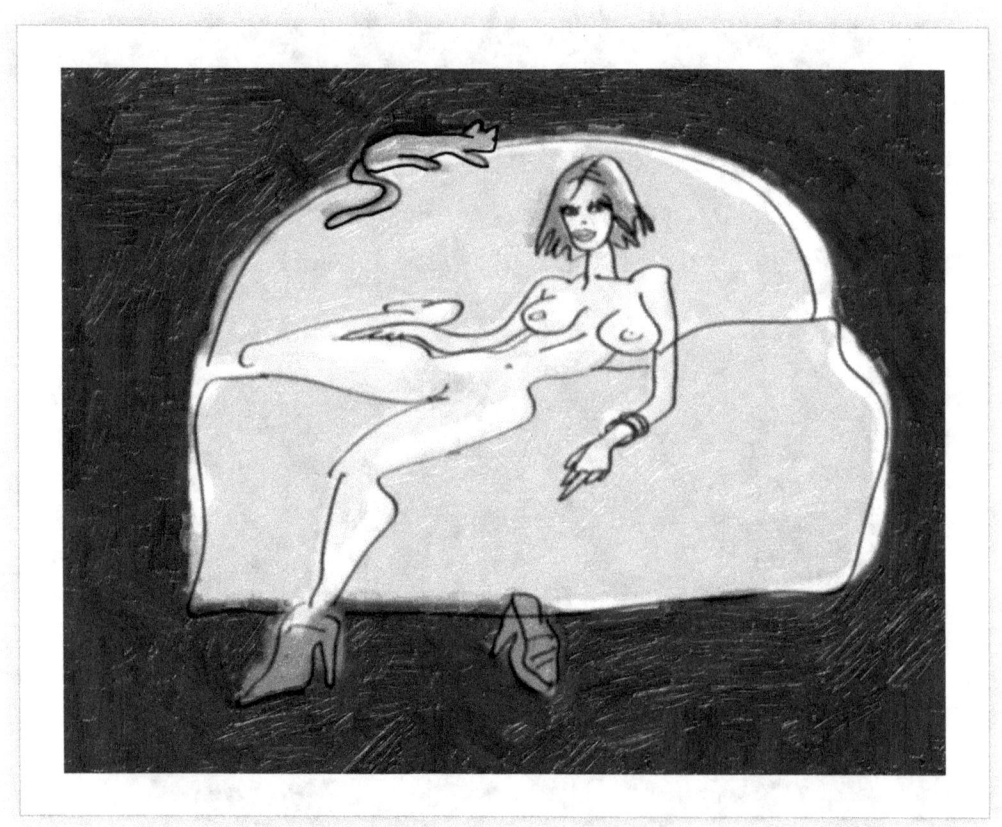

Cat on a couch.

This woman has one leg on the floor just in case.

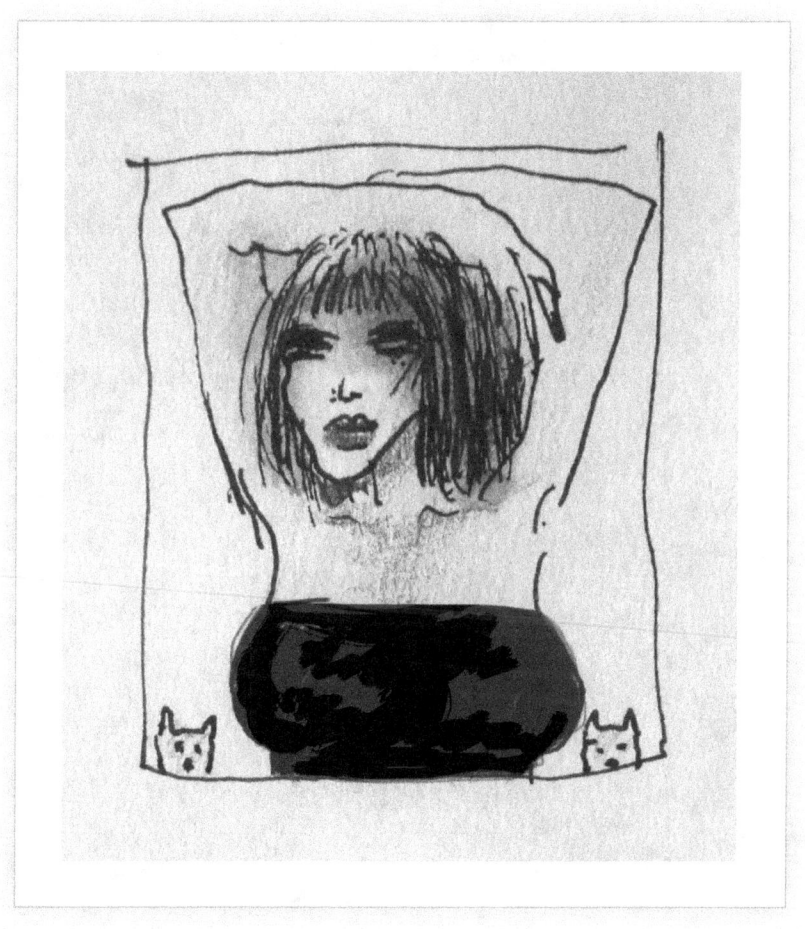

Double dogs.

Man's best friends.

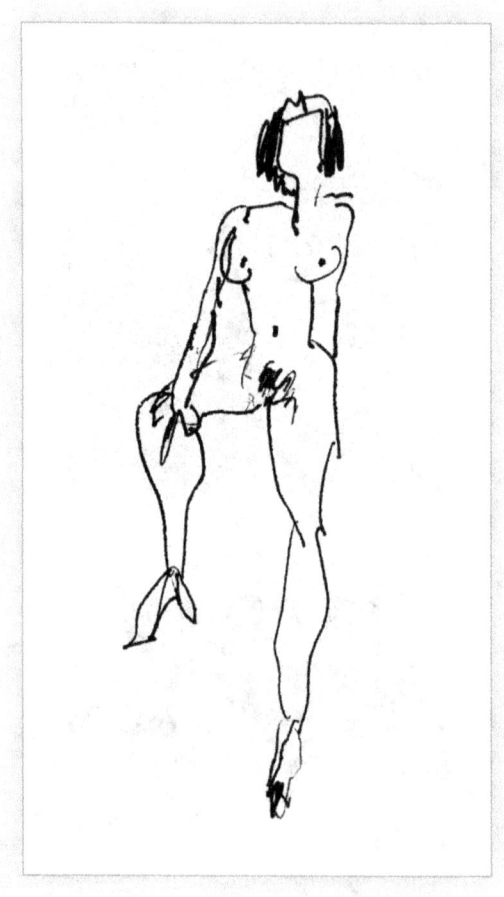

Quick Friday nude.

Drawn on a Friday.

Took about 4.5 seconds to complete.

Had a cup of tea afterwards.

I needed it.

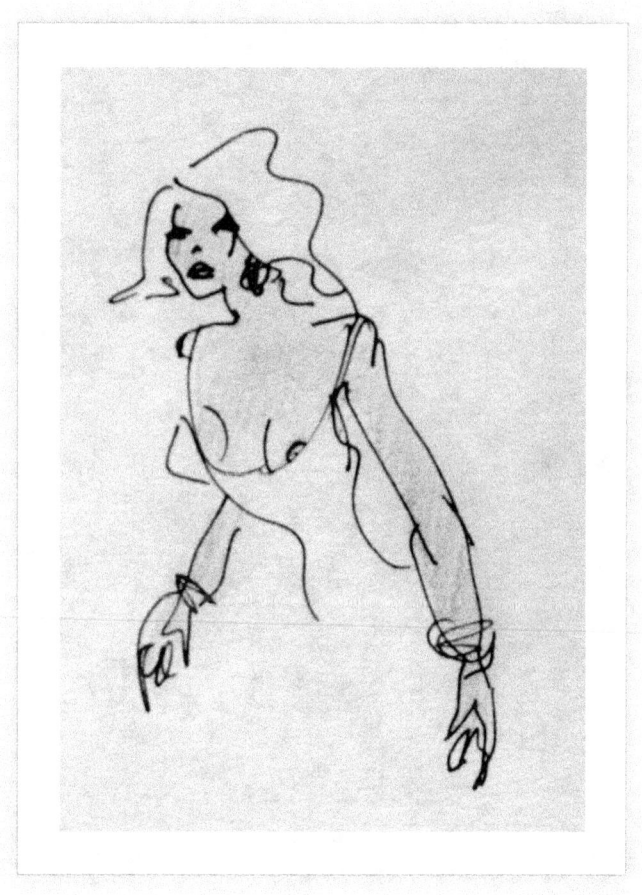

Slight wardrobe malfunction.

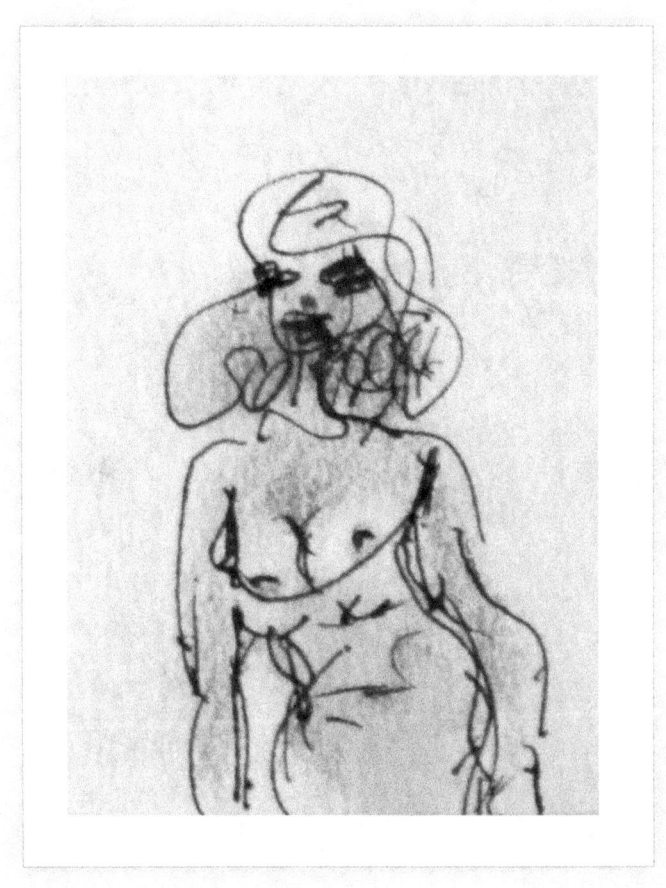

Major wardrobe malfunction.

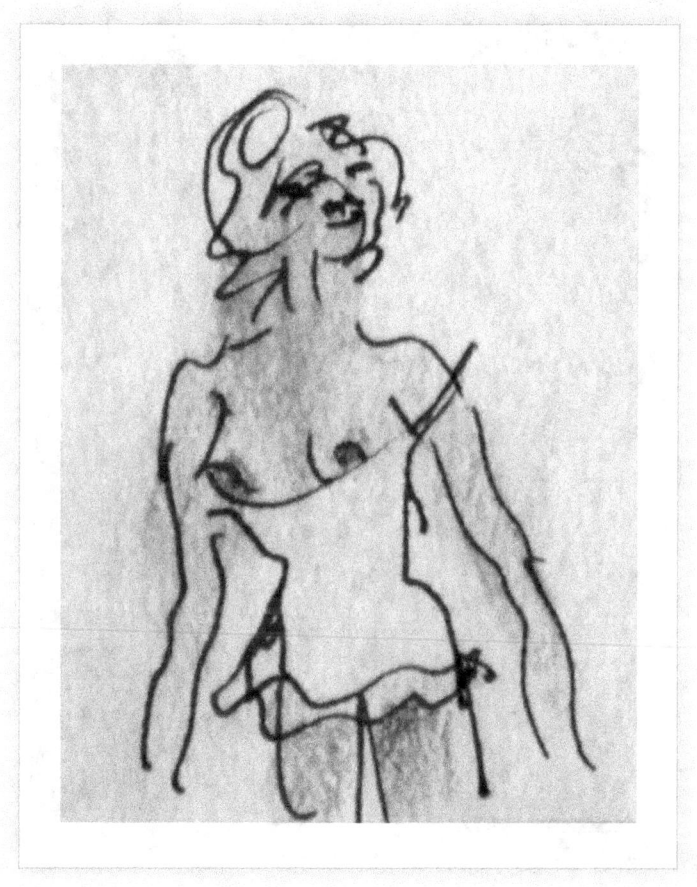

Catastrophic wardrobe malfunction.

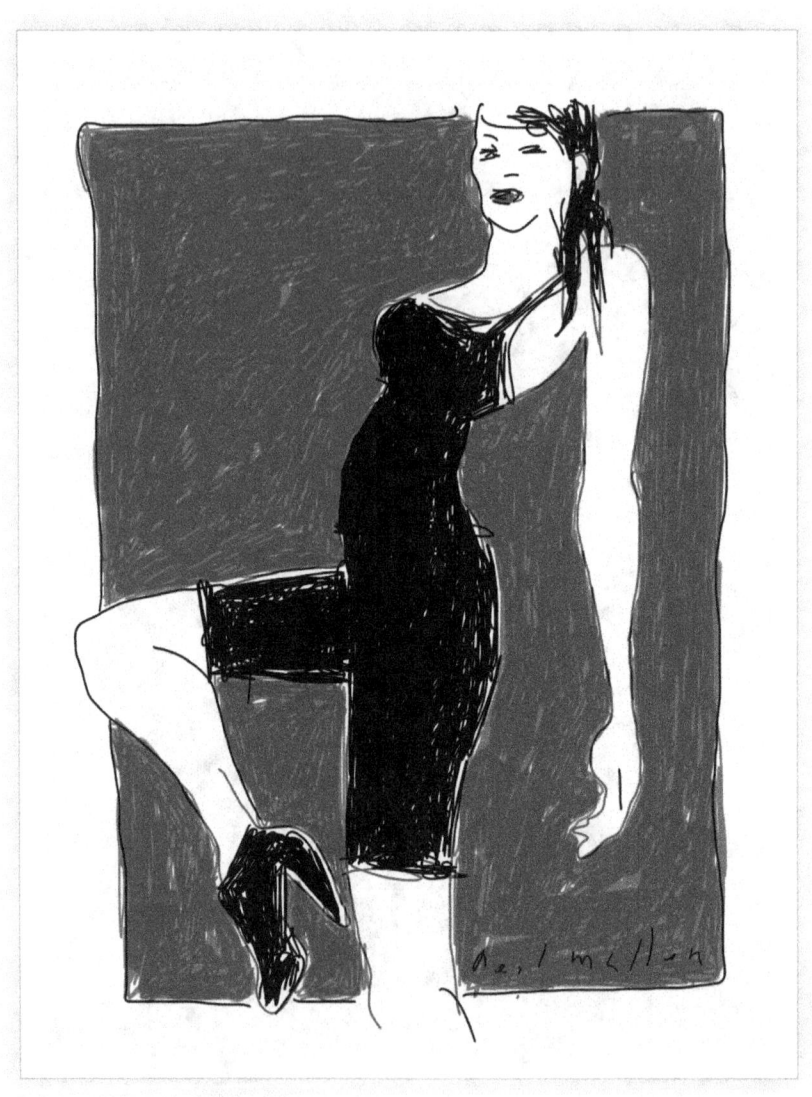

Taking a step in the right direction.

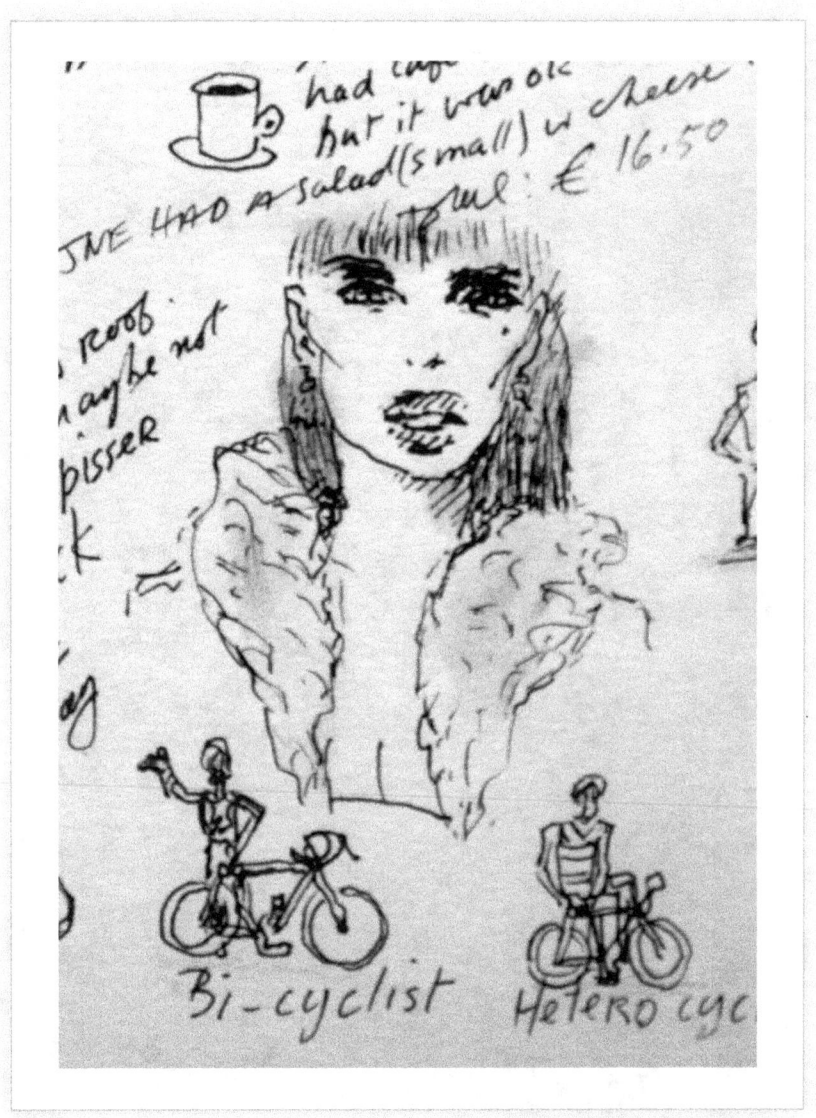

She had a small salad with cheese.

This drawing comes with 2 extra bicyclists.

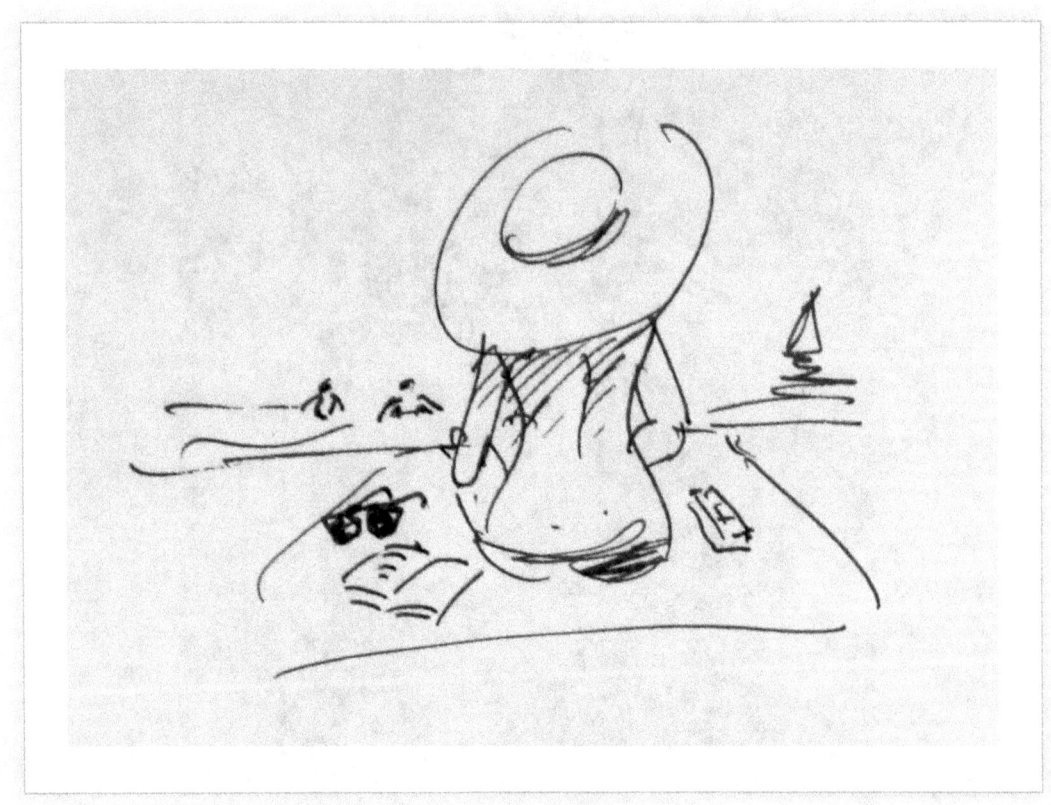

Well undressed.

On the beach in the South of France.

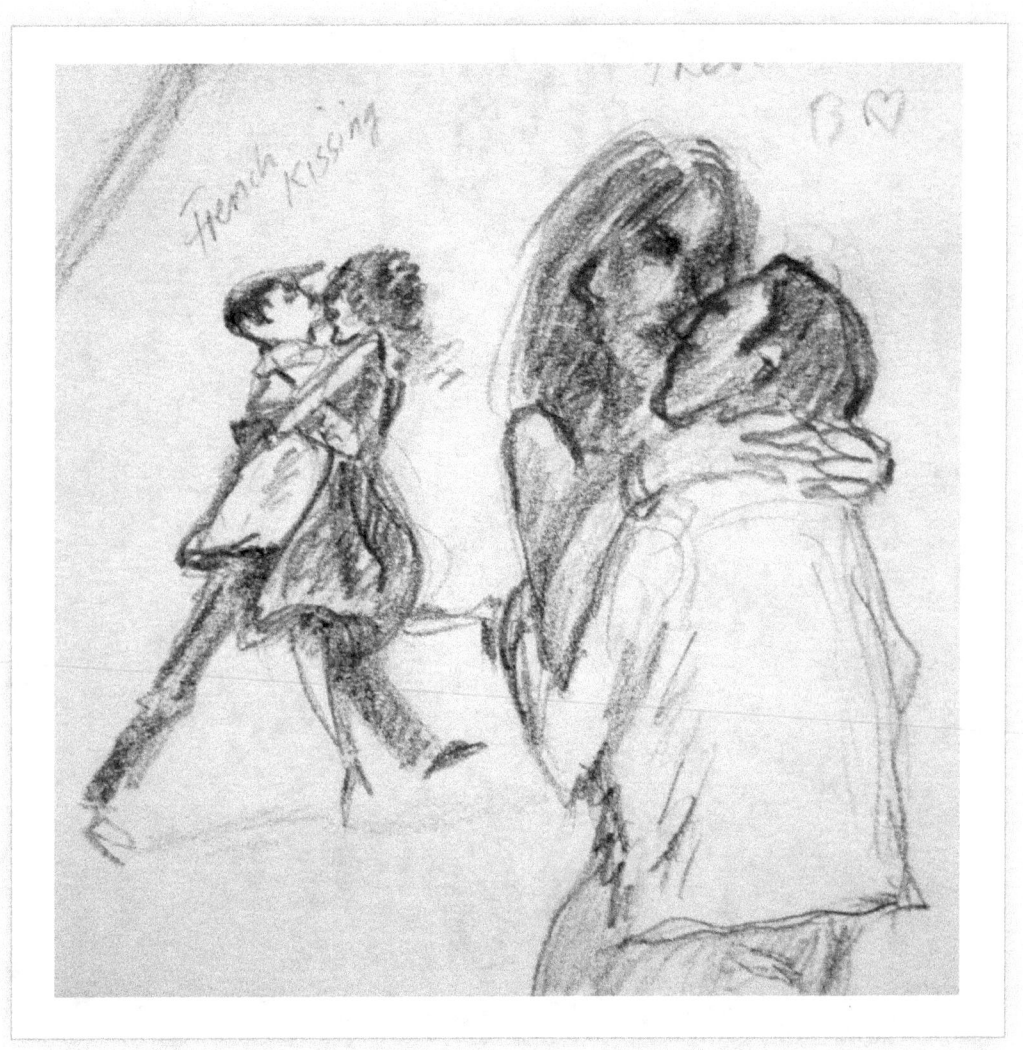

French, kissing.

Often practised by the French.

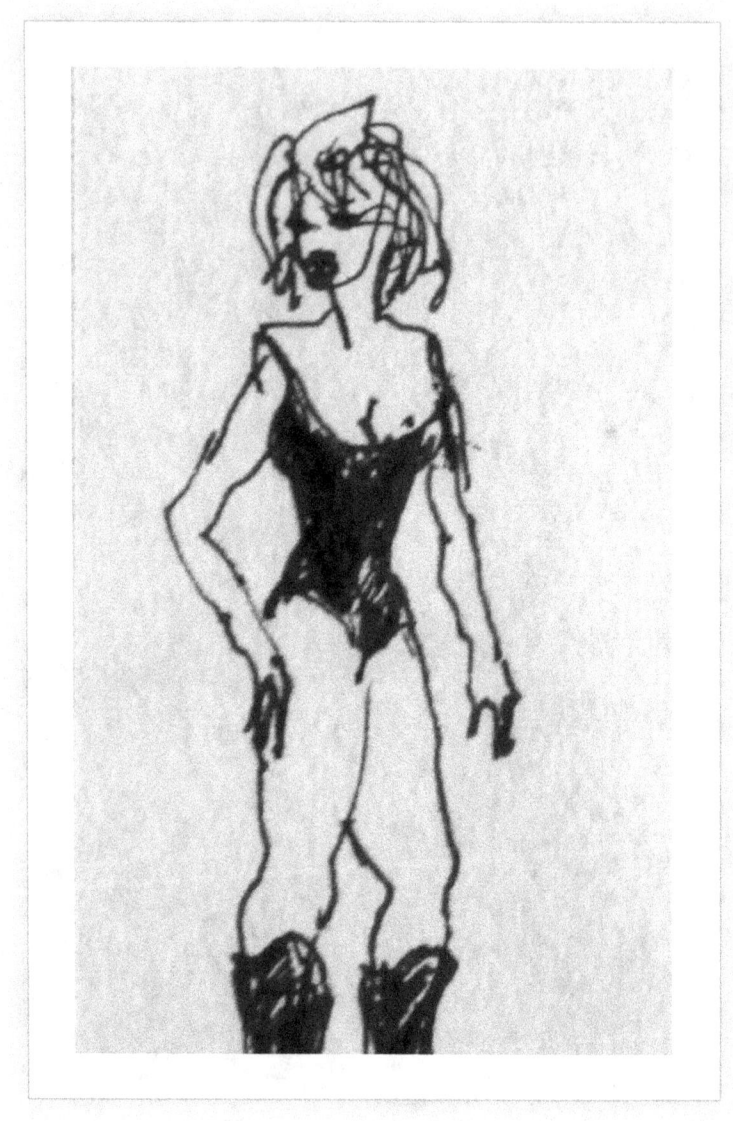

Puss in cowboy boots.

What is it about cowboy boots?

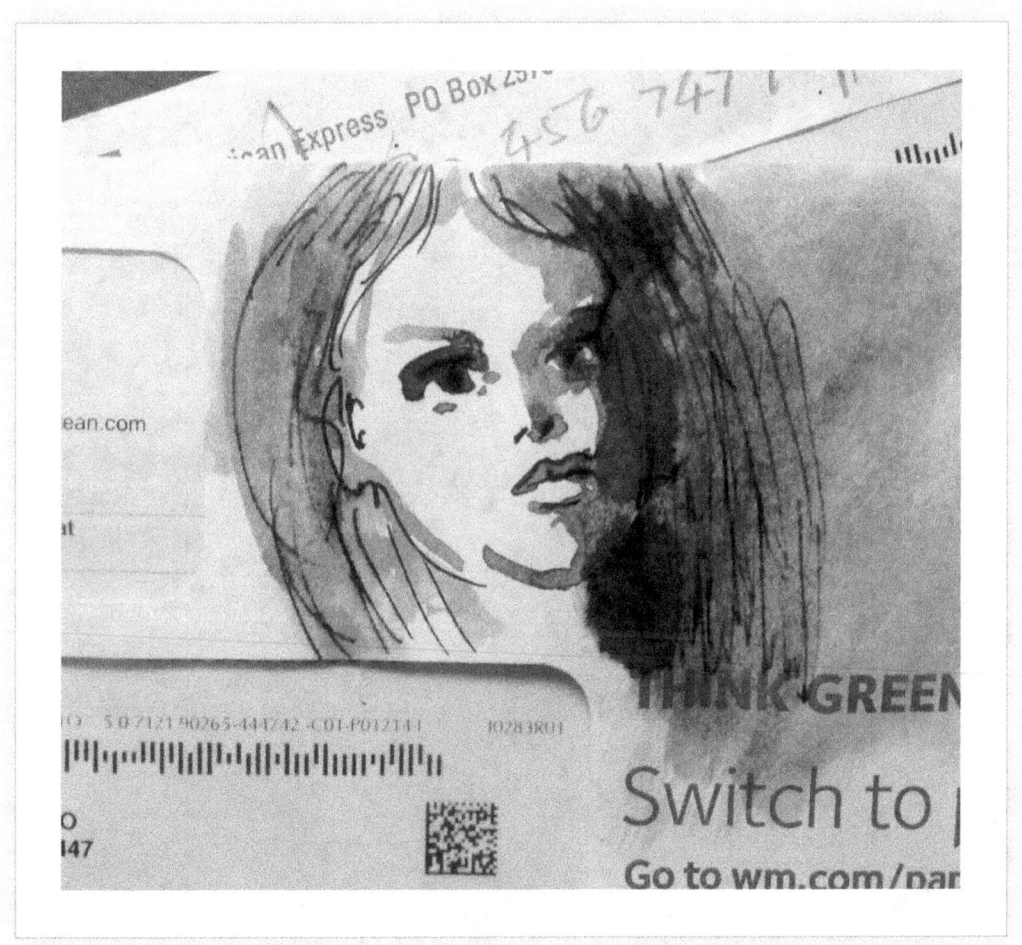

Girl on a bill.

That reminds me. Pay up or else.

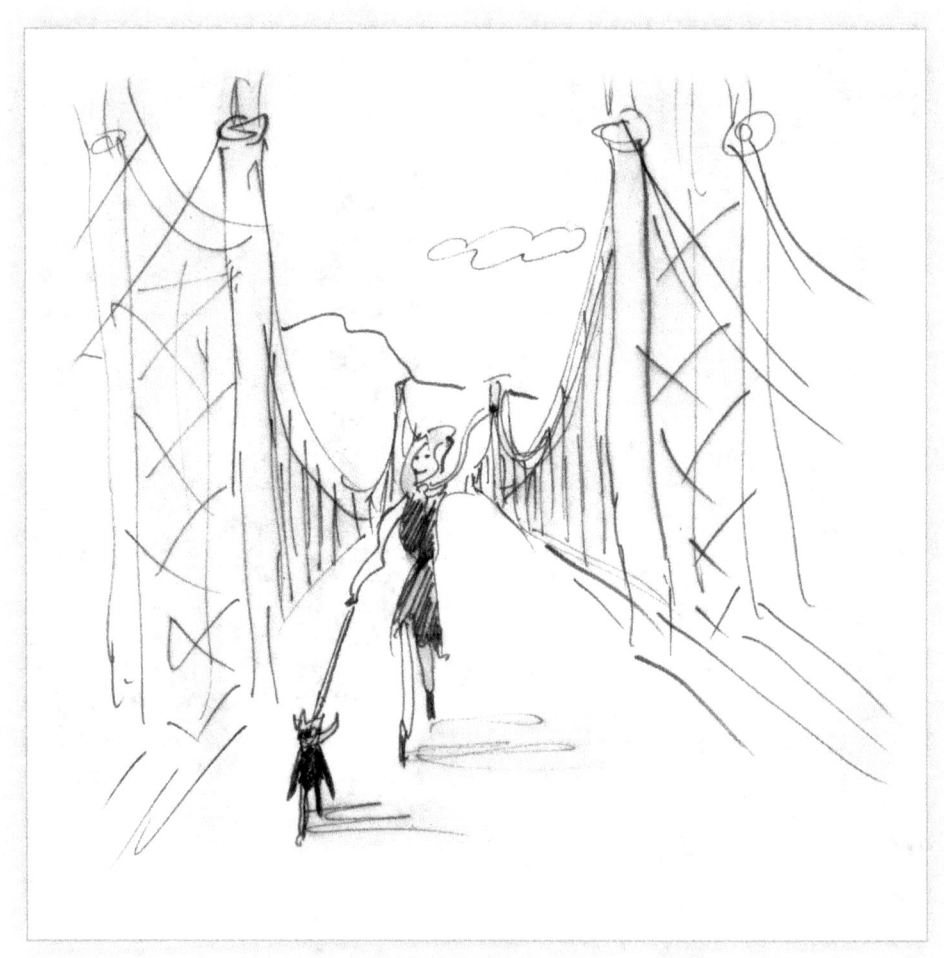

A golden gait.

Nothing prettier than seeing a woman walk the walk.

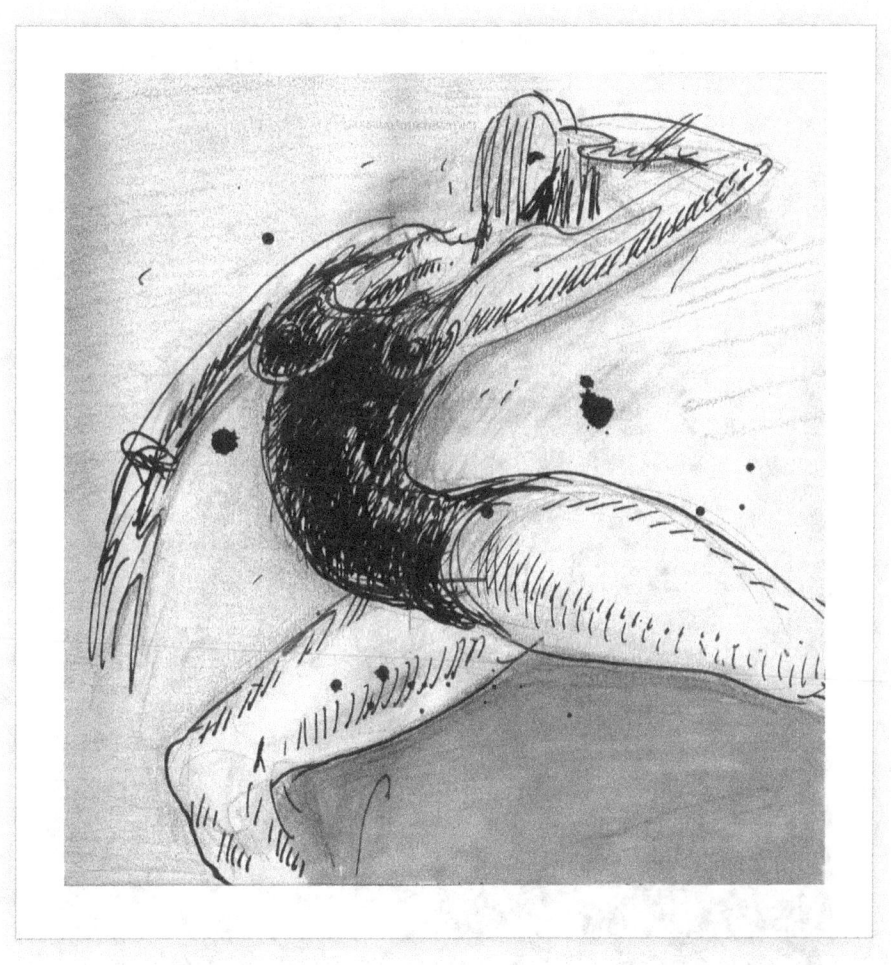

Stretch sketch.

She said: "My thighs need work"

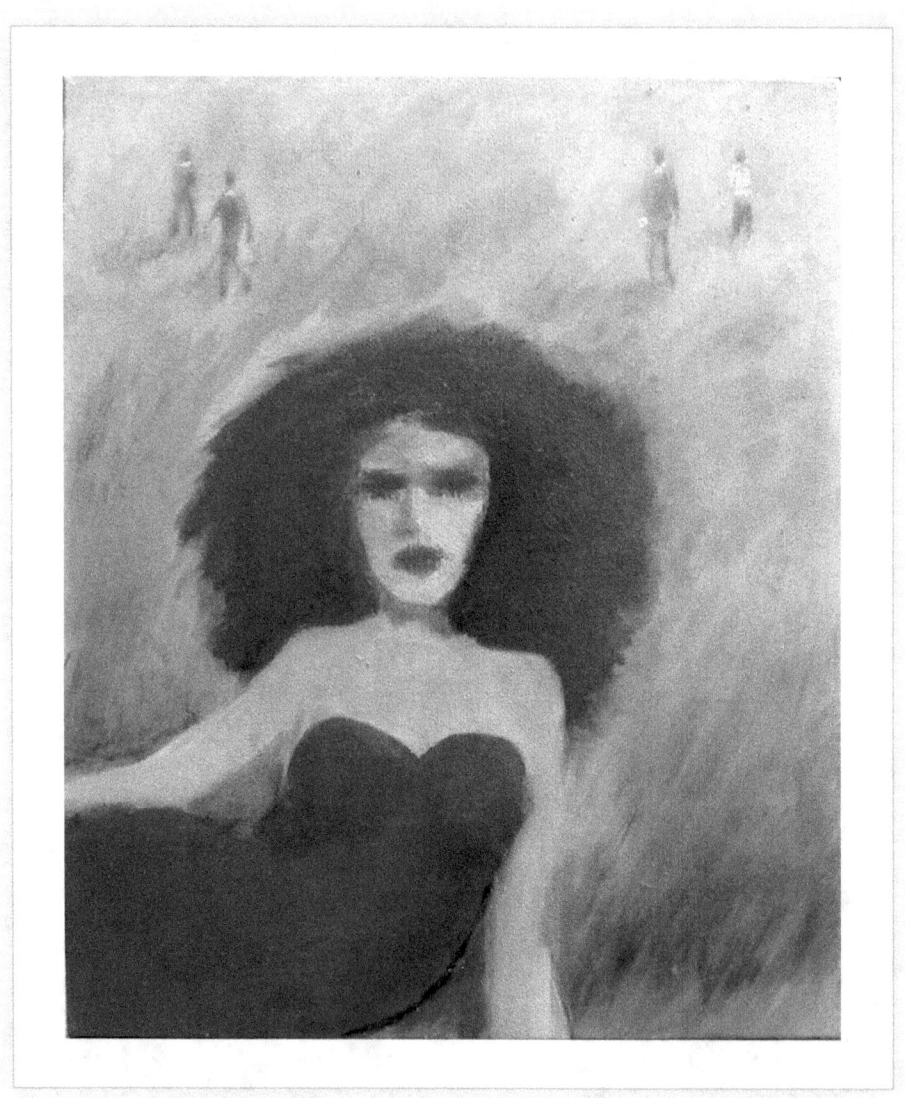

Waiting for her to do something.

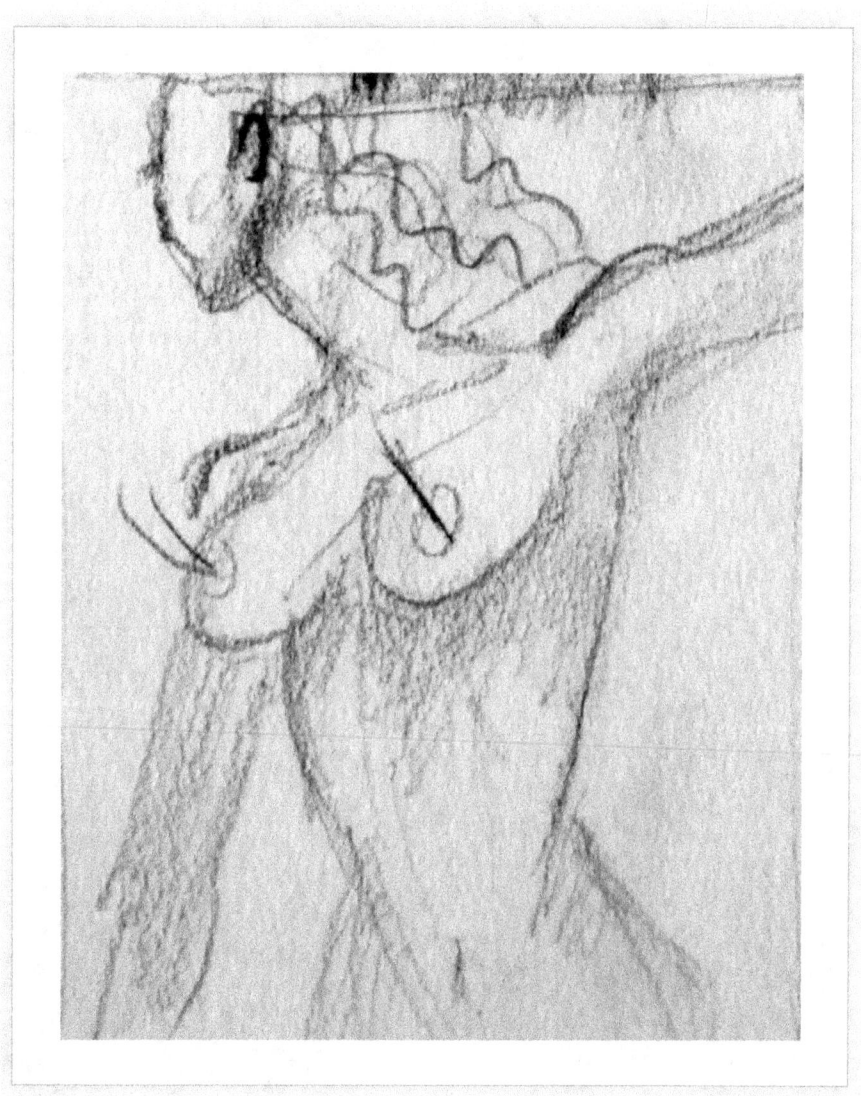

Perky nude.

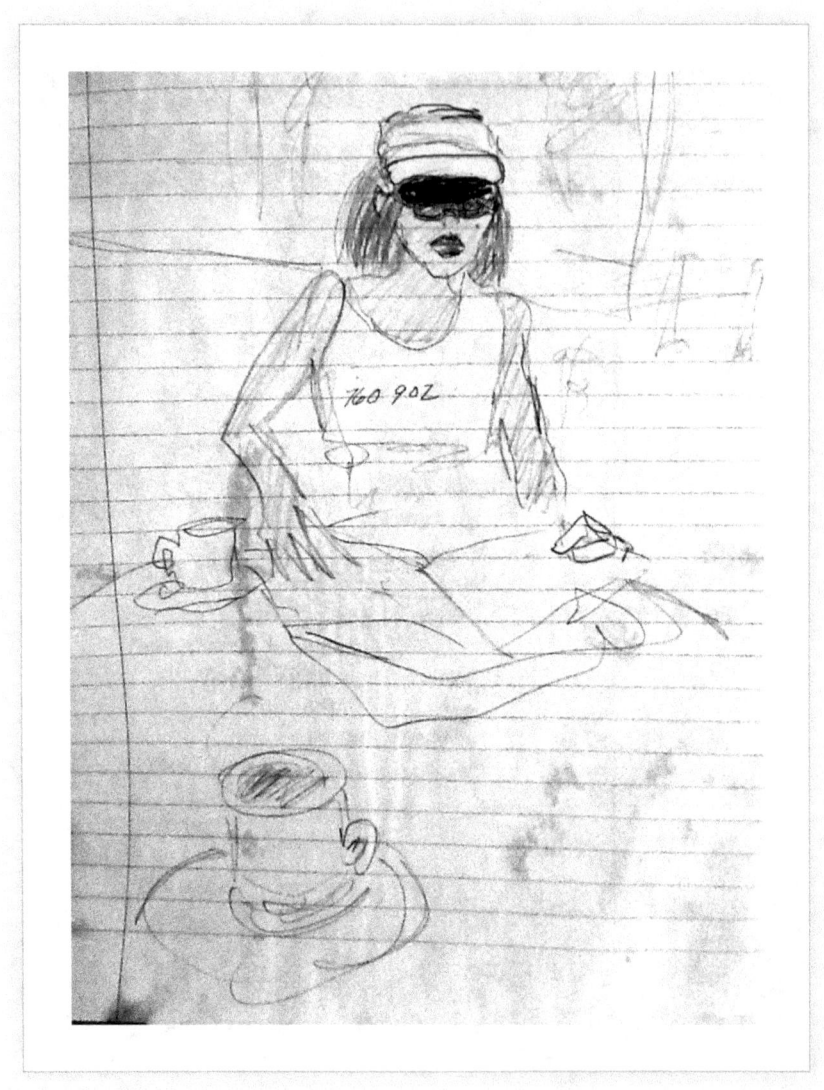

2 Lattes with Jennie.

She ordered hers with extra foam, as she always does.

Mine arrived with extra foam too, but it did not upset me too much.

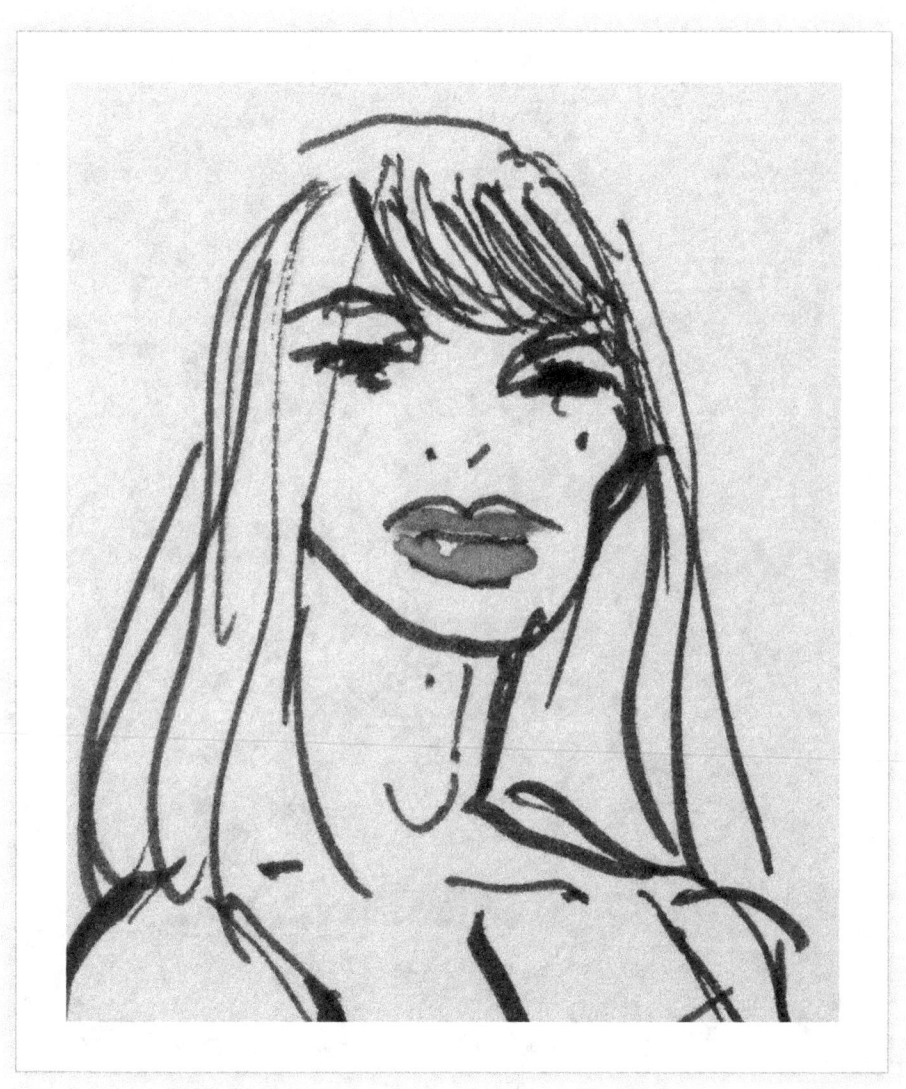

If lips could talk.

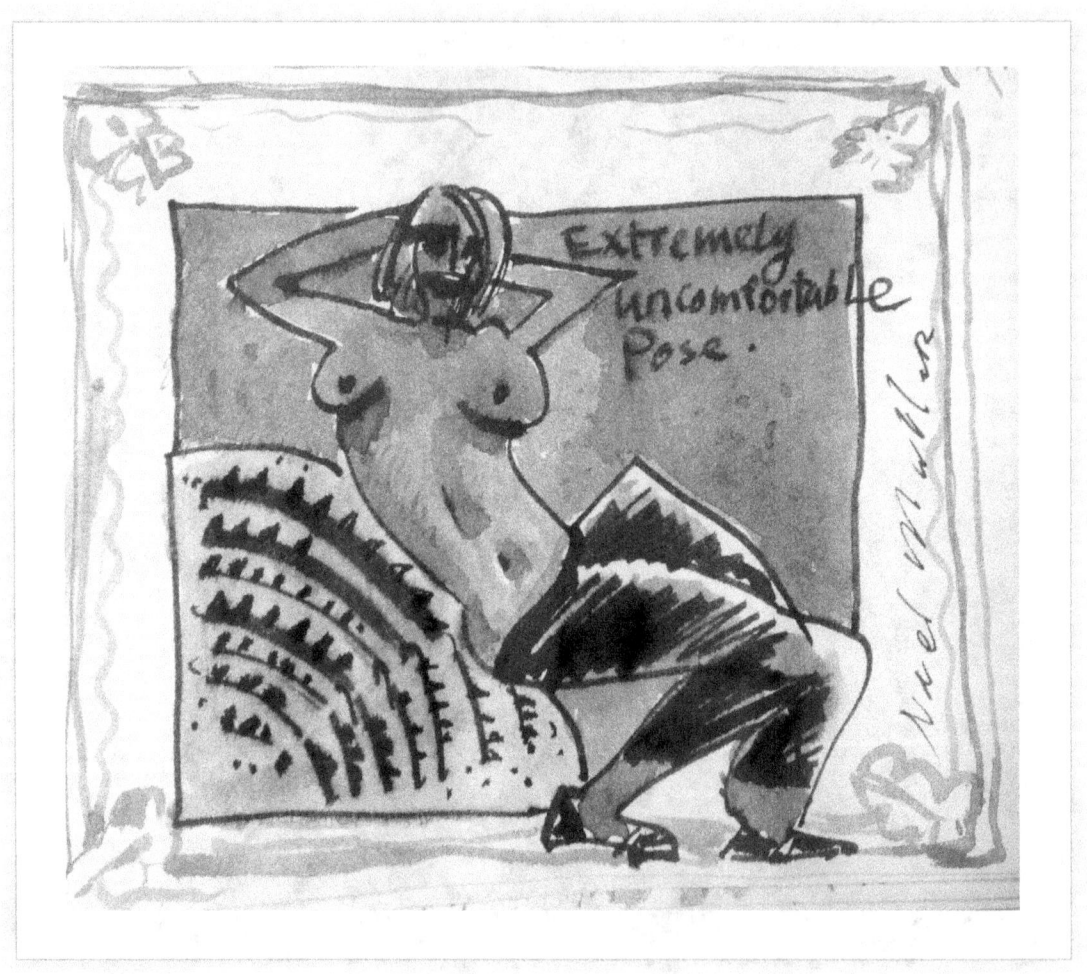

Extremely uncomfortable pose.

Thank God she had a secret extra muscle to keep this pose under control.

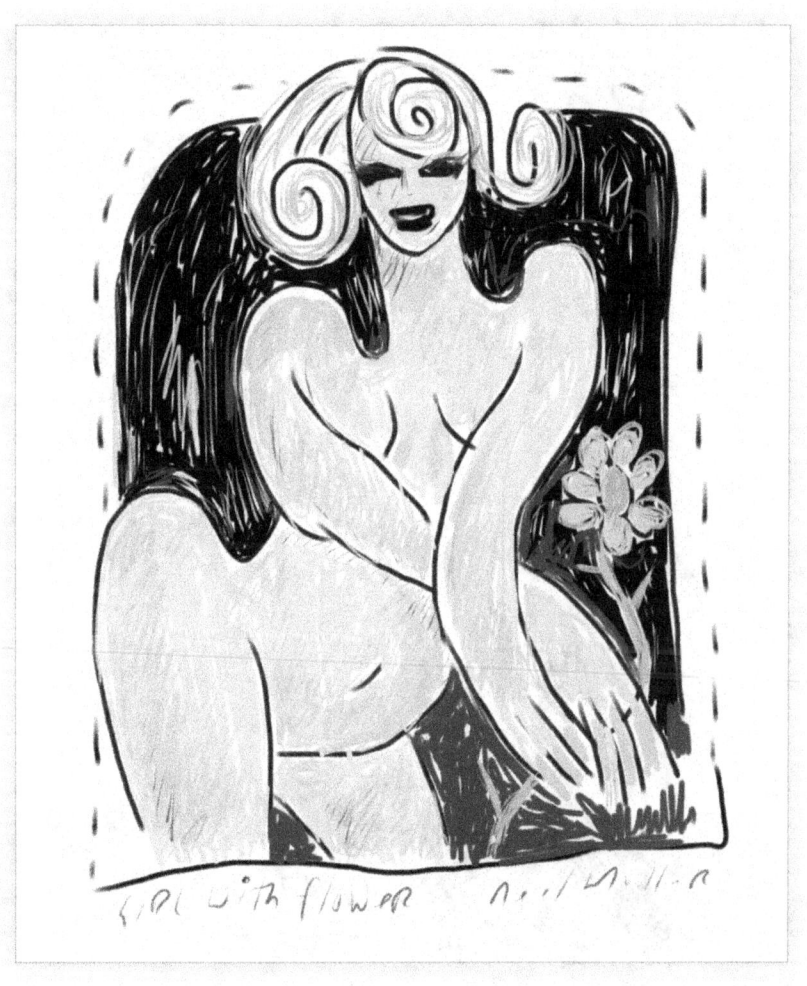

Women love flowers.

A simple fact of life.

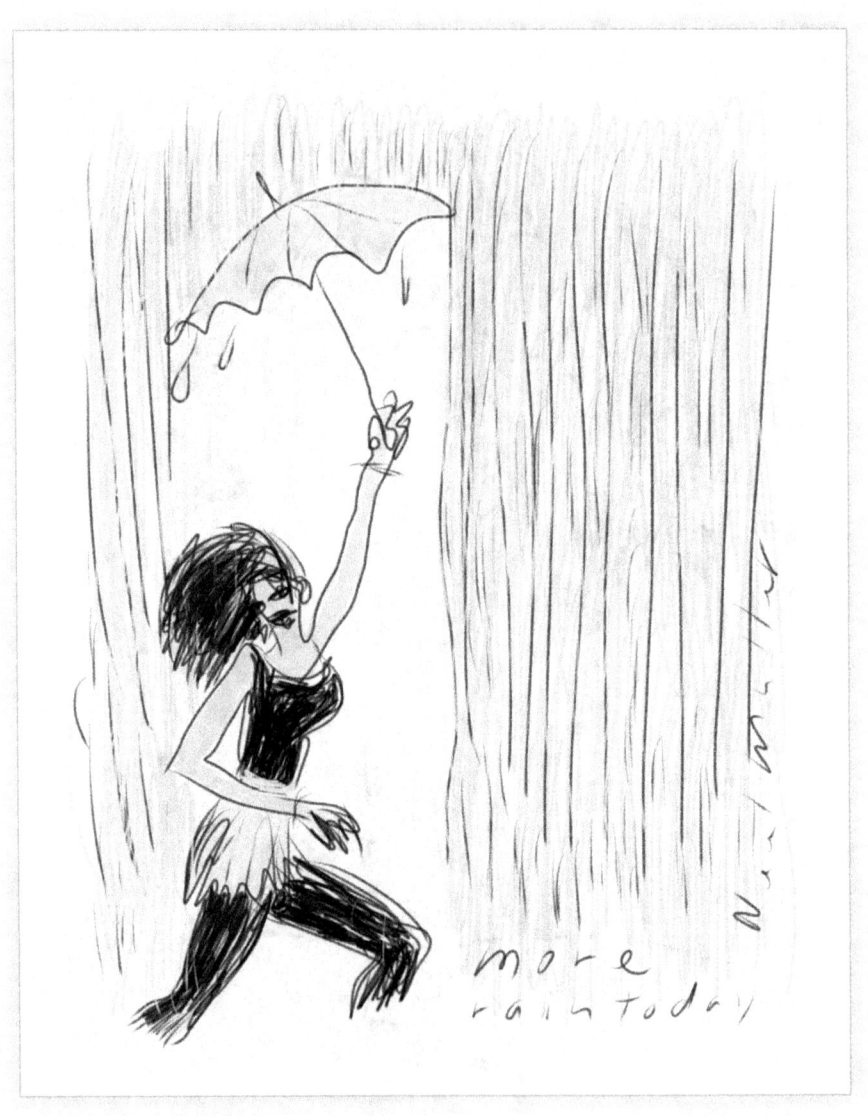

More rain today.

Not a problem..

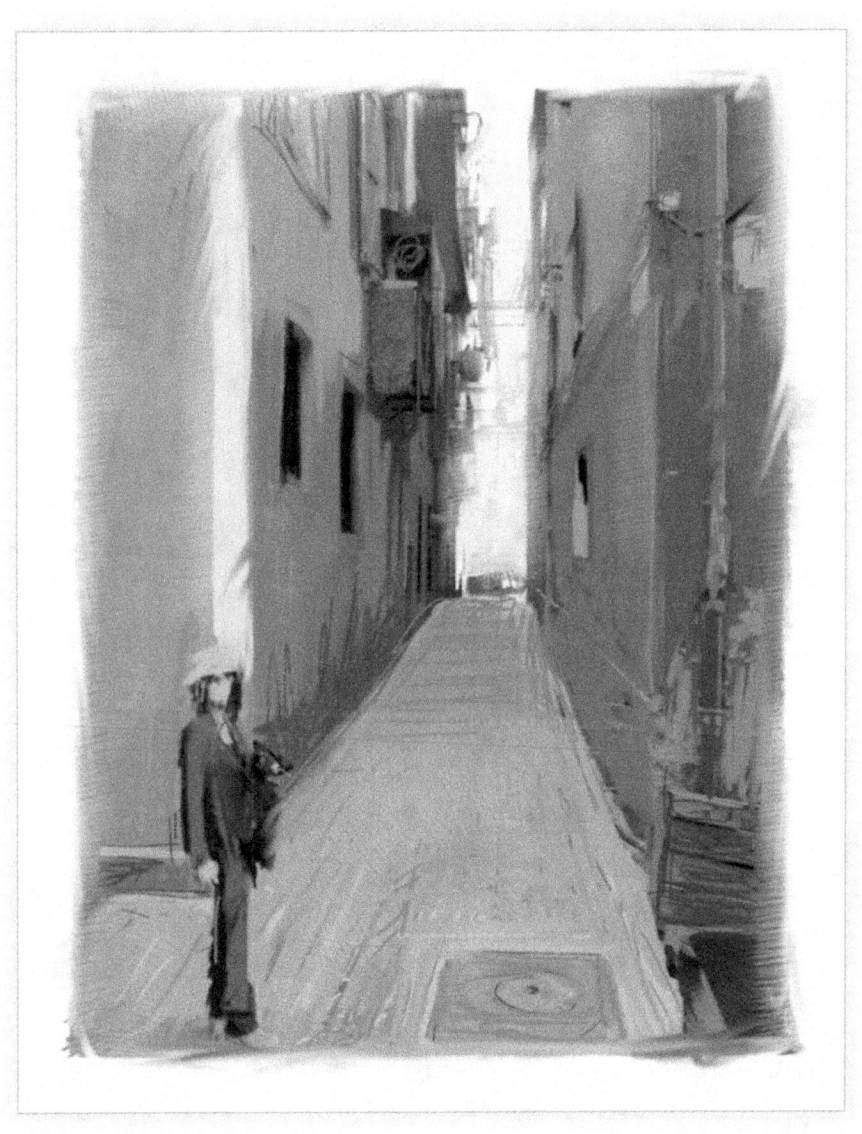

Nice woman in Nice.

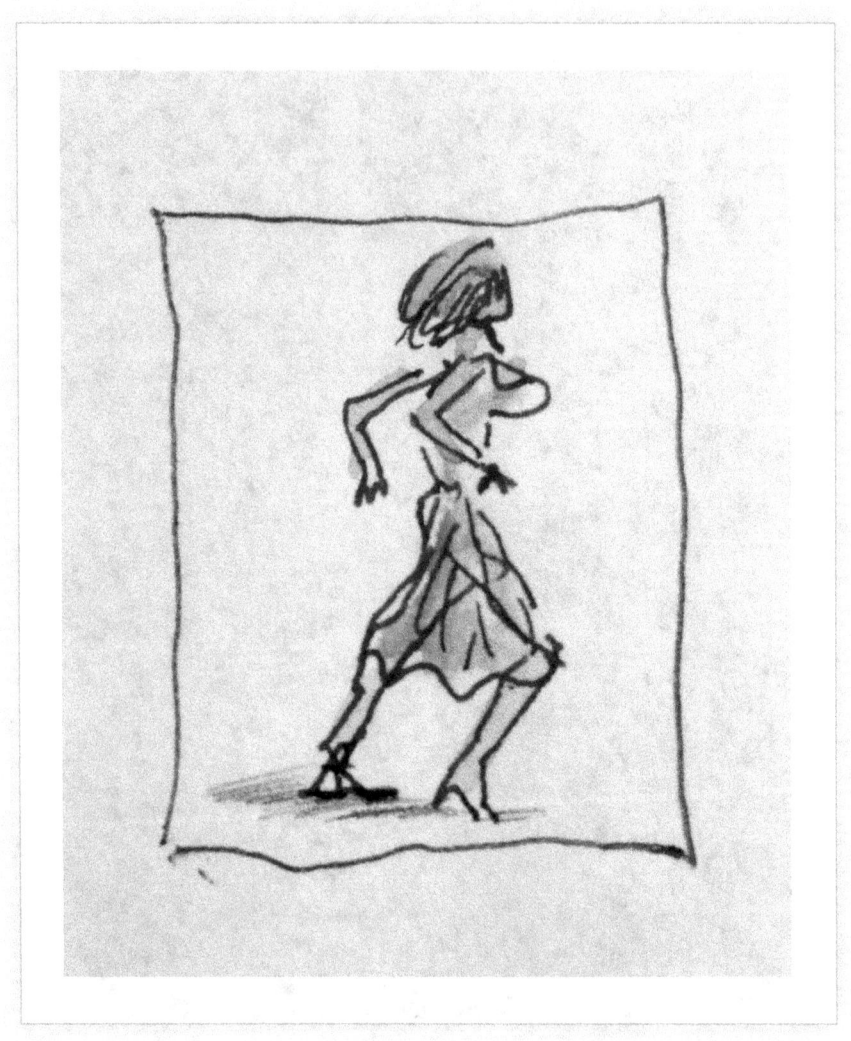

Woman demonstrating her excellent motor skills.

Essential in this day and age.

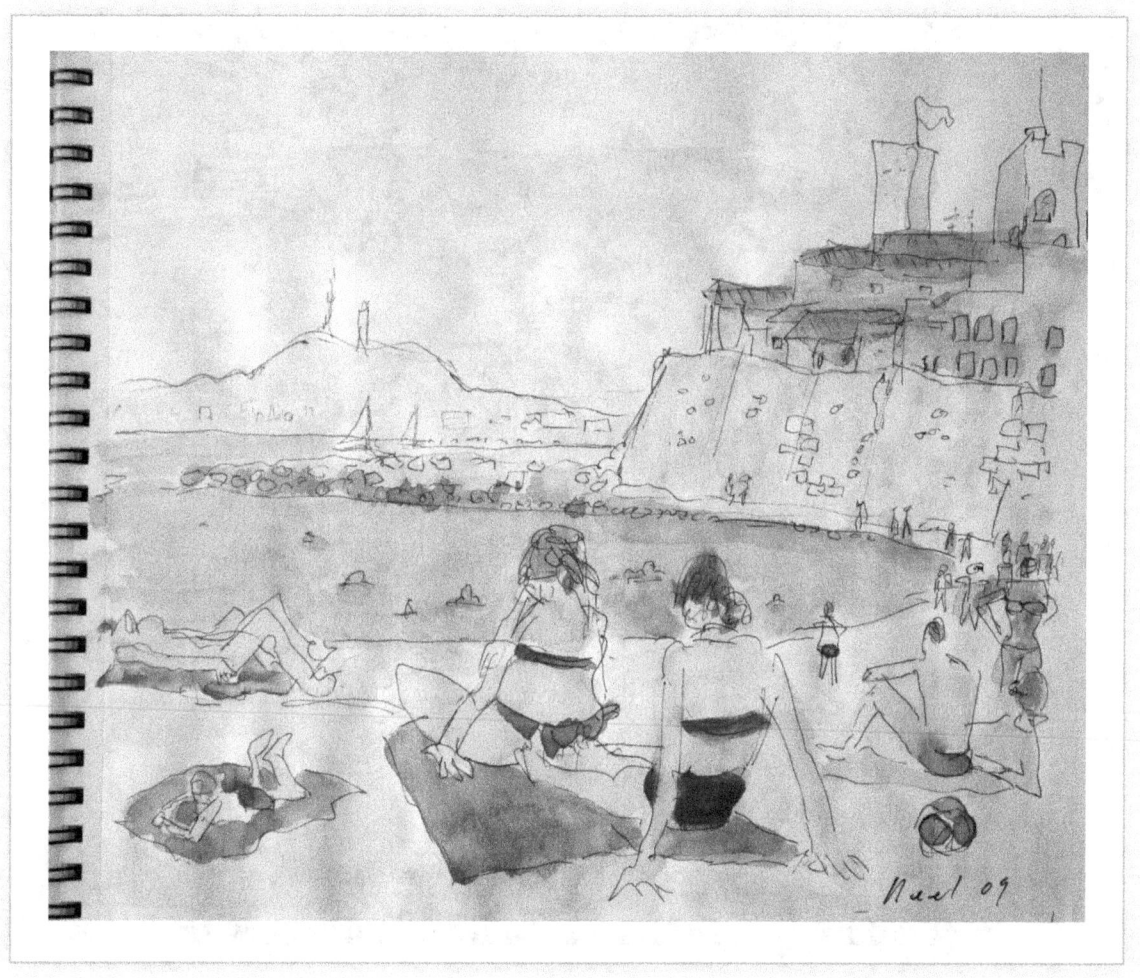

Ladies on the beach.

Chatting up a storm, no doubt.

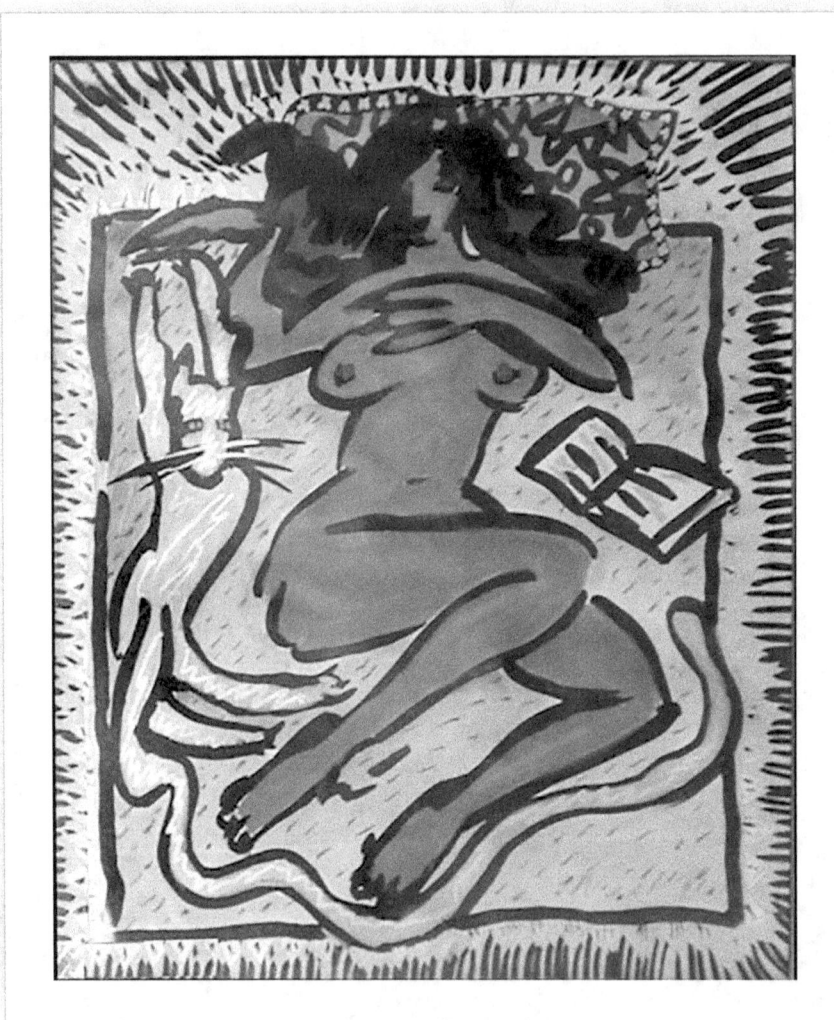

Cat nappers.

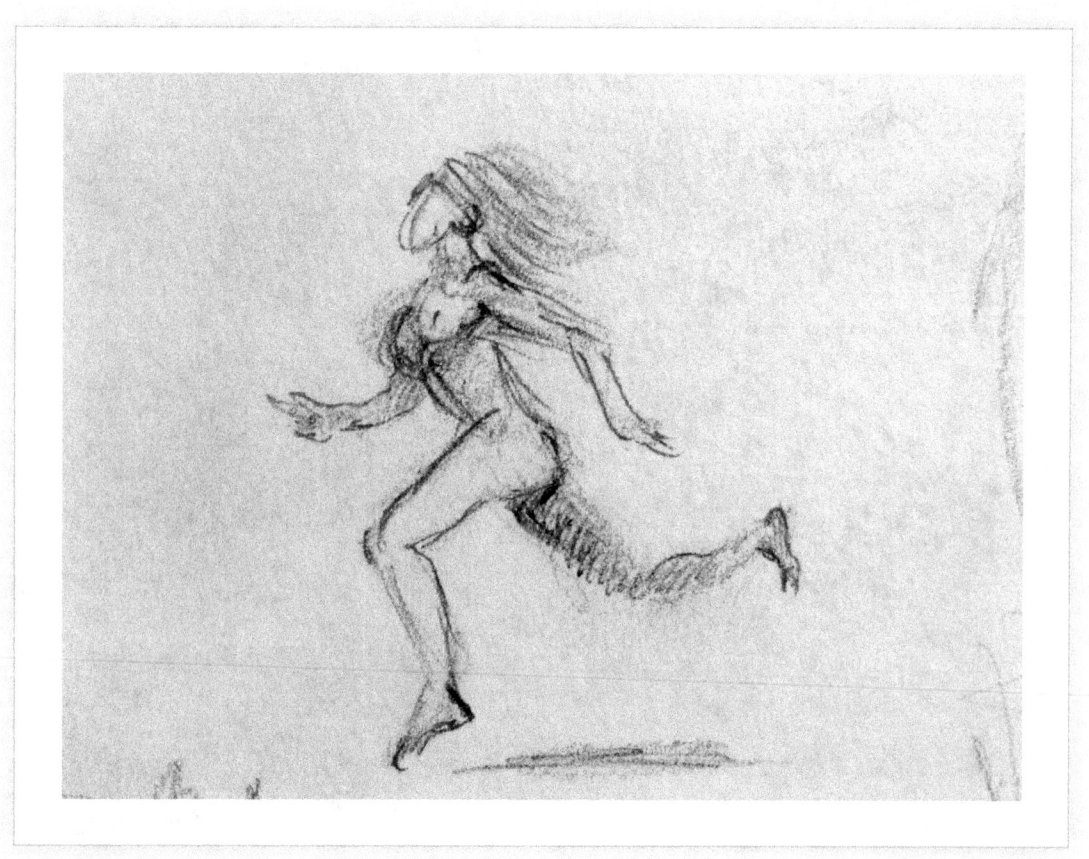

Nude on the run.

She made a sharp right turn right after I drew this.

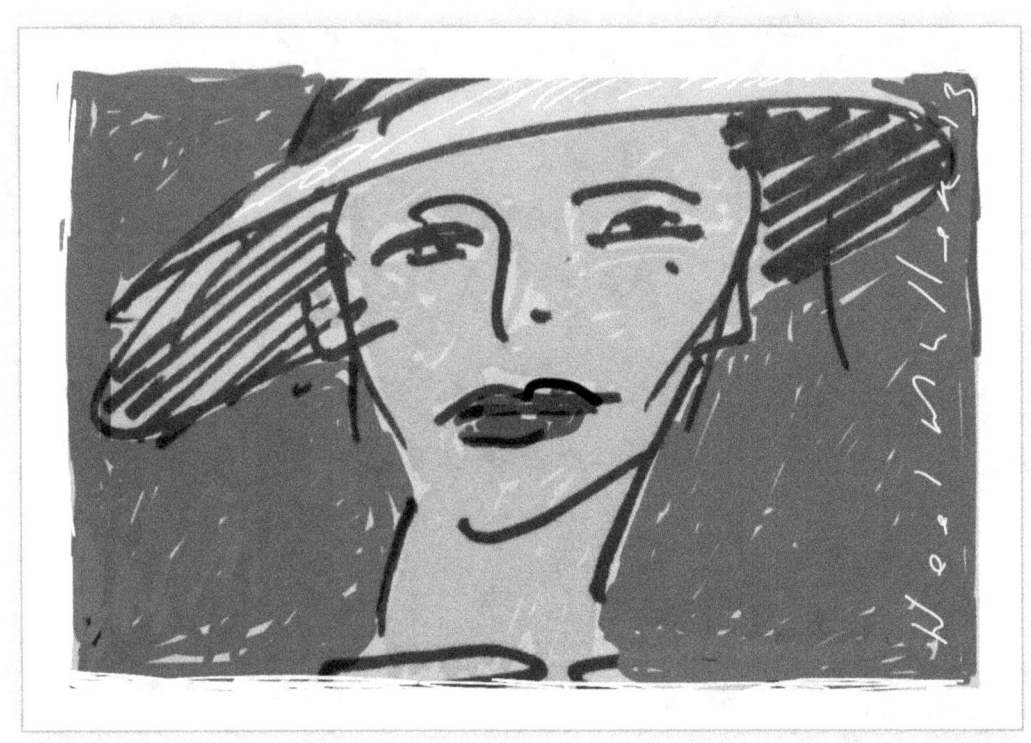

The hat wears her well.

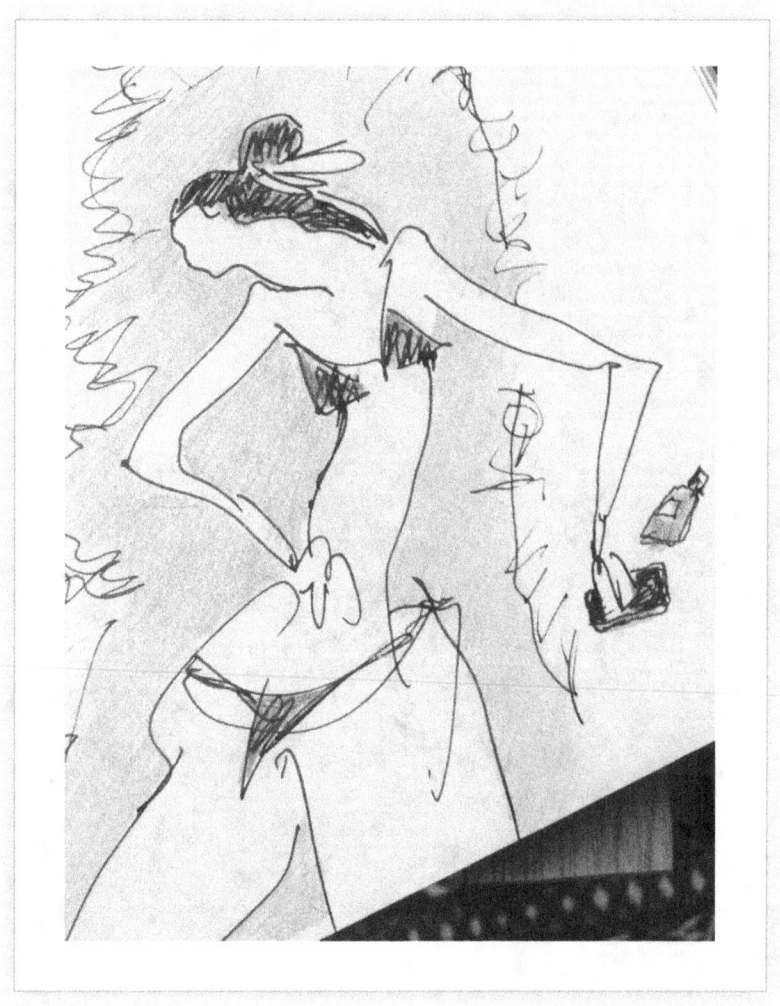

Woman about to maker a phone call on her smart phone.

Does that mean she's smart?

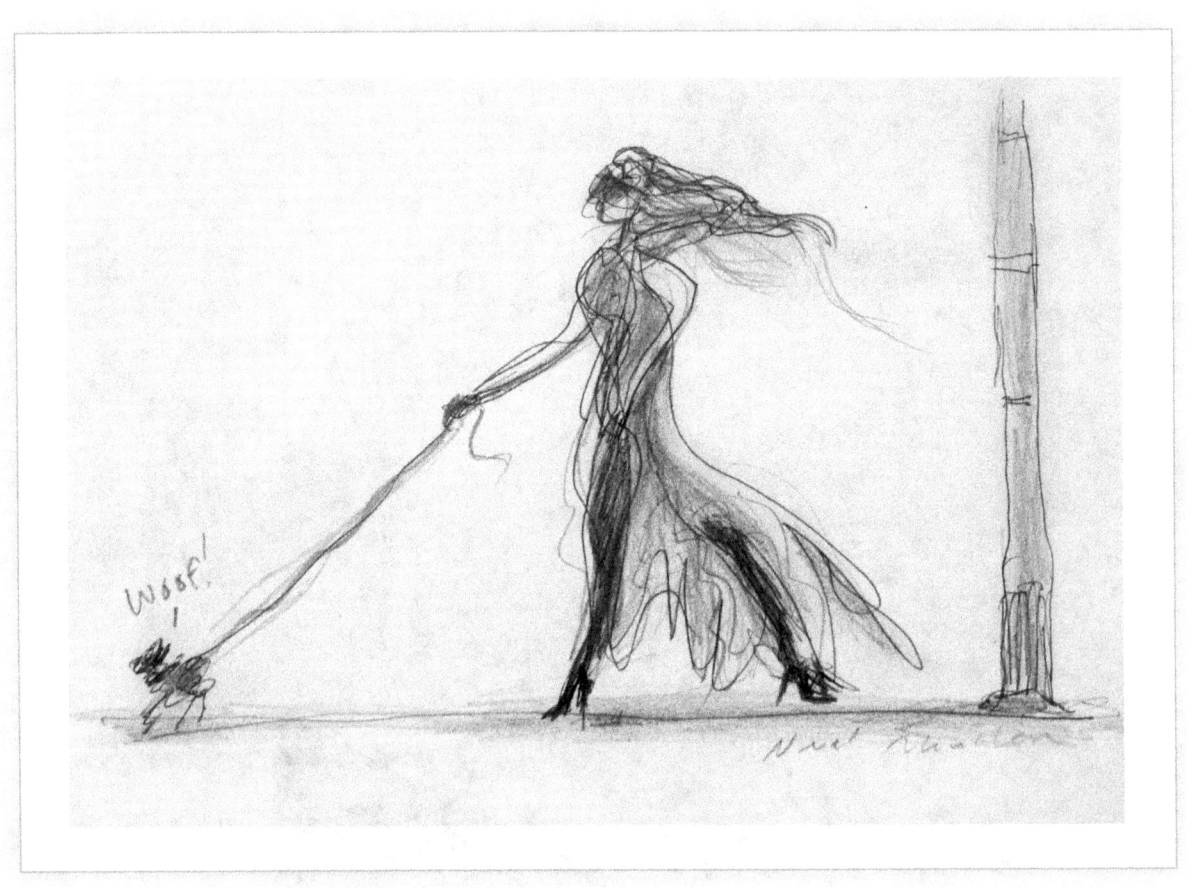

Woman waiting for her dog to stop barking.

She's a yapper. The dog I mean.

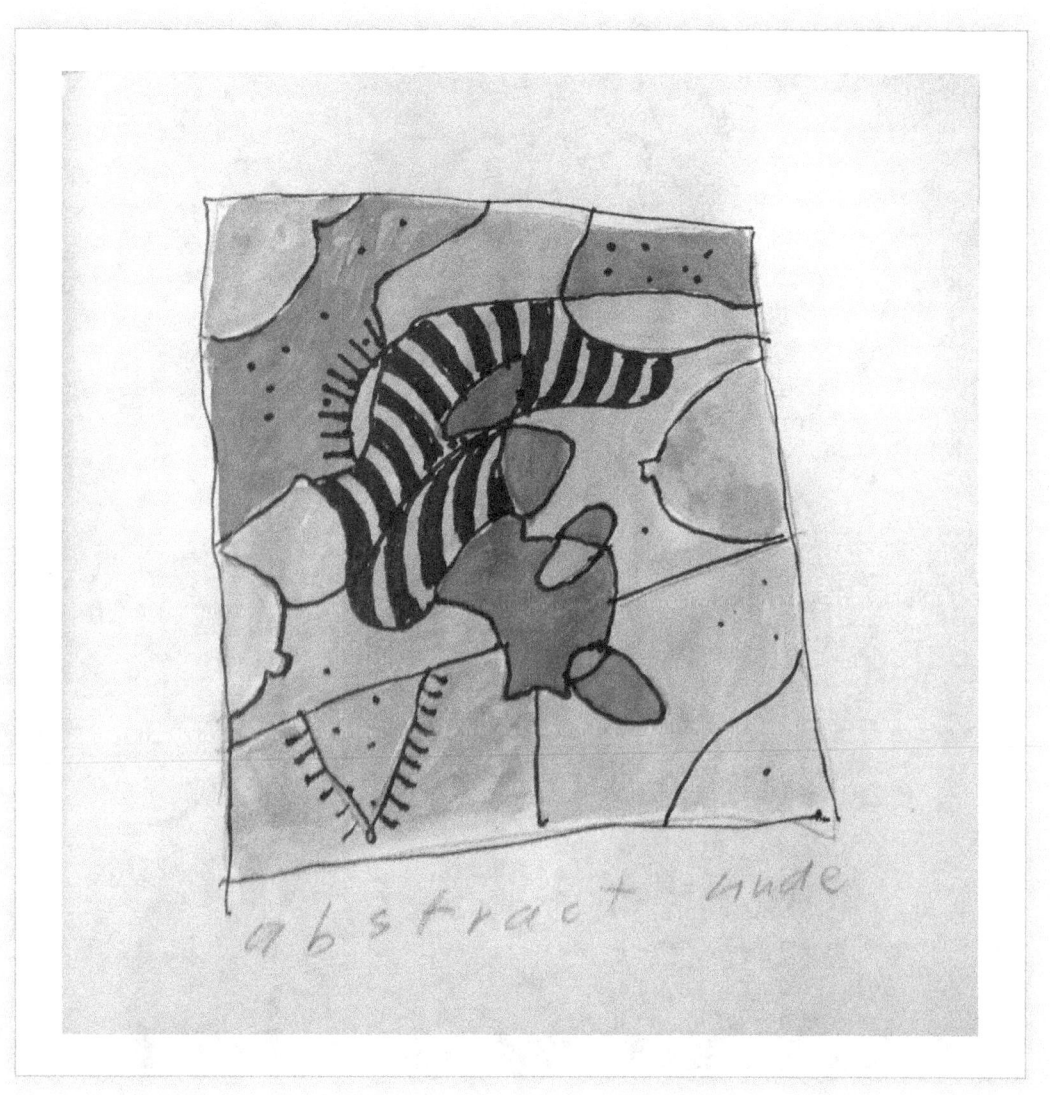

Abstract nude.

Did I leave off any parts?

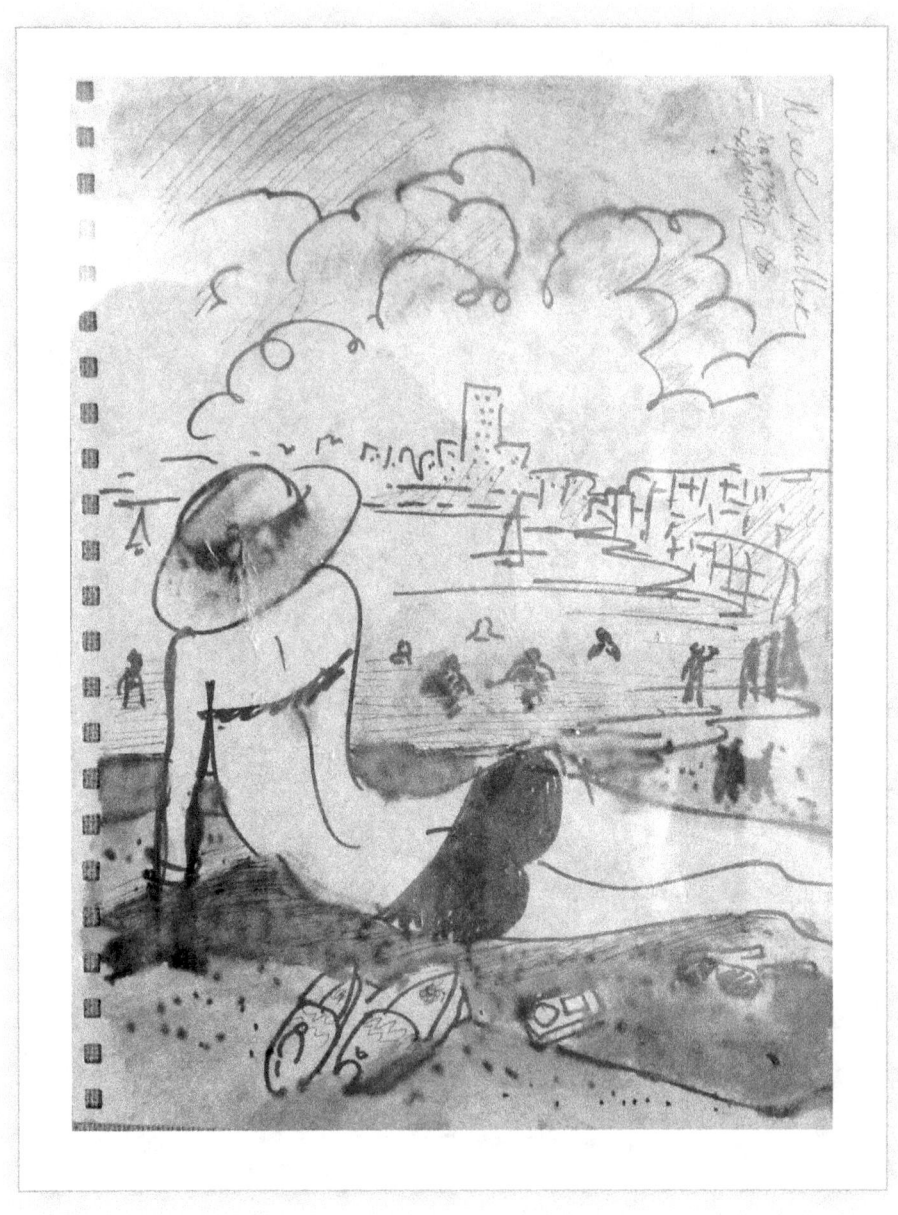

Beached girl.

Someone said her sandals look fishy.

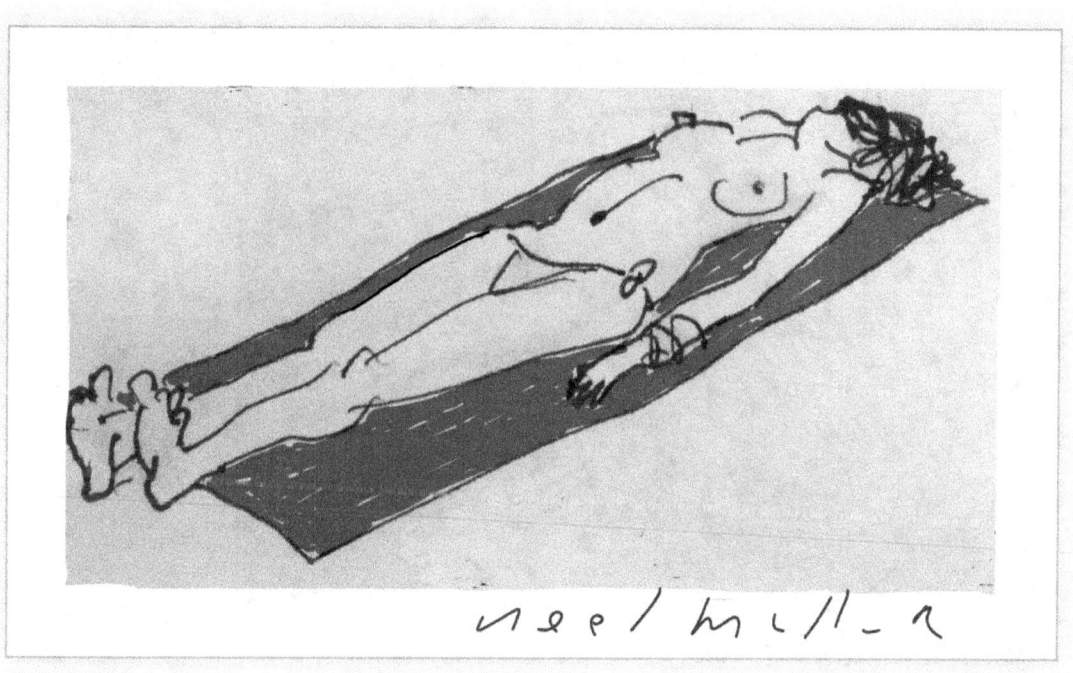

Flat on her back in the back.

What are backyards for?

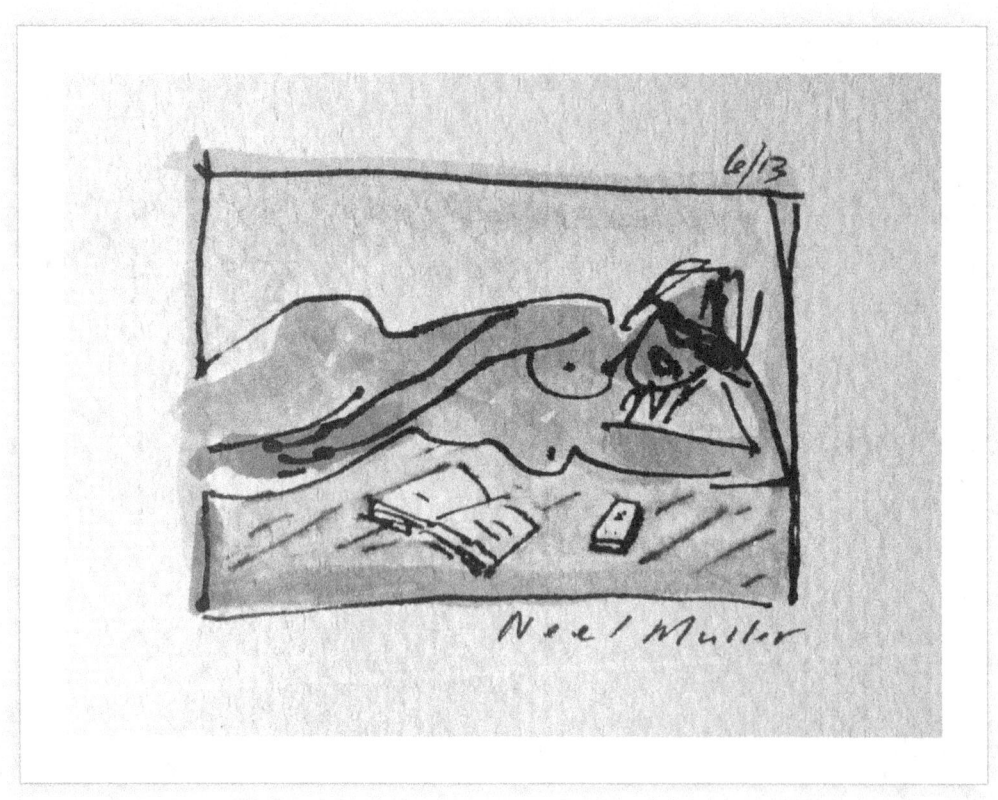

Bookworm.

Some women read a lot.

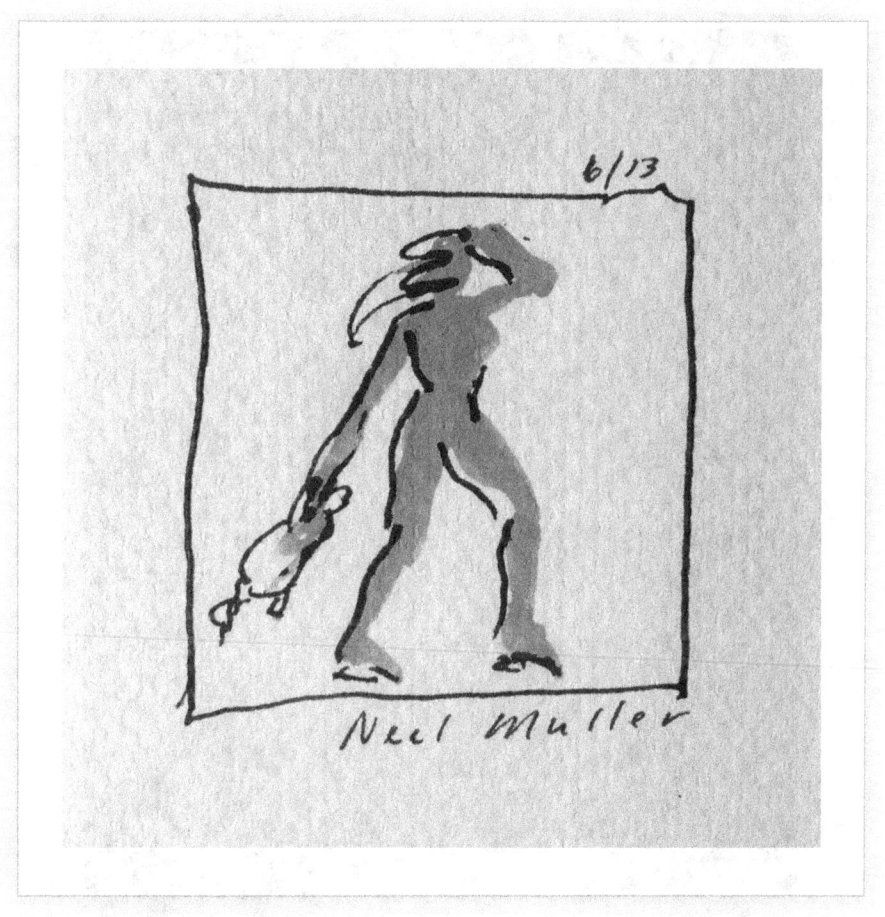

Nude holding something.

Not sure what she's holding. Could be a rabbit.

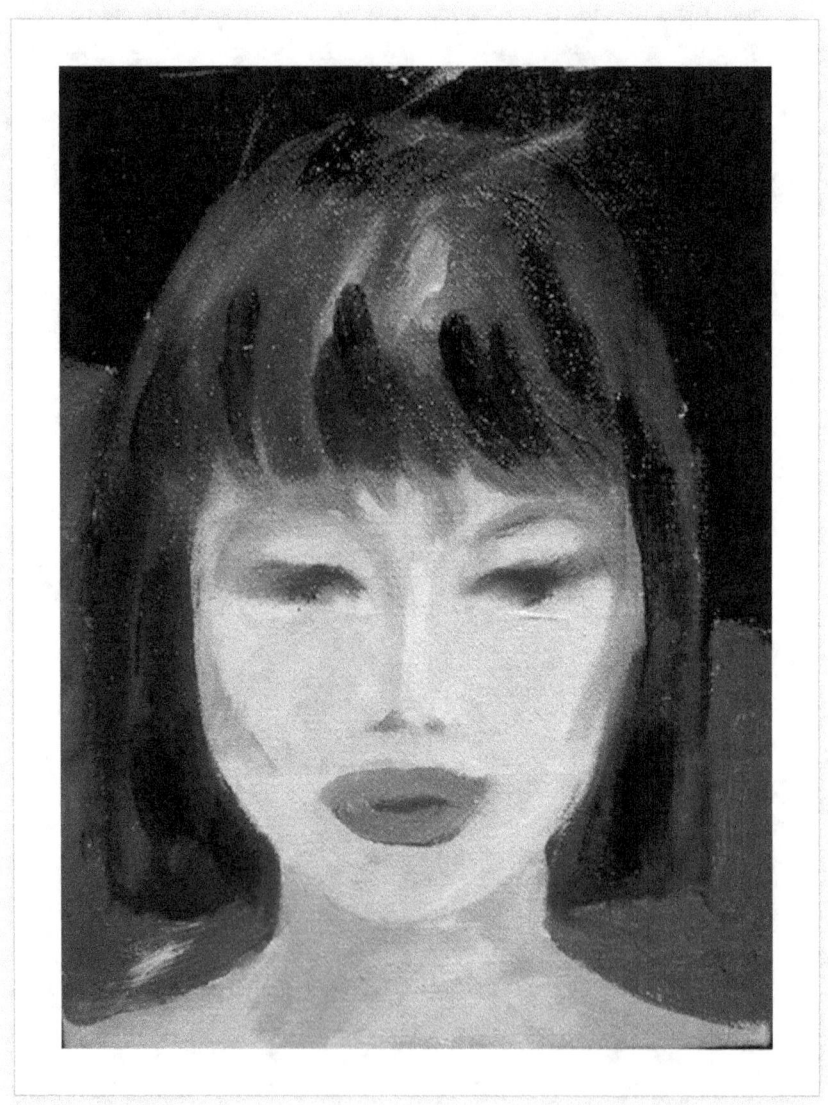

Wife in oil.

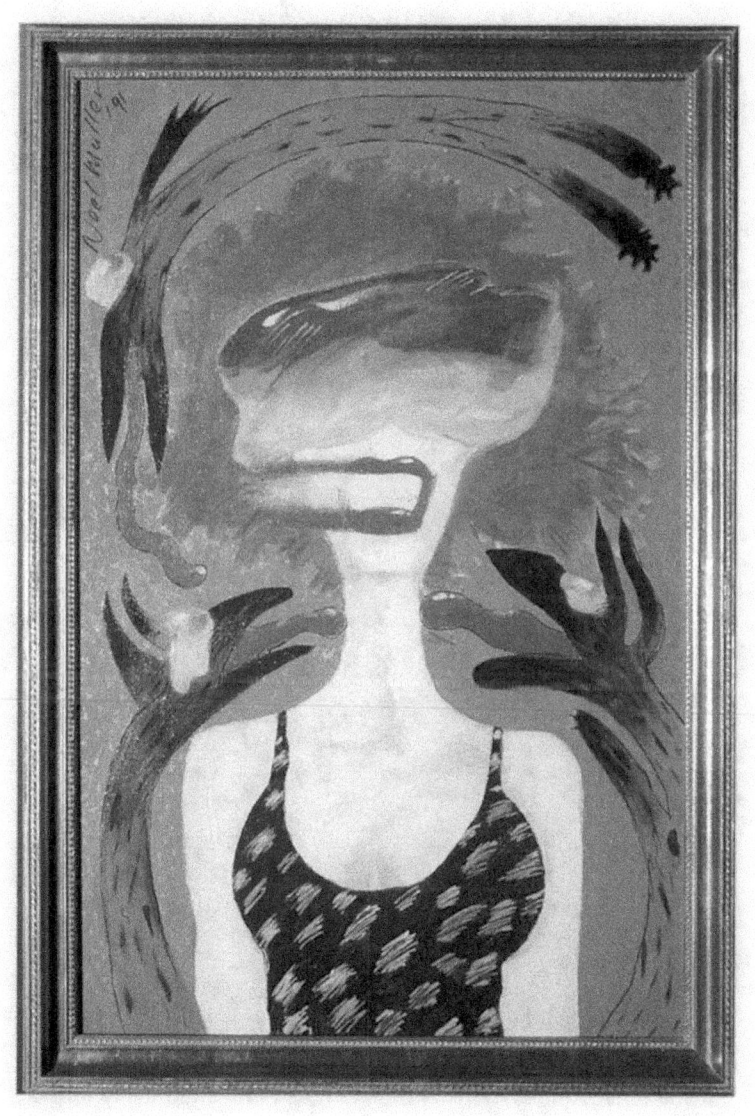

Ex wife in acrylic.

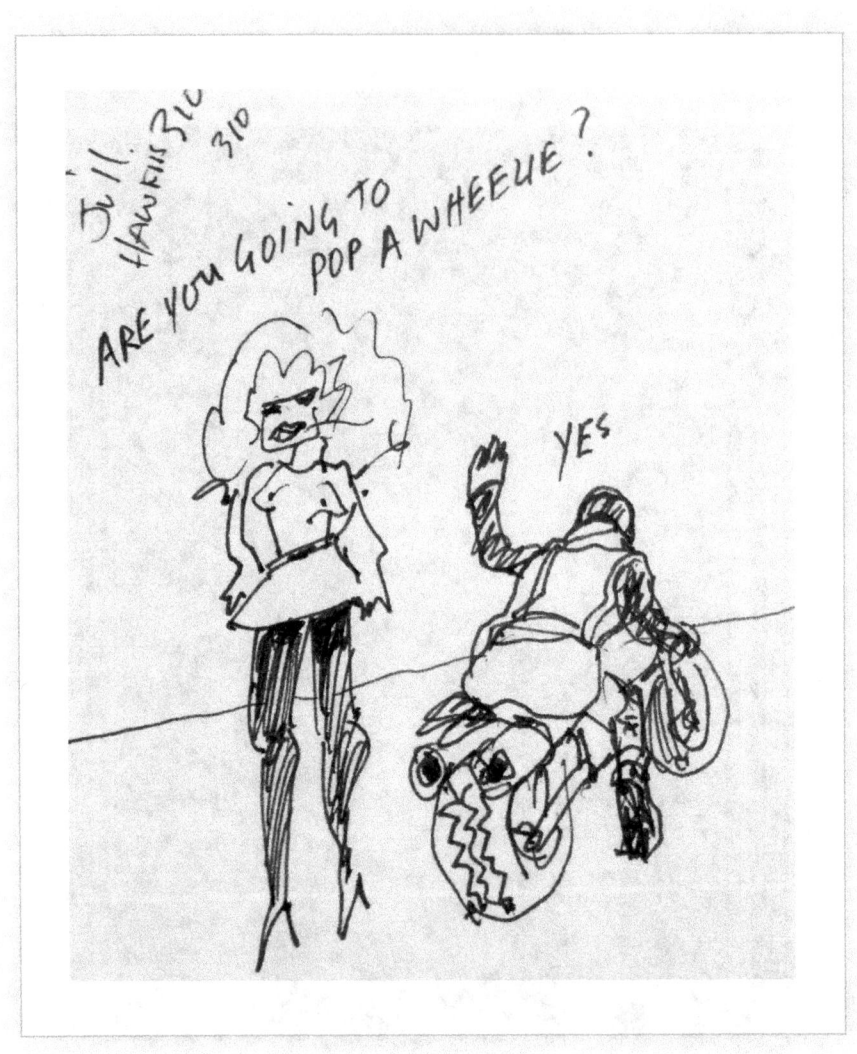

A good question.

And a good answer.

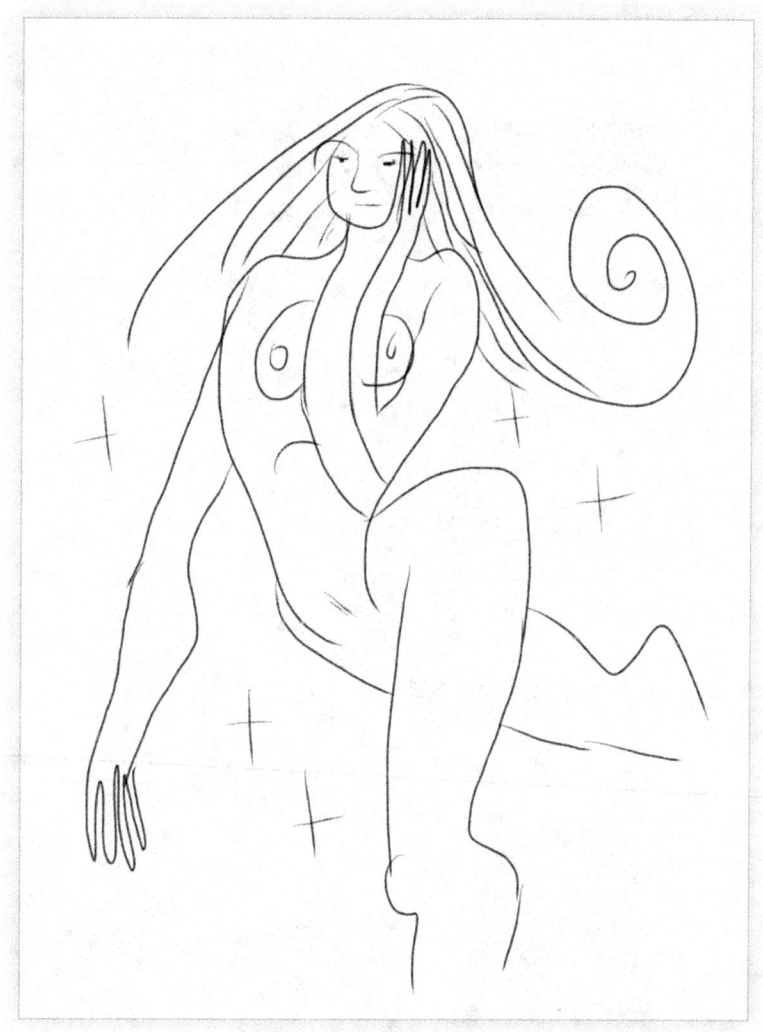

Pensive nude.

Is she talking on her phone? Hard to know sometimes.

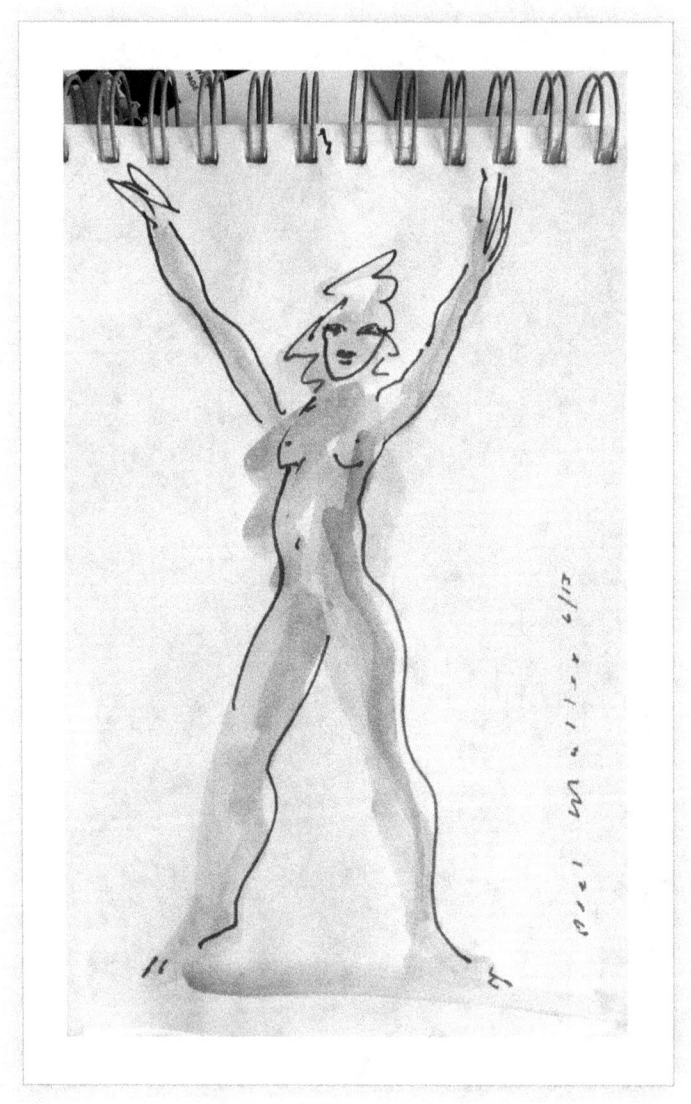

Spiral bound nude.

Unwinding herself.

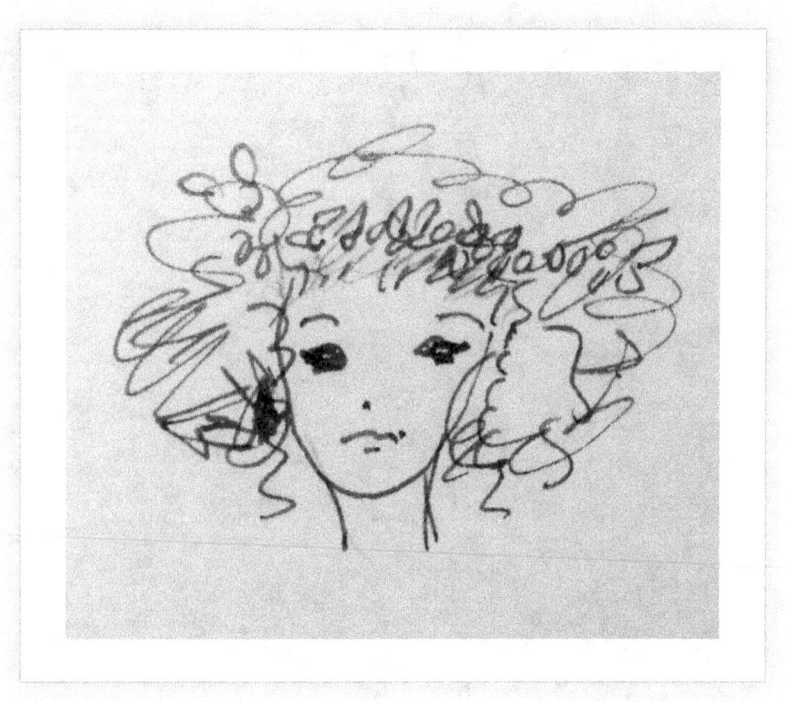

A woman to be.

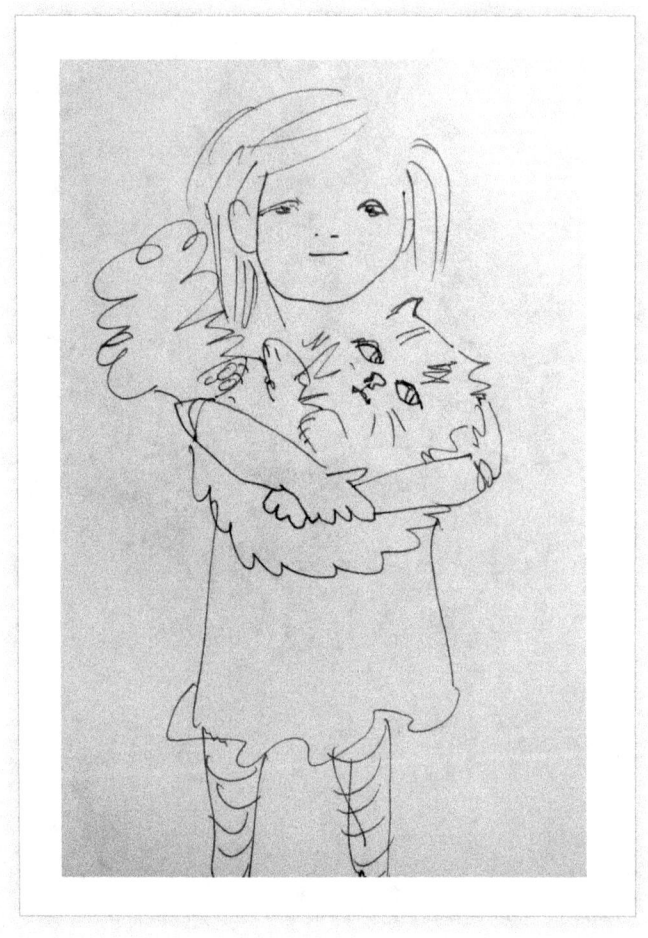

Little girl with cat.

The cat was not too happy with the situation.

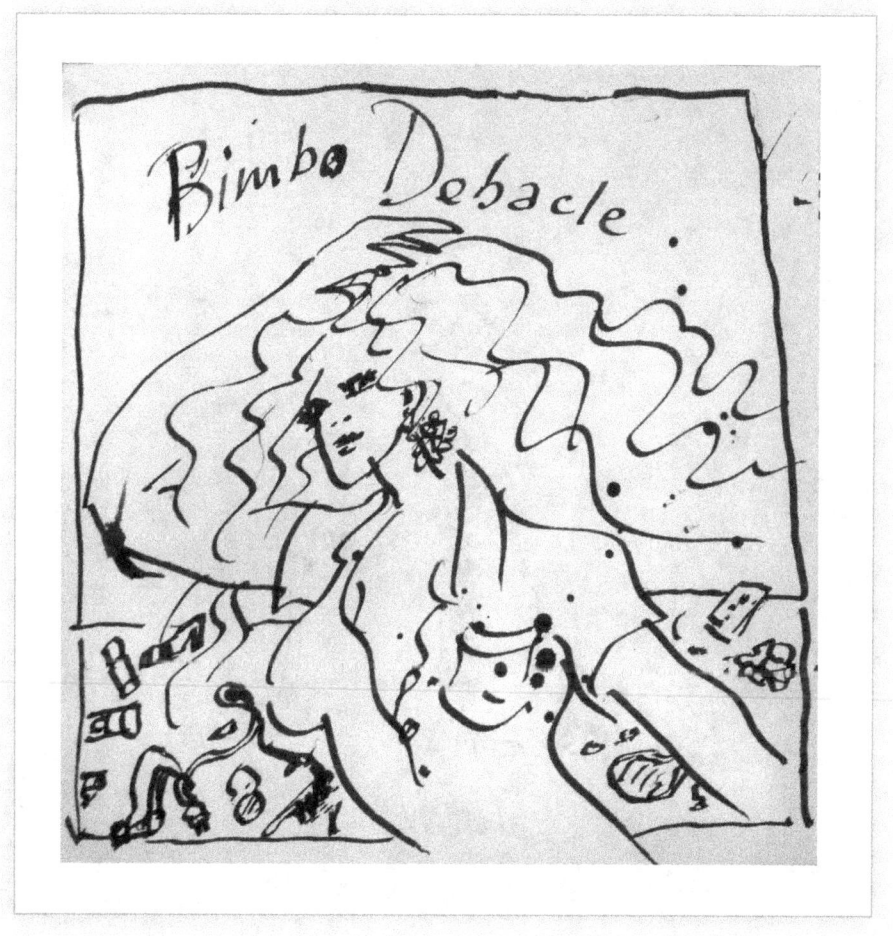

Bimbo debacle.

Nothing serious. Just a small make-up flare-up.

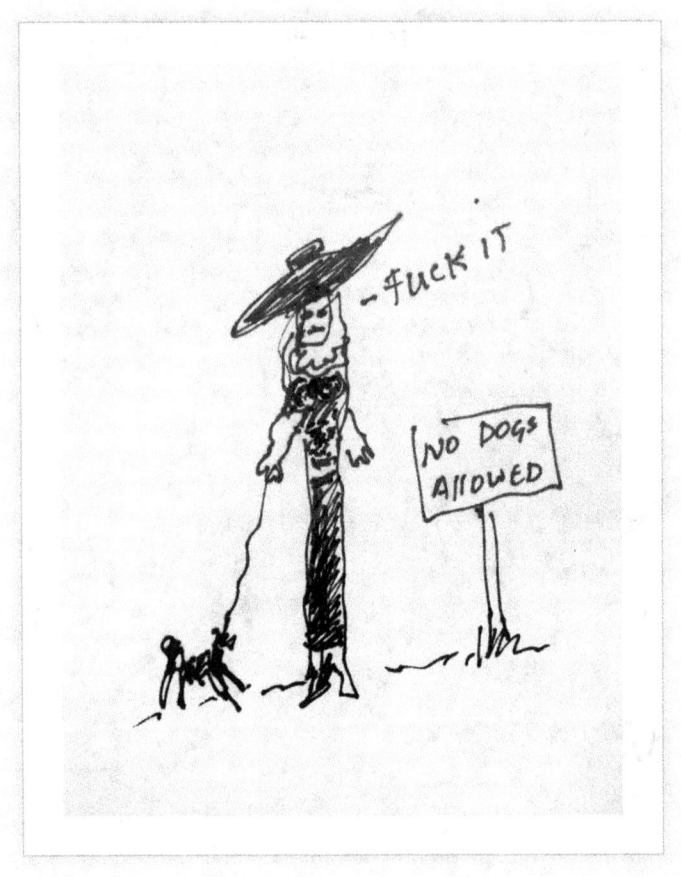

No dogs allowed.

Women get away with a lot more.

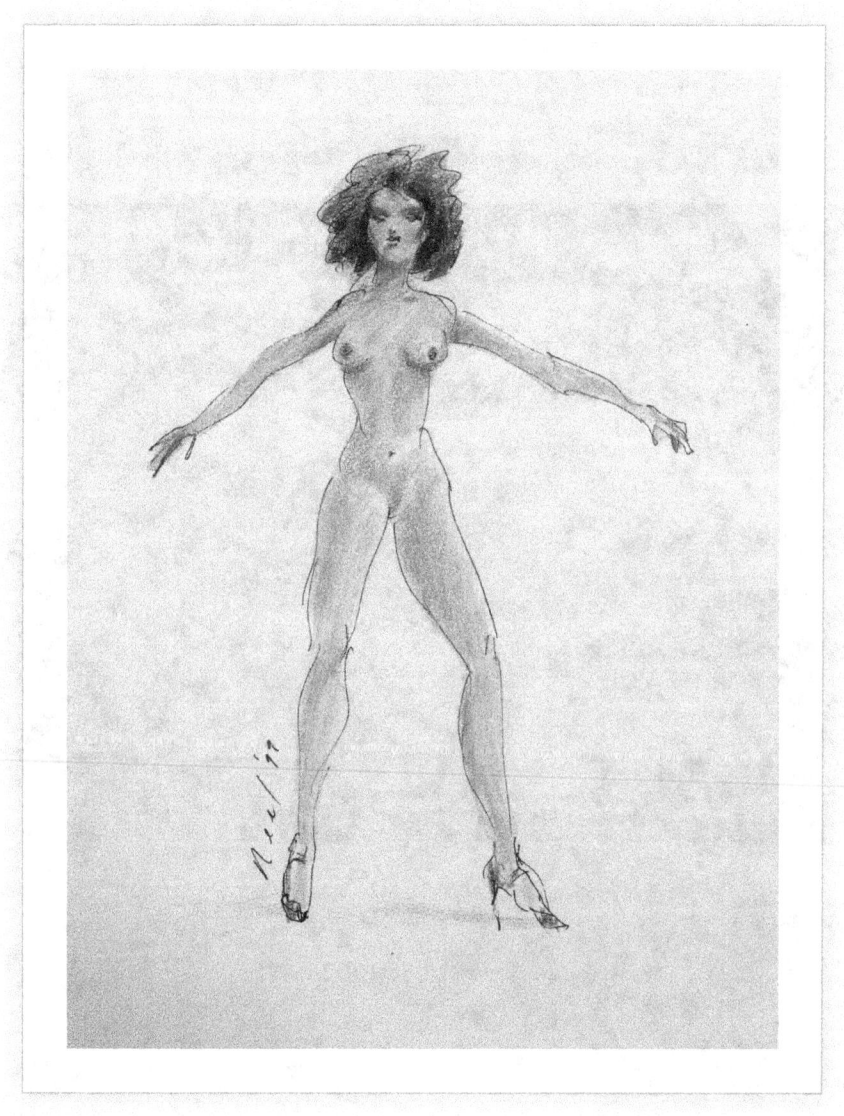

Striking a pose for the betterment of mankind.

Everyone has to do their share.

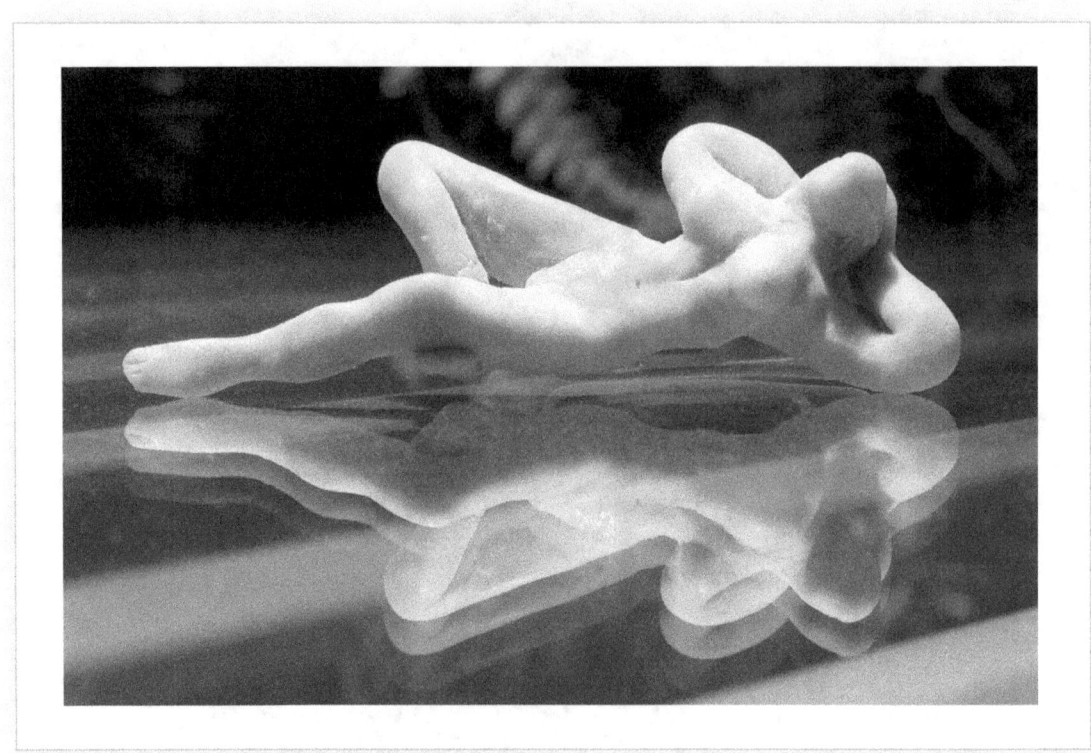

Solidly built nude.

I know because I built her myself.

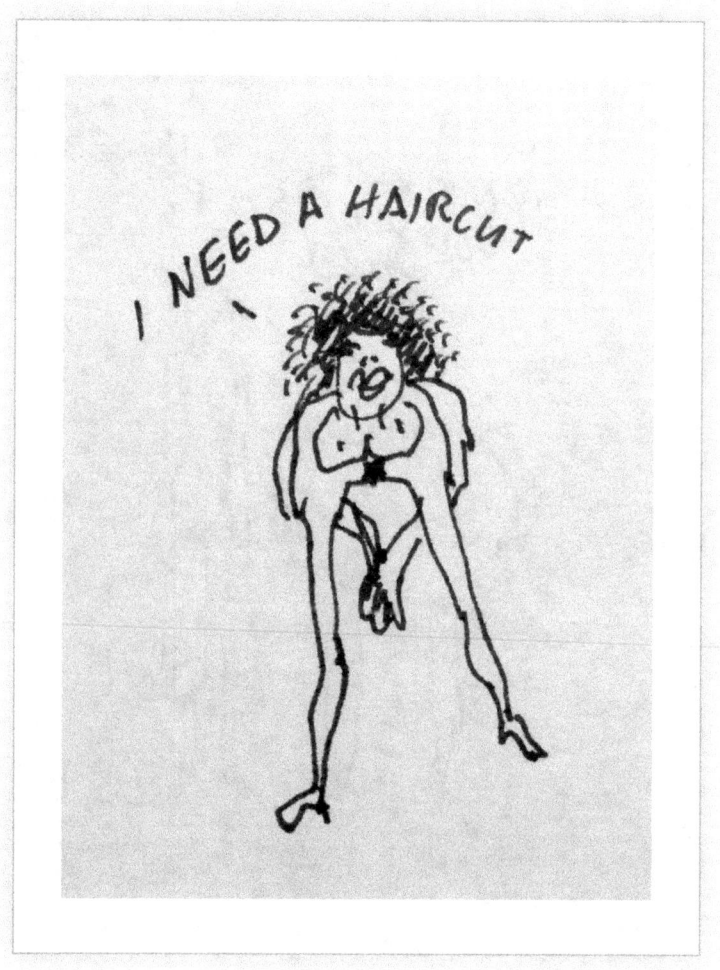

Needy woman.

Not always a pretty sight.

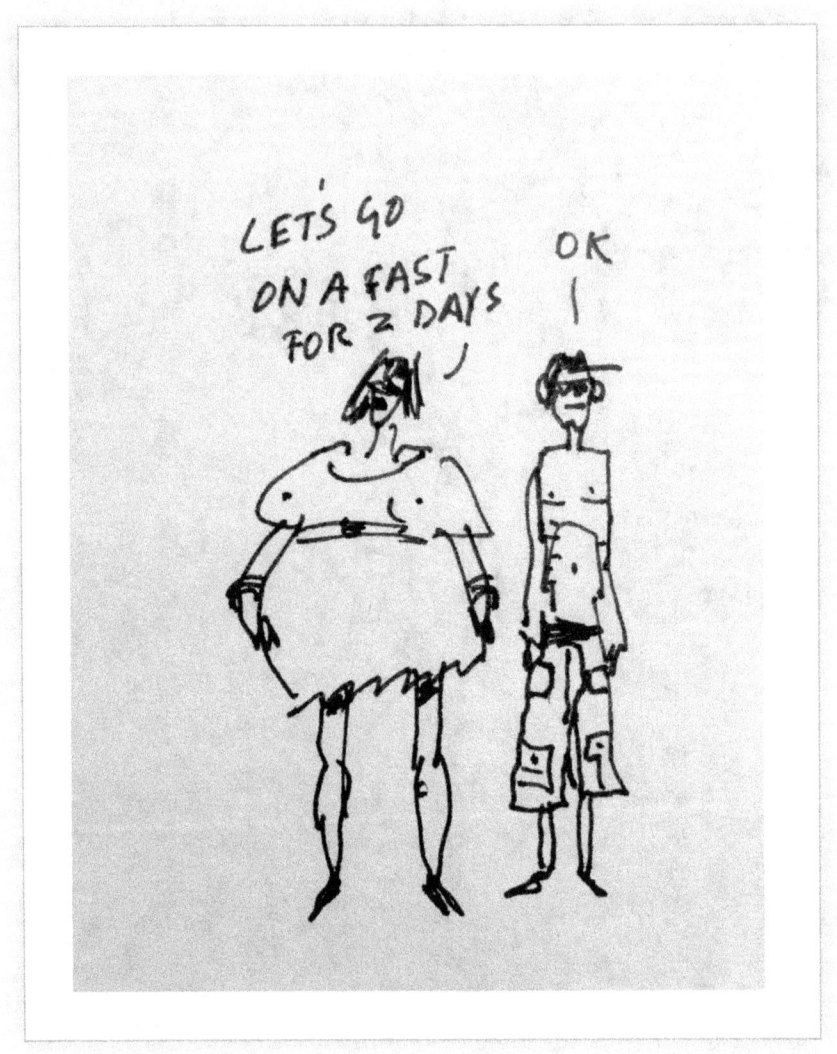

A good suggestion.

And a good response I might add.

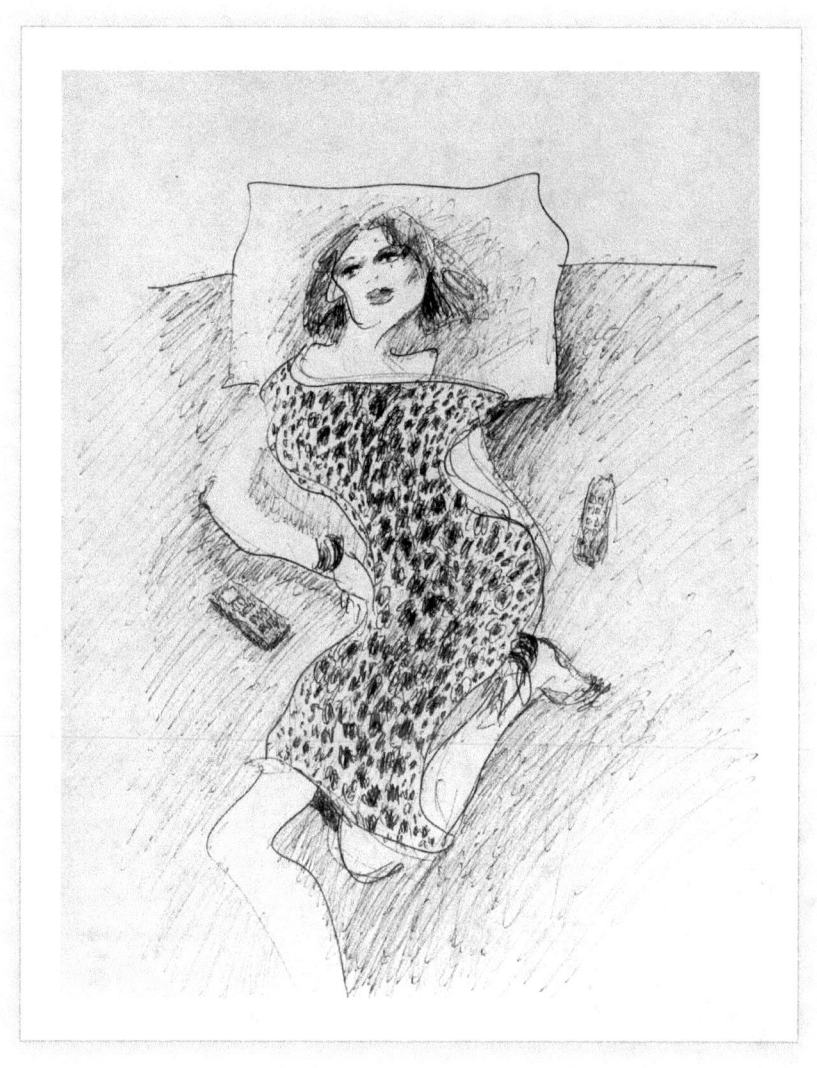

Waiting for her phones to ring.

A dumb and a smart phone.

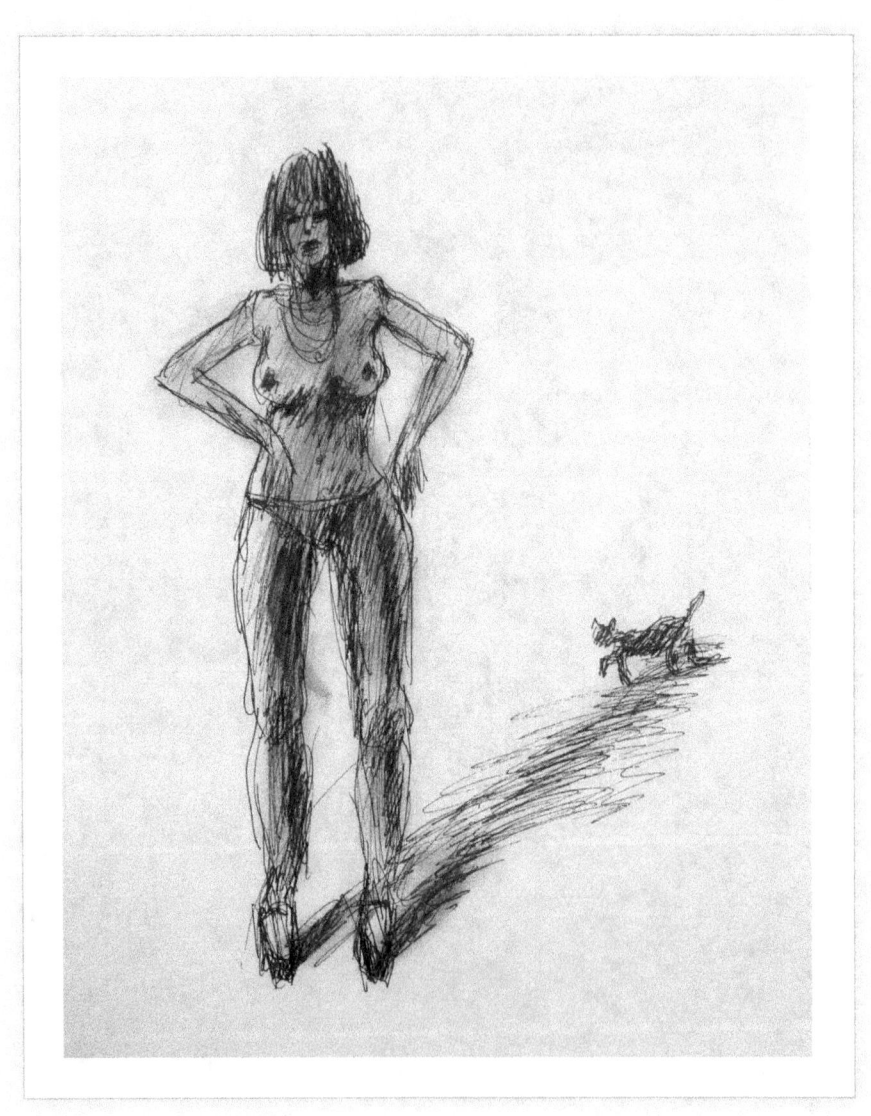

Cat sneaking by without being seen.

She had no idea.

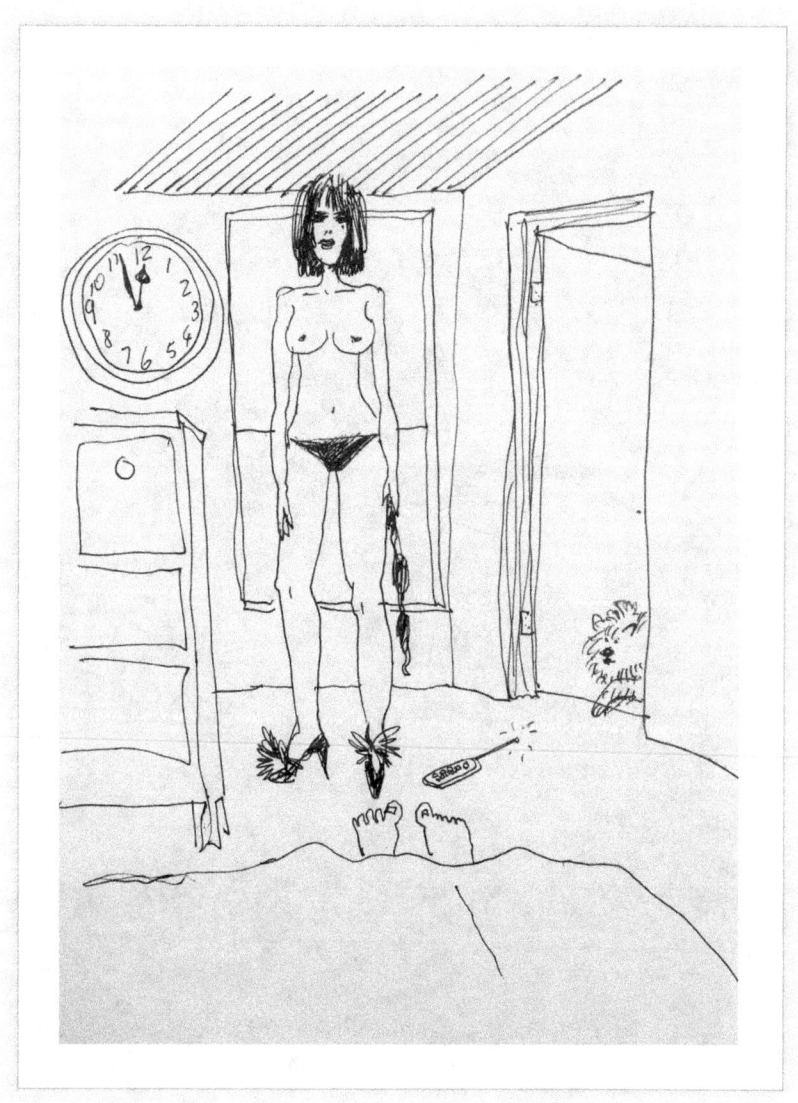

Almost noon.

Thank God it was a Sunday.

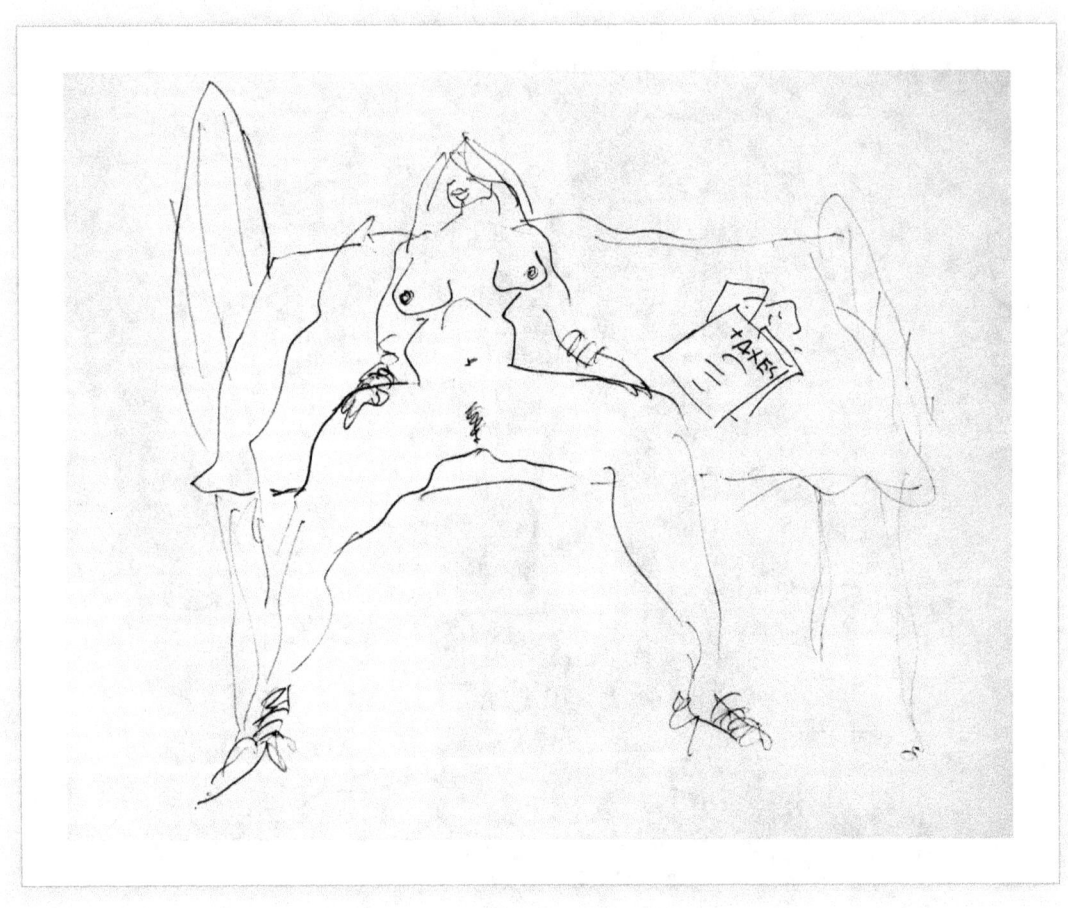

Nude getting ready to do her tax returns.

In early April.

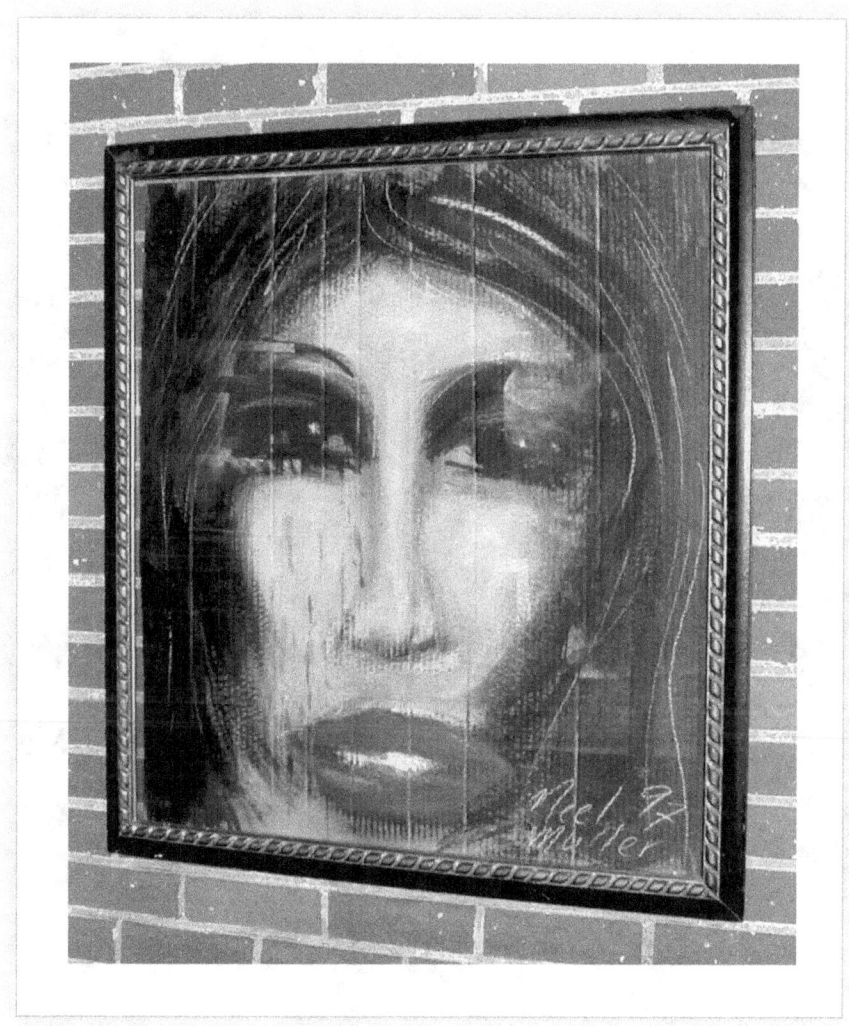

Lips in sync.

On cardboard. Done quick. Large.

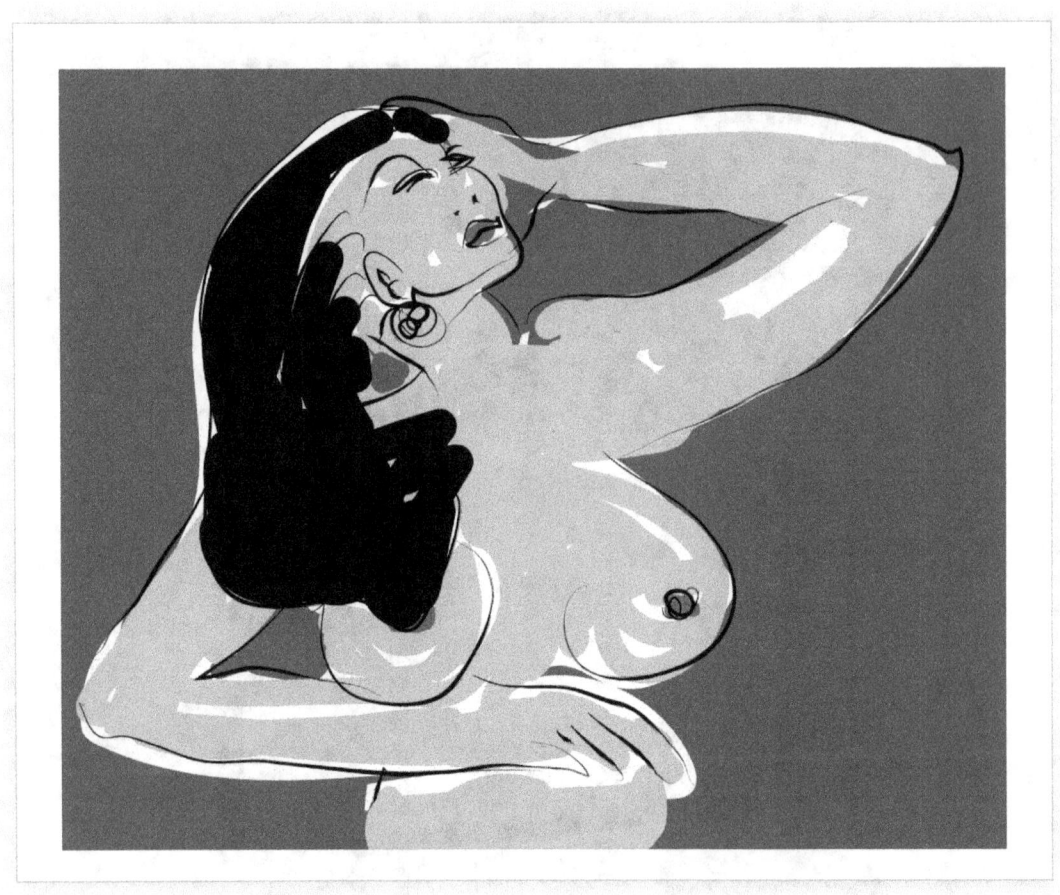

Drama Queen.

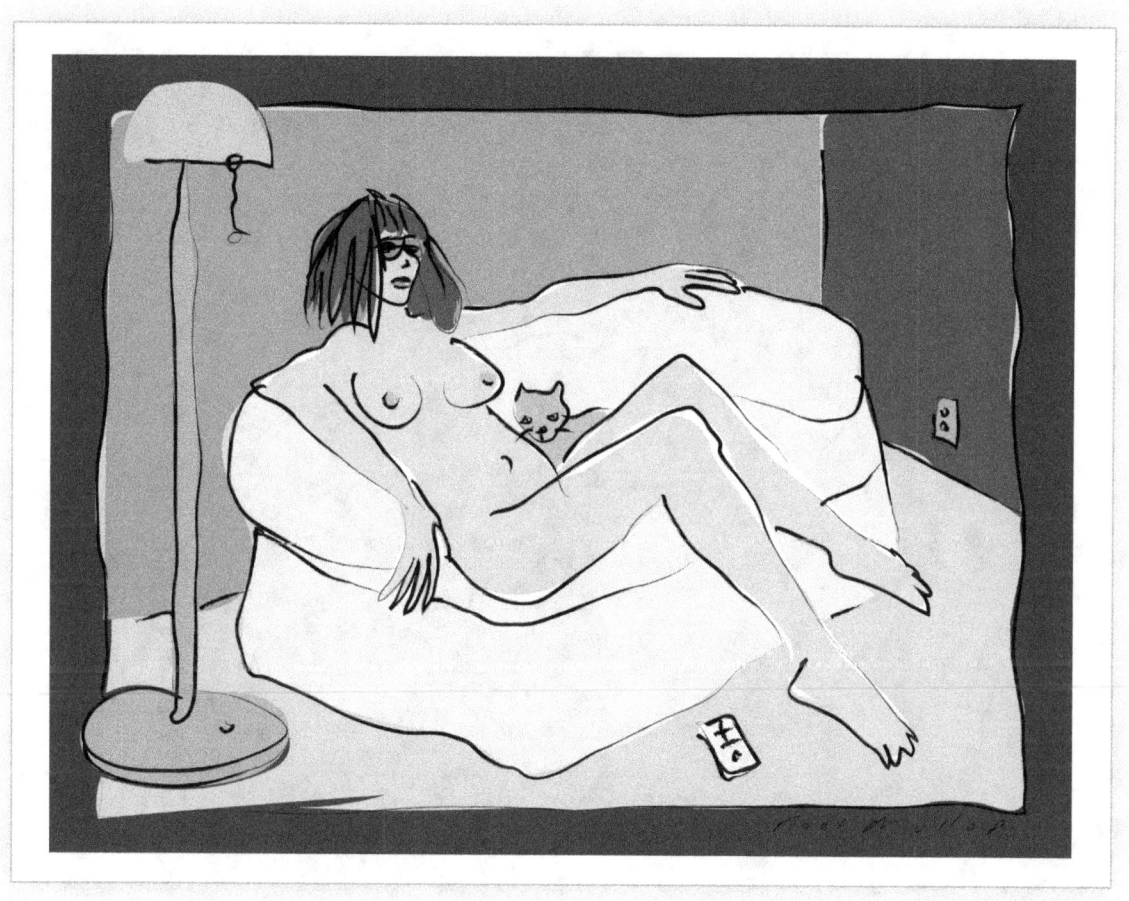

Purring girls.

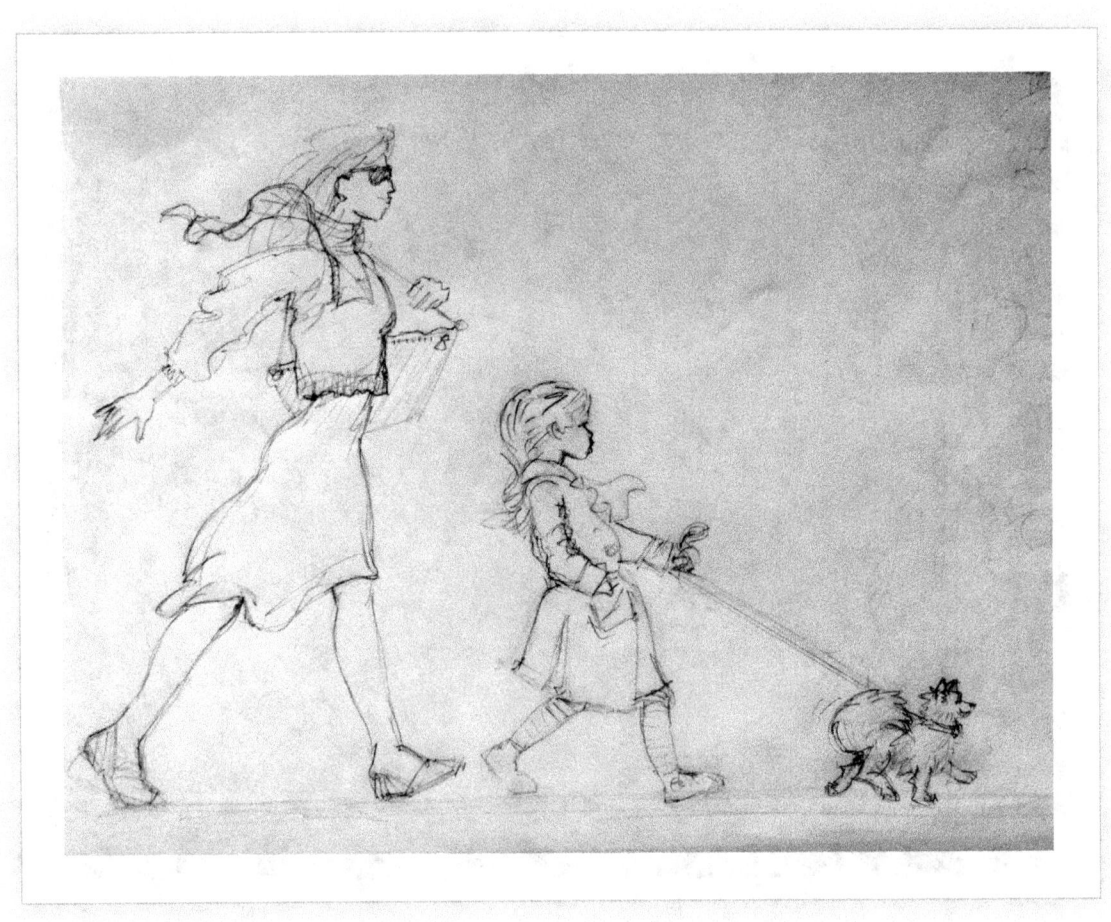

Girls day out.

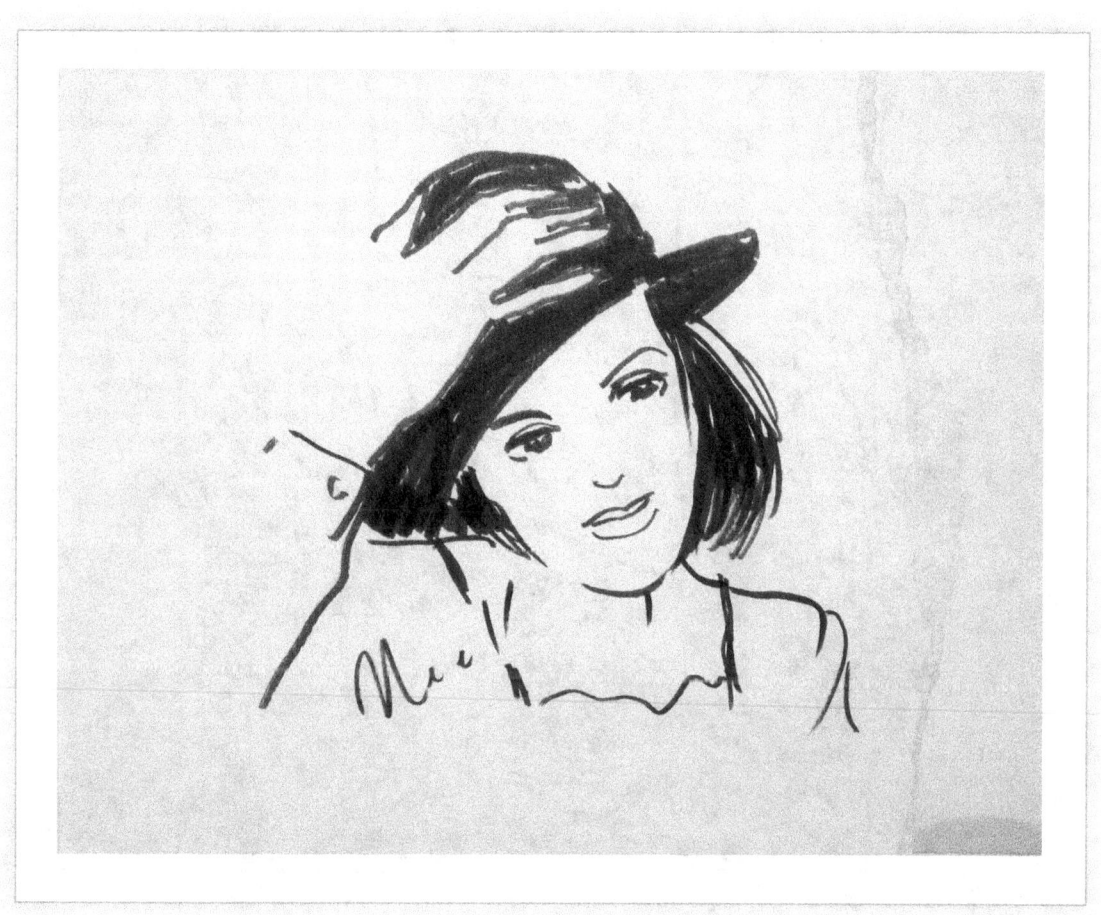

Holding onto her hat.

Just in case.

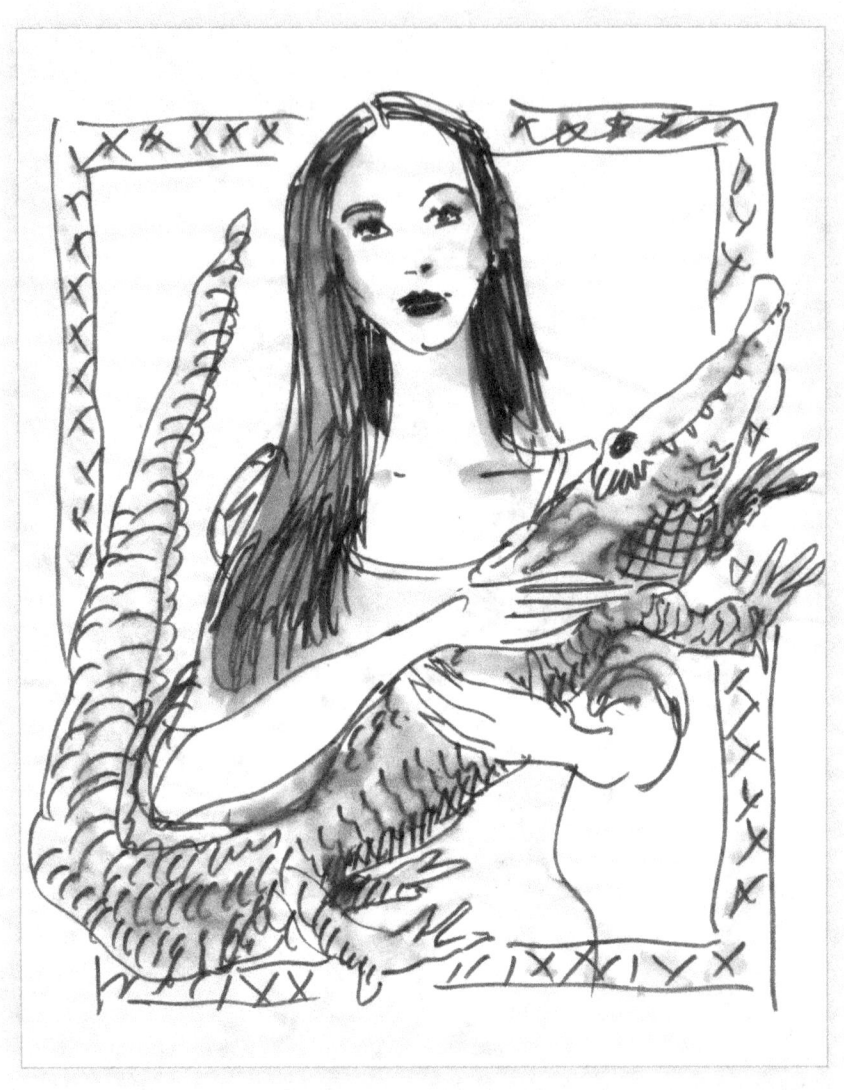

Woman with alligator.

She had a calming effect.

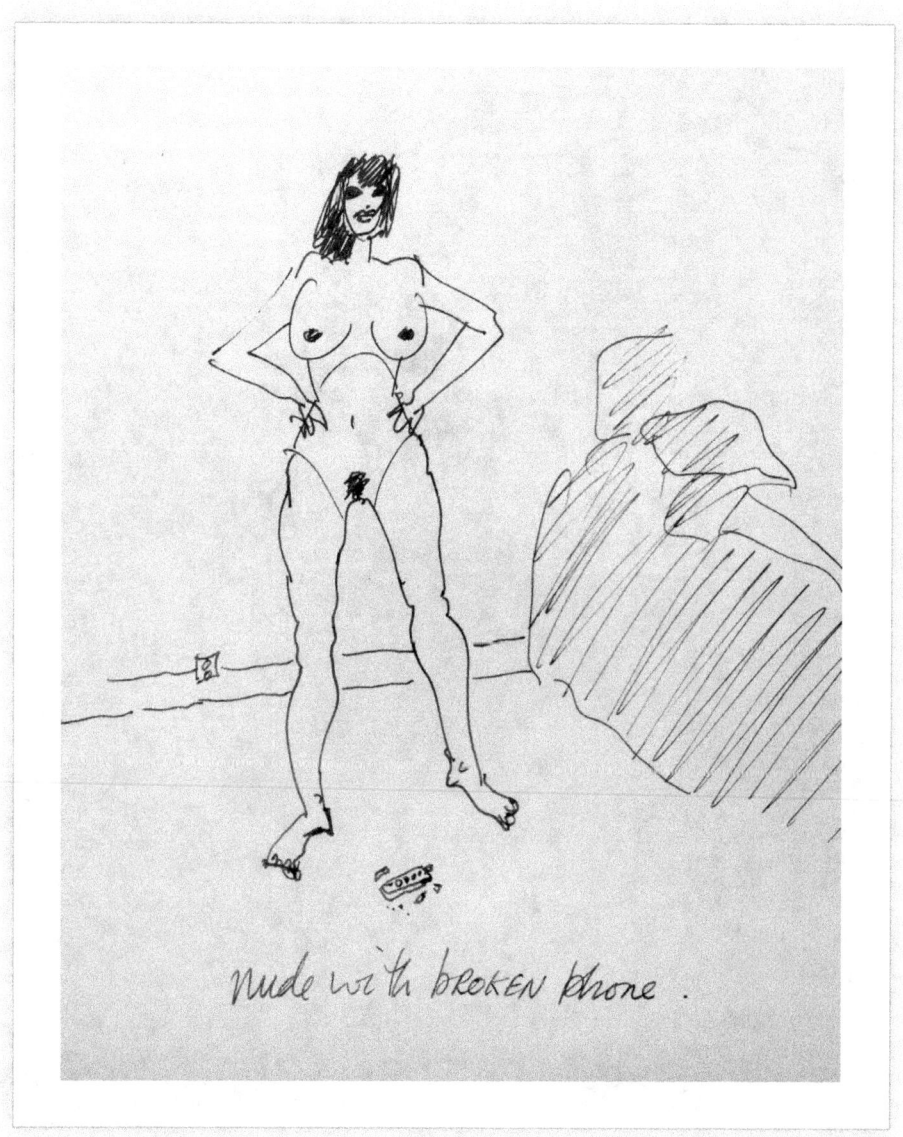

Nude with broken phone.

She dropped it in a fit of anger but soon got over it when she realized

it was time to upgrade to a new one.

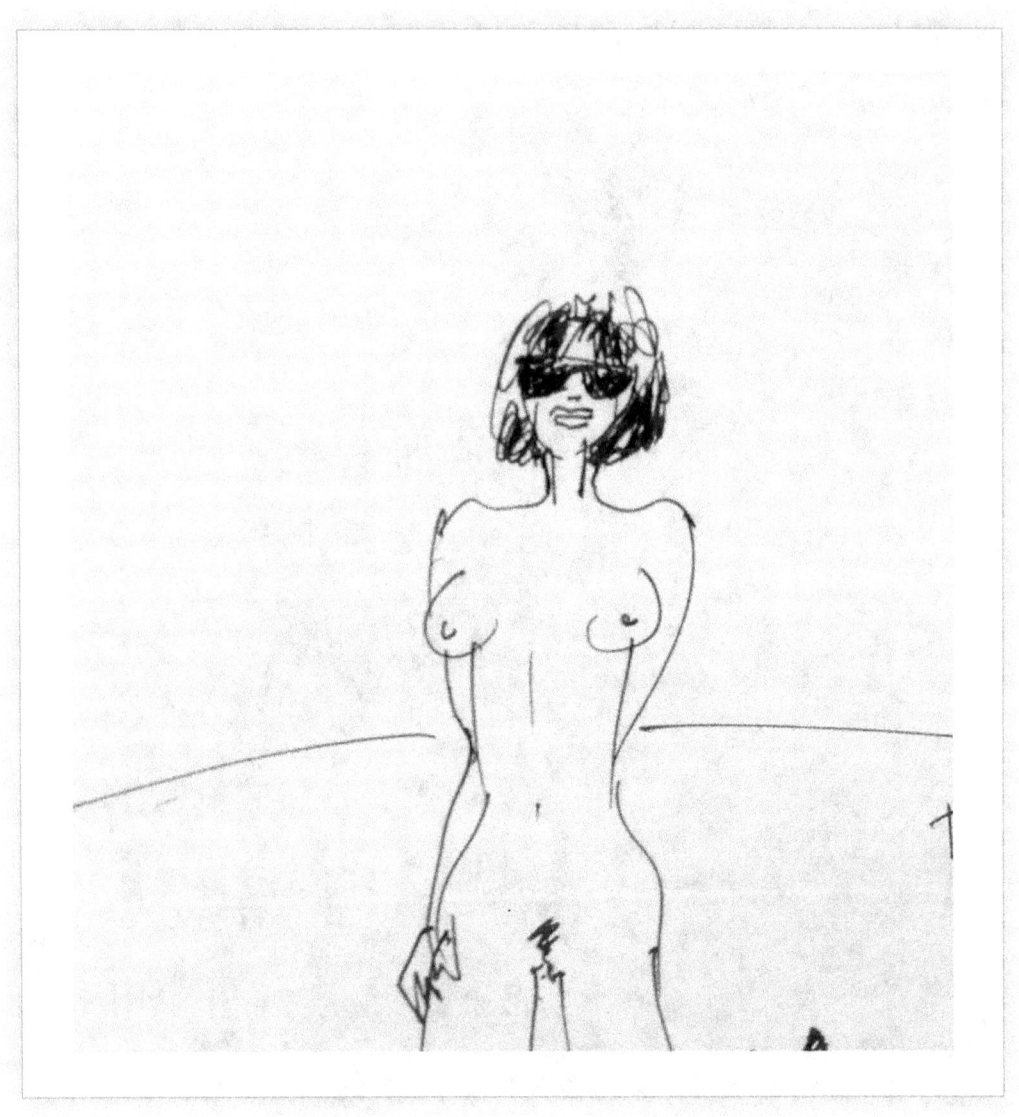

She felt naked without her sunglasses.

And who can blame her?

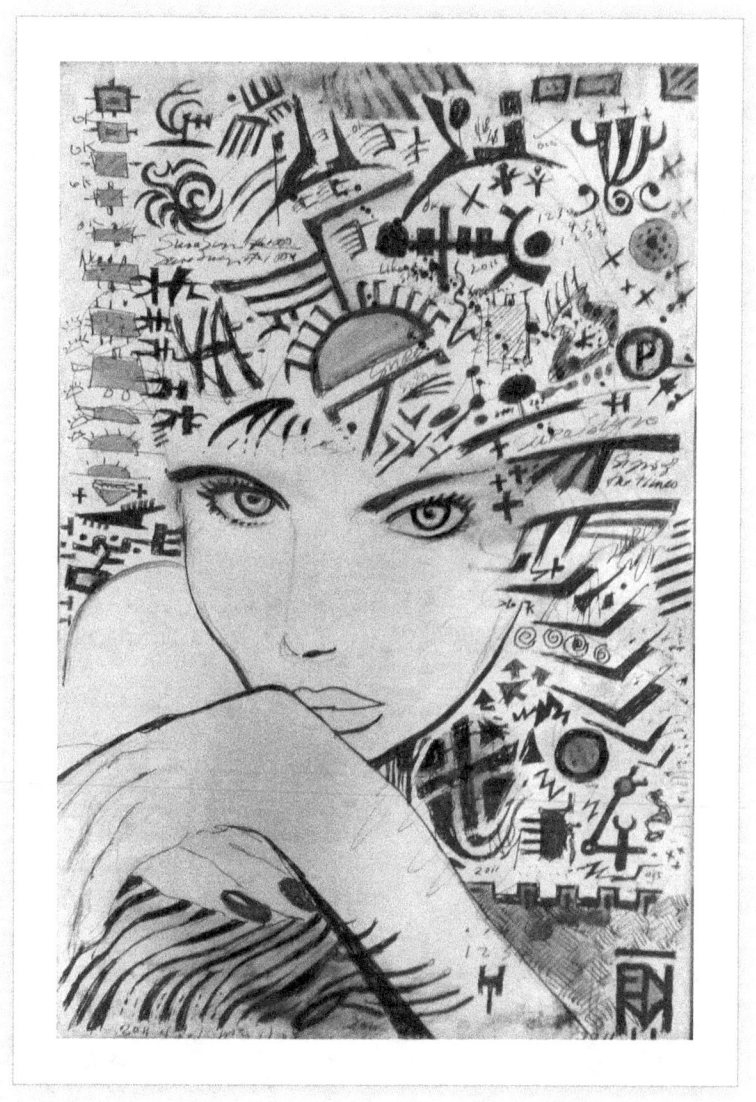

Metallic woman.

Drawn on a piece of metal of course.

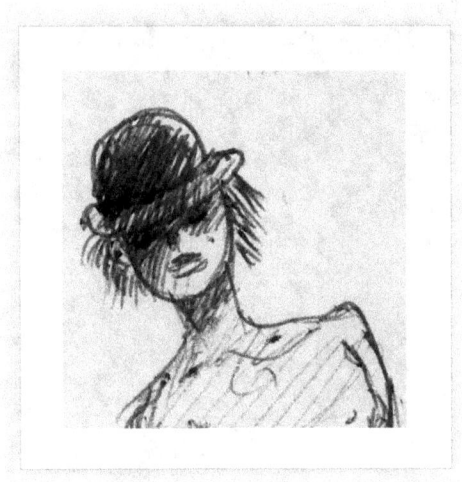

Girl in bowler hat.

Very fitting.

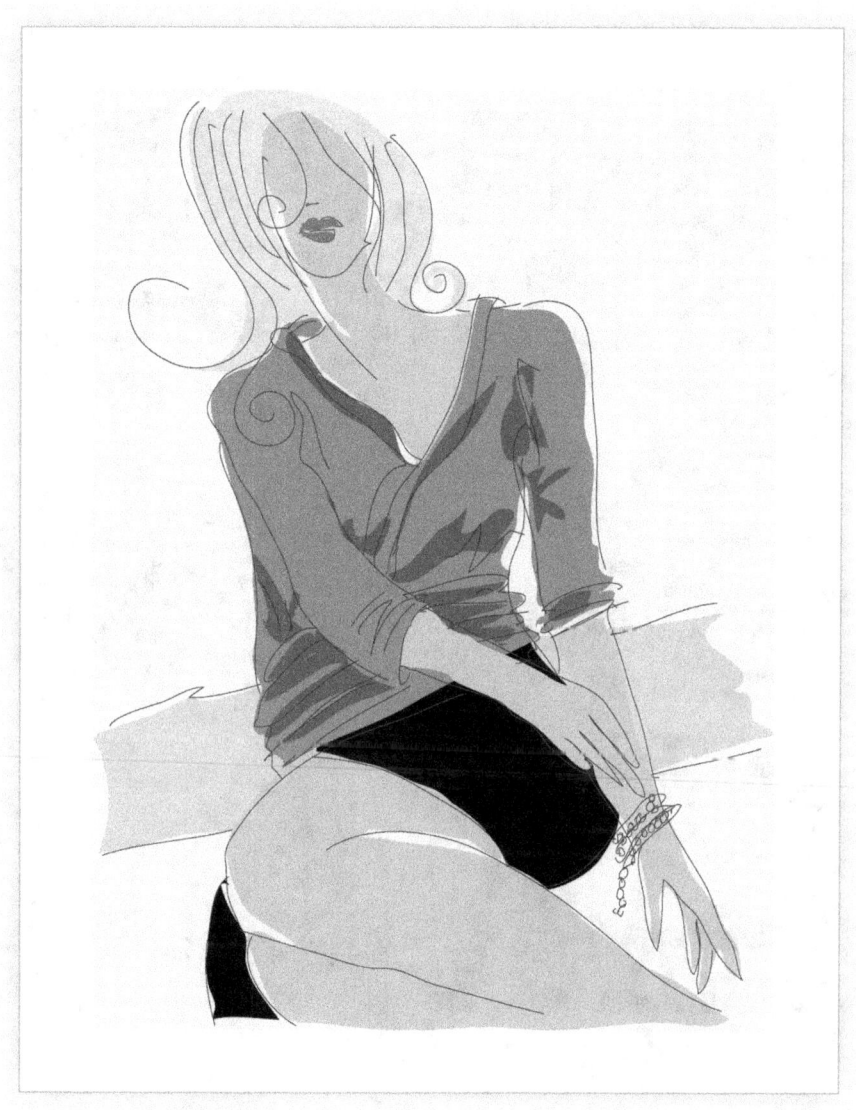

Sitting pretty.

I drew this under duress for some stupid Sony Pictures ad project that never materialized.

At least I got paid for it.

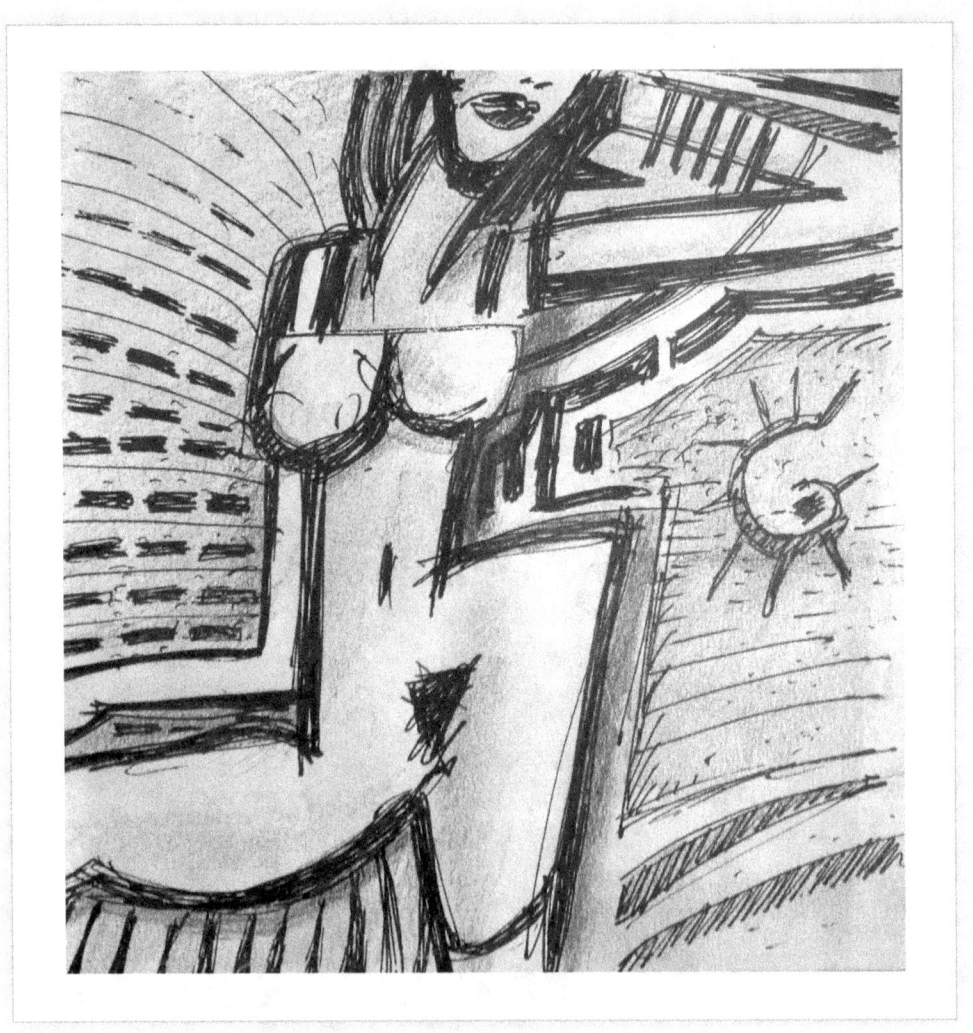

Woman with a slight edge.

She seemed straight forward and to the point.

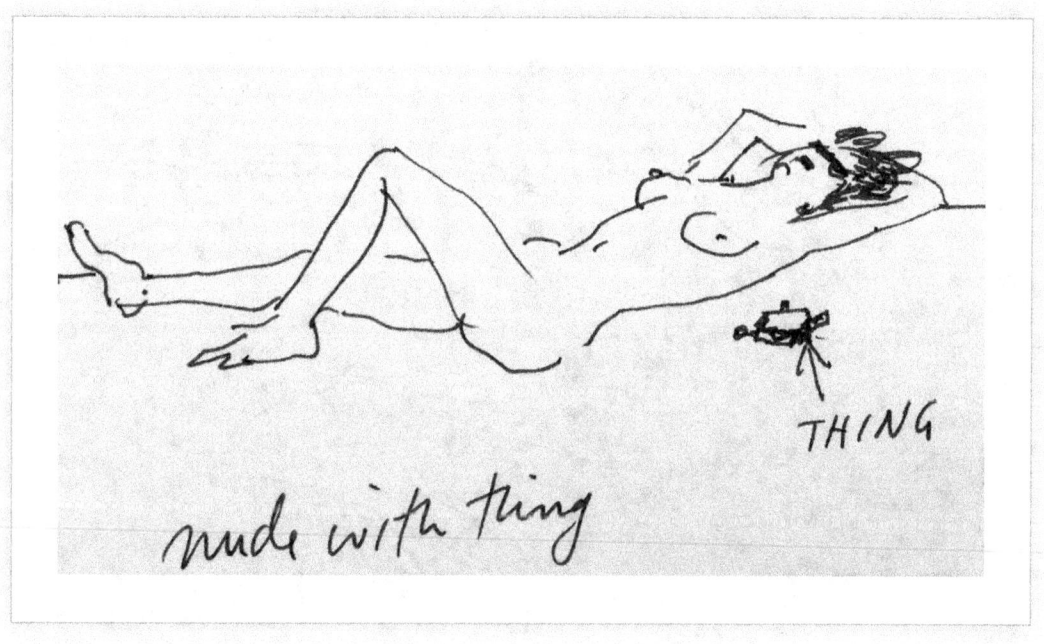

Nude with thing.

To her left was a thing.

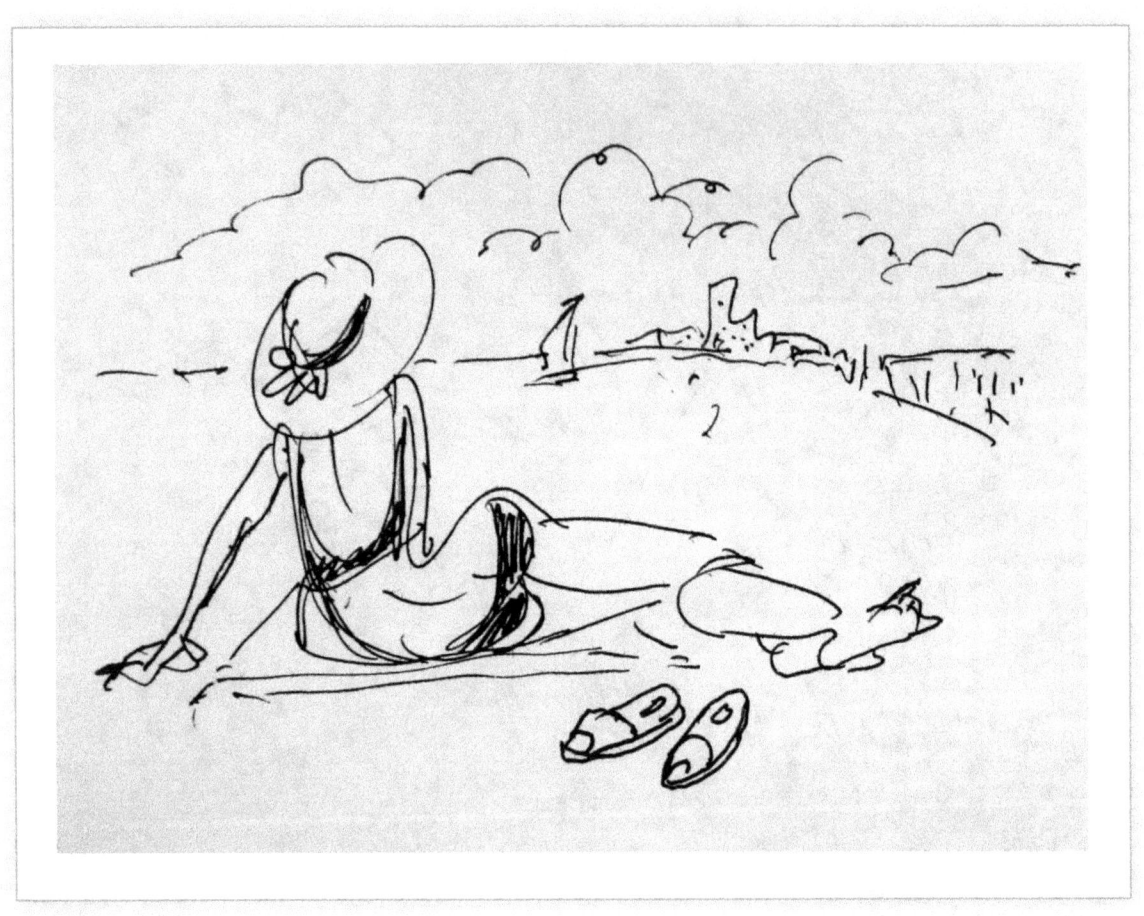

Bathing beauty.

She never got into the water knowing that the luxury yachts nearby
flushed their waste into the ocean.

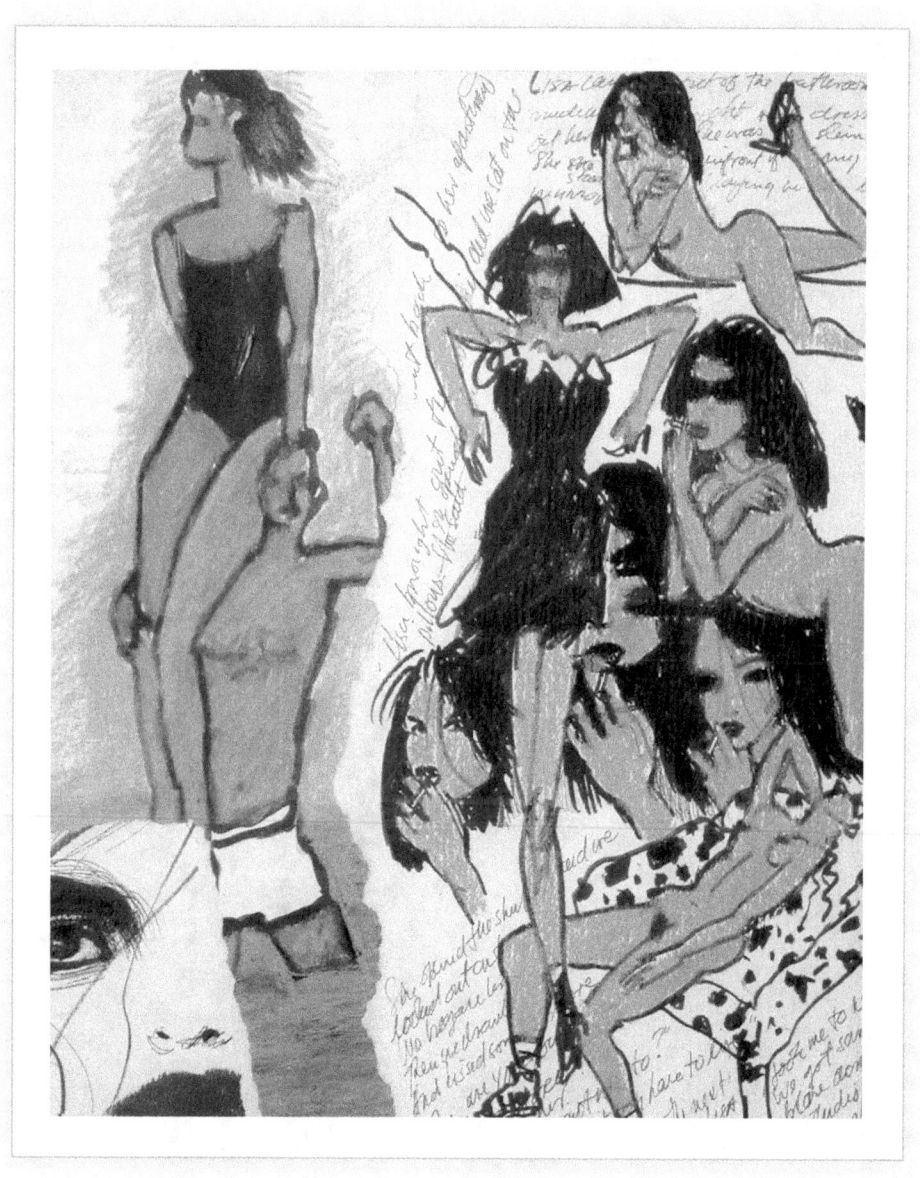

Loose women.

Loosely drawn.

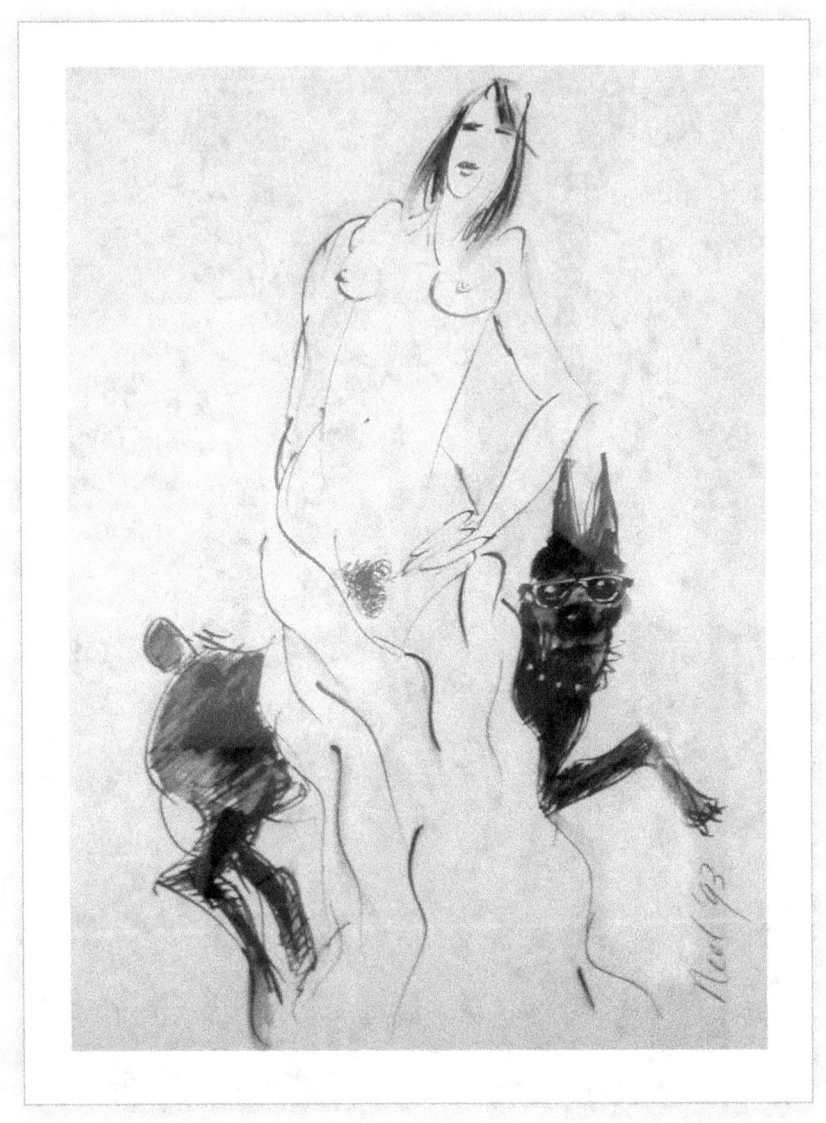

Great Danes.

I sold this drawing to a friend of mine for very cheap.

Then one day I saw it for sale at a store and bought it back.

Now my son has it. A long story, I know.

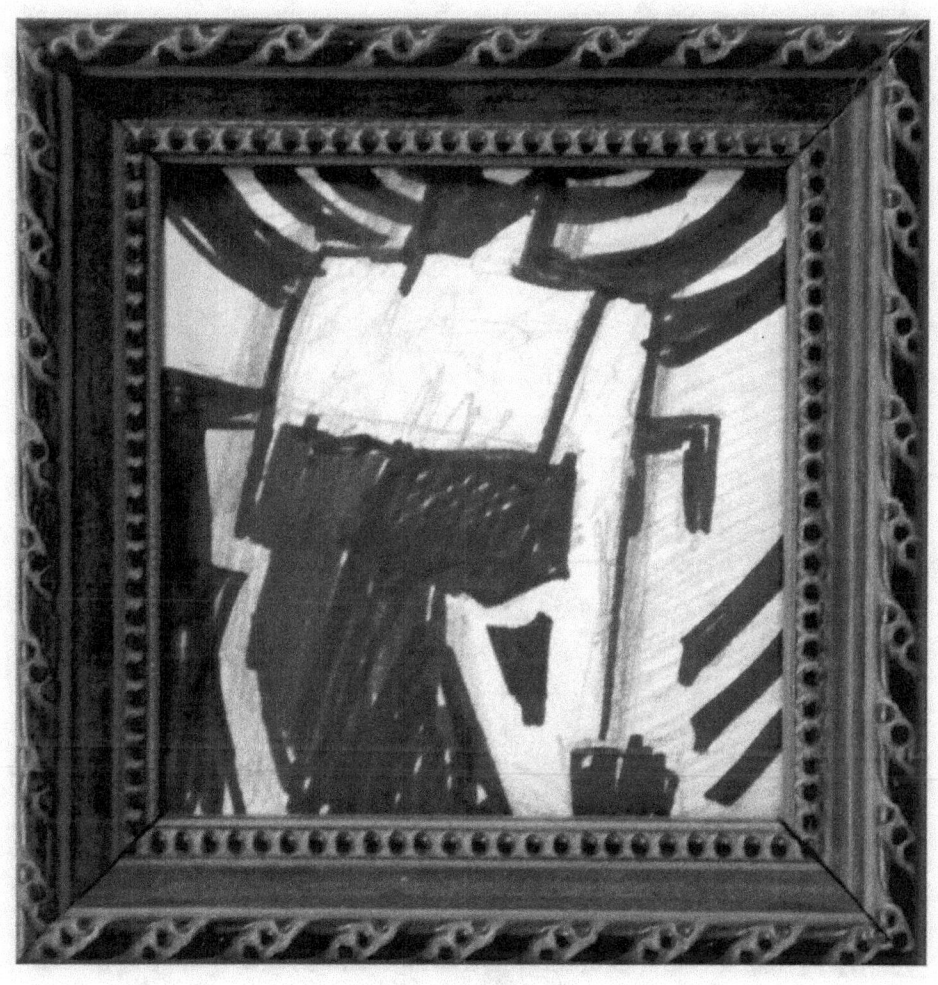

Woman in black.

Her mood was the same color.

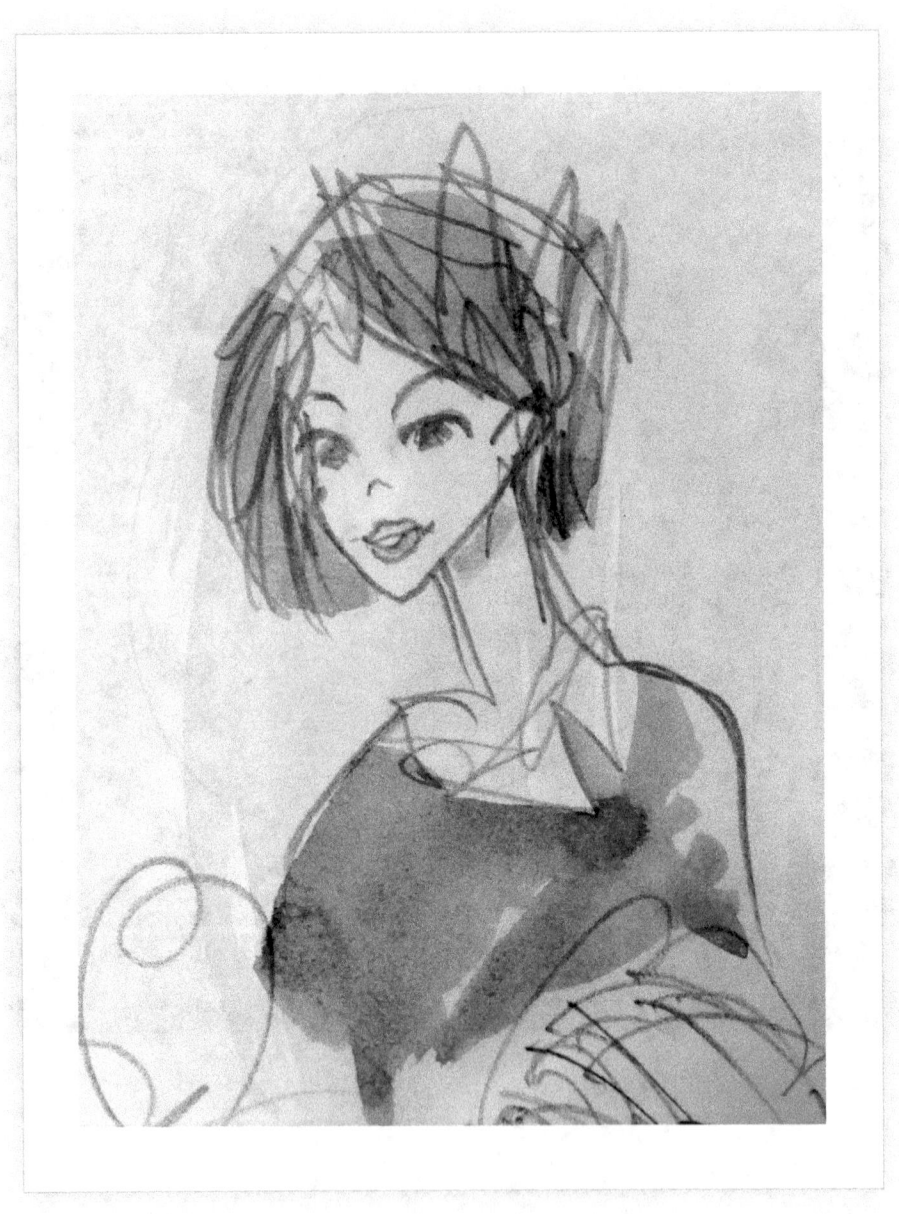

Young Aubergene.

Lest not we forget her.

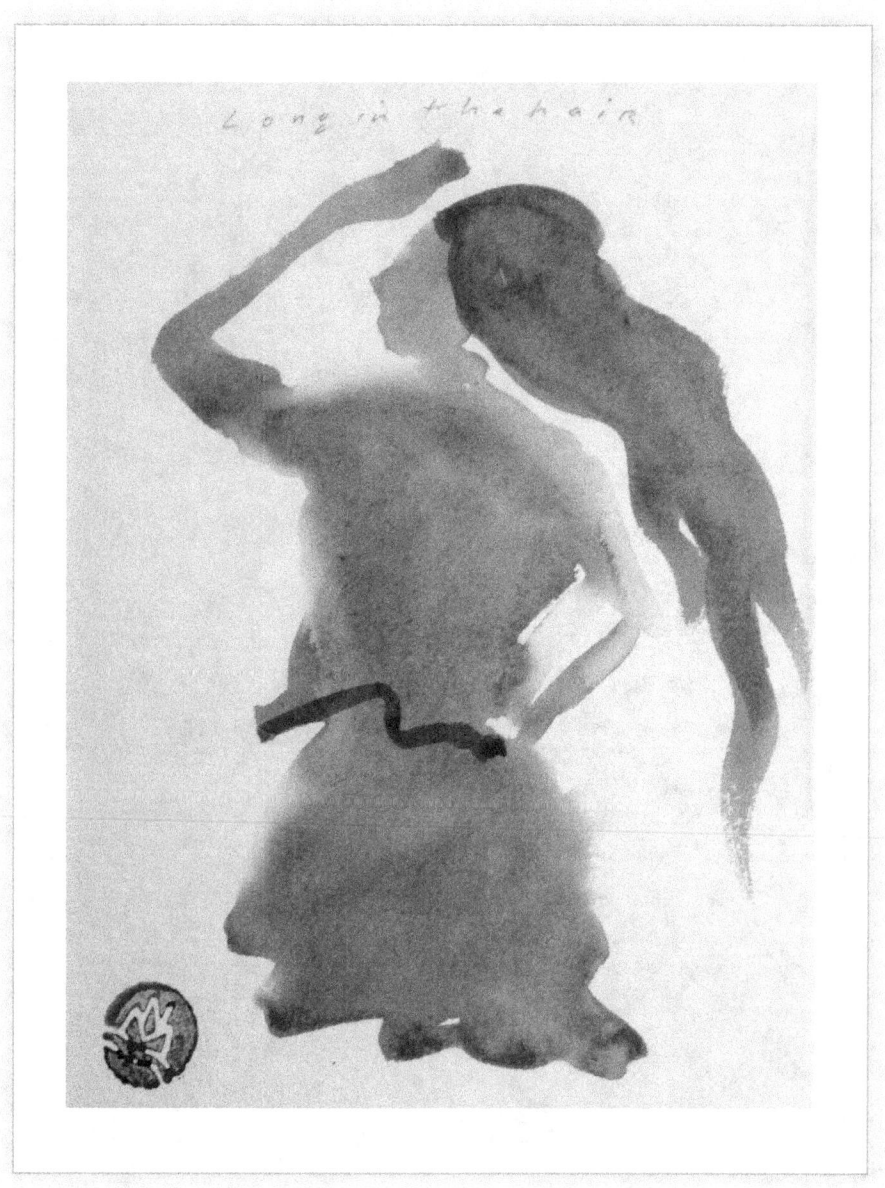

Long in the hair.

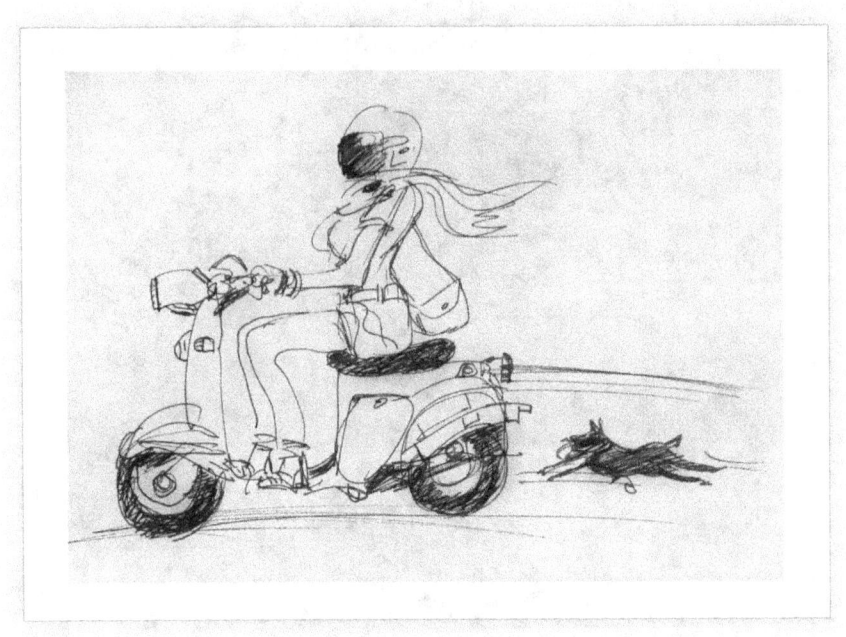

Fast woman on a Vespa.

Noisy. The Vespa, not the woman.

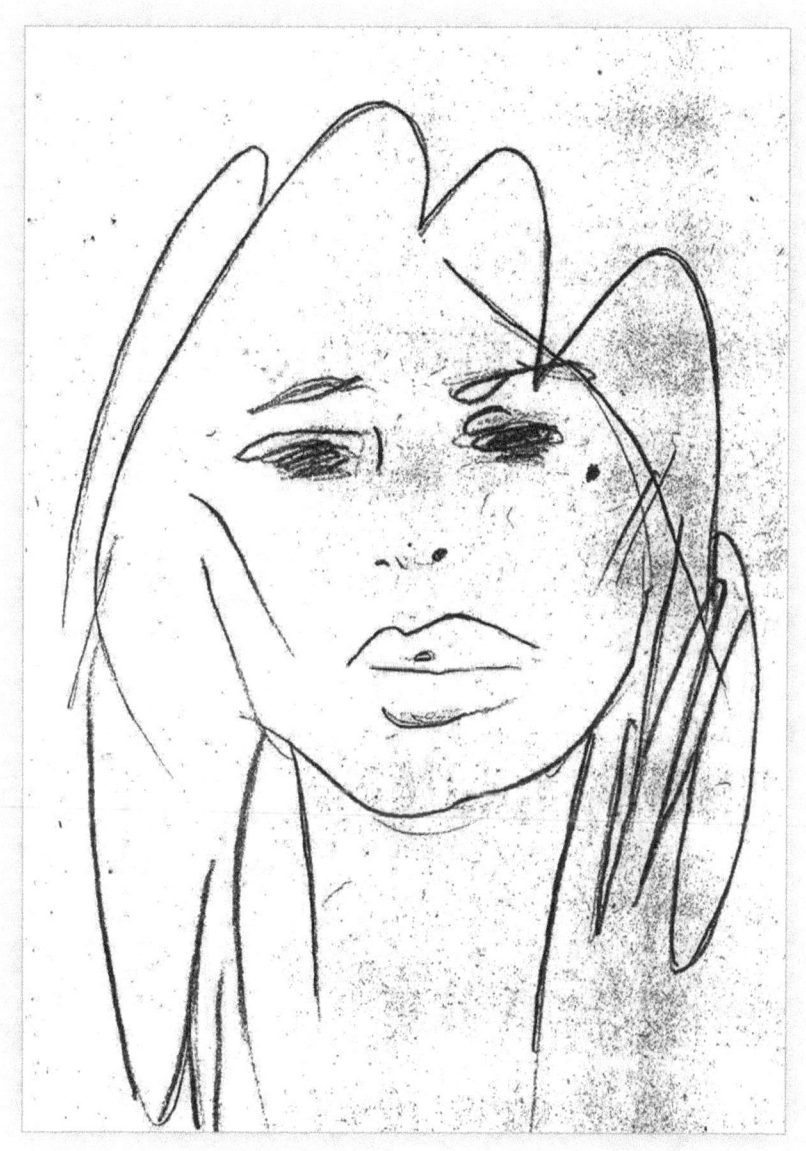

Wife.

Quick sketch of my wife.

I had to draw fast. She will not sit still.

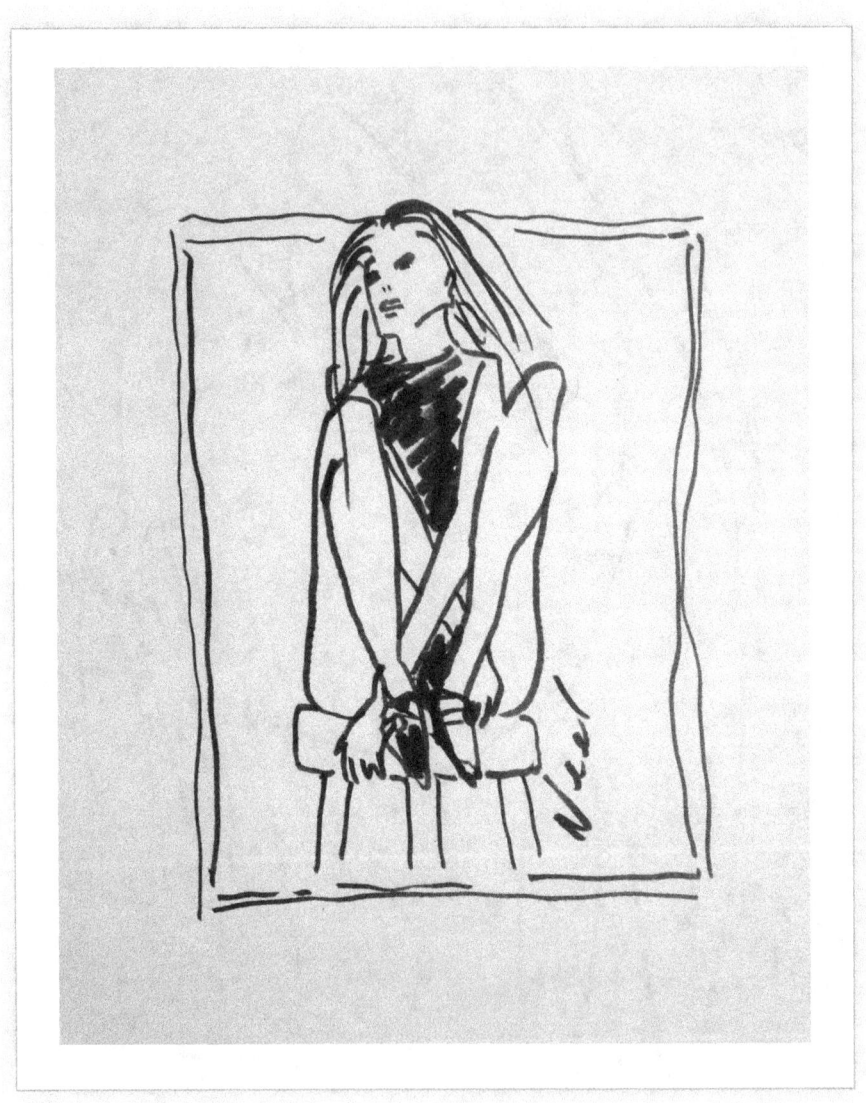

Sitting pretty.

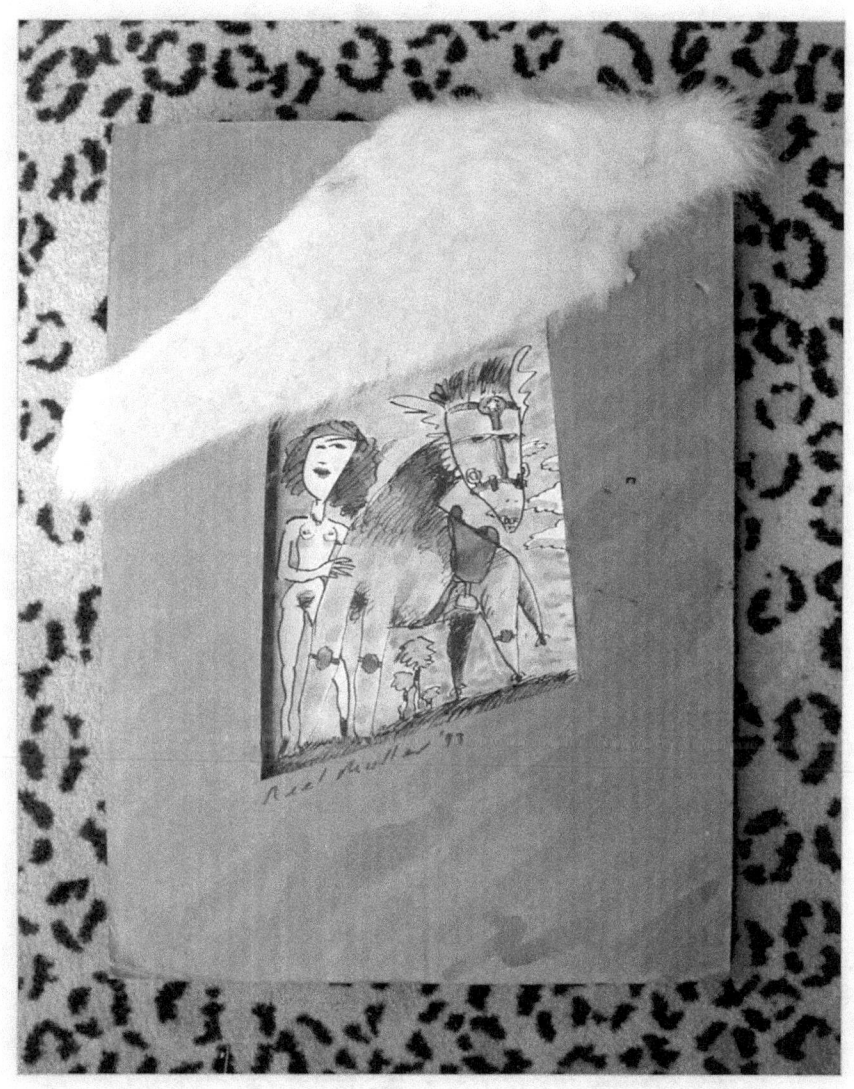

Horsing around.

Like there's no tomorrow.

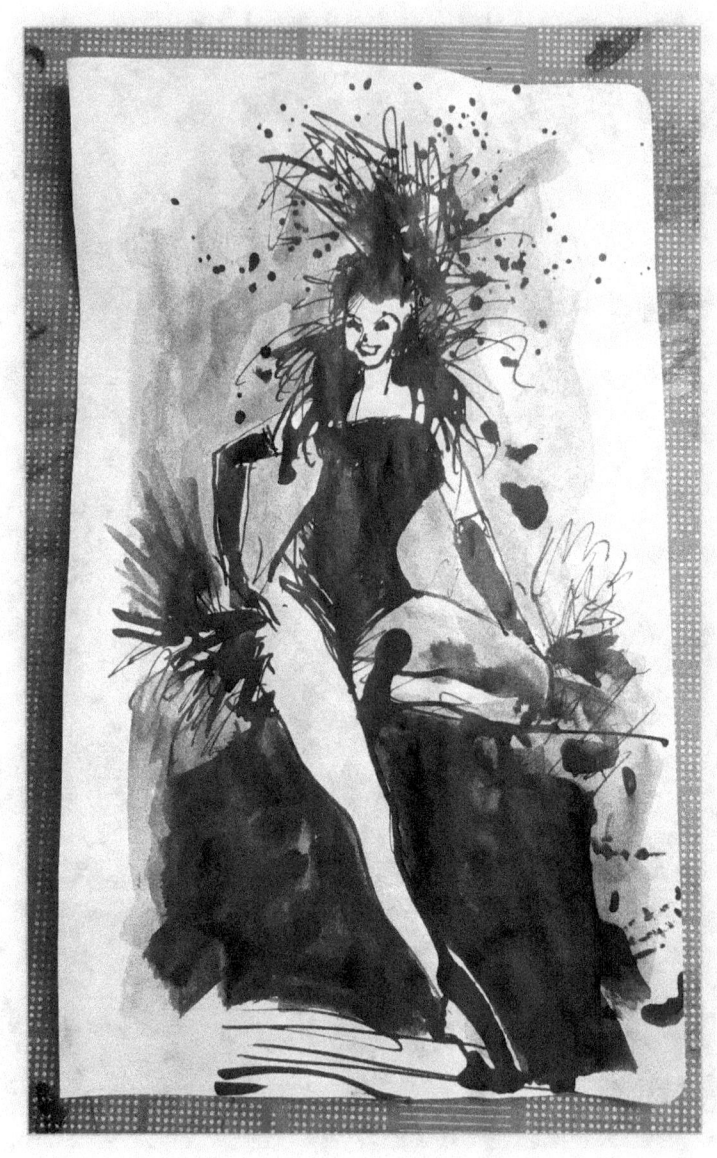

Chorus girl.

With legs to match.

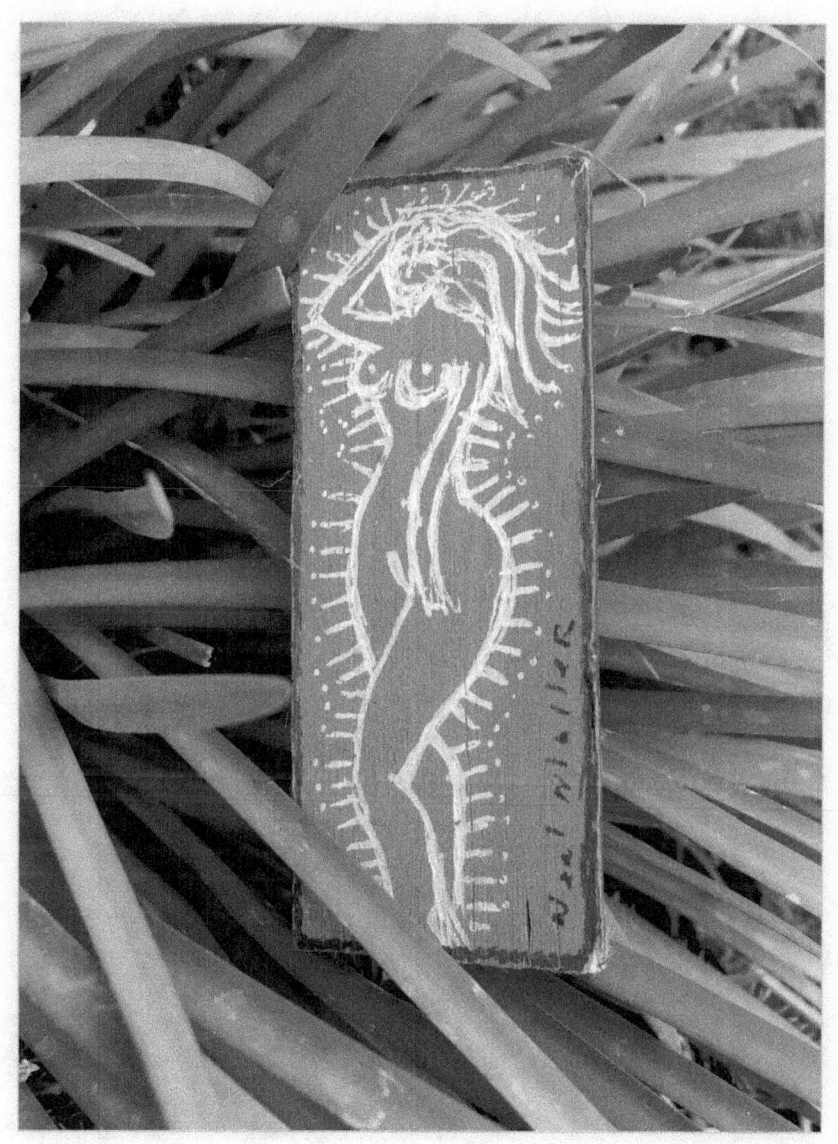

A nude in the front yard.

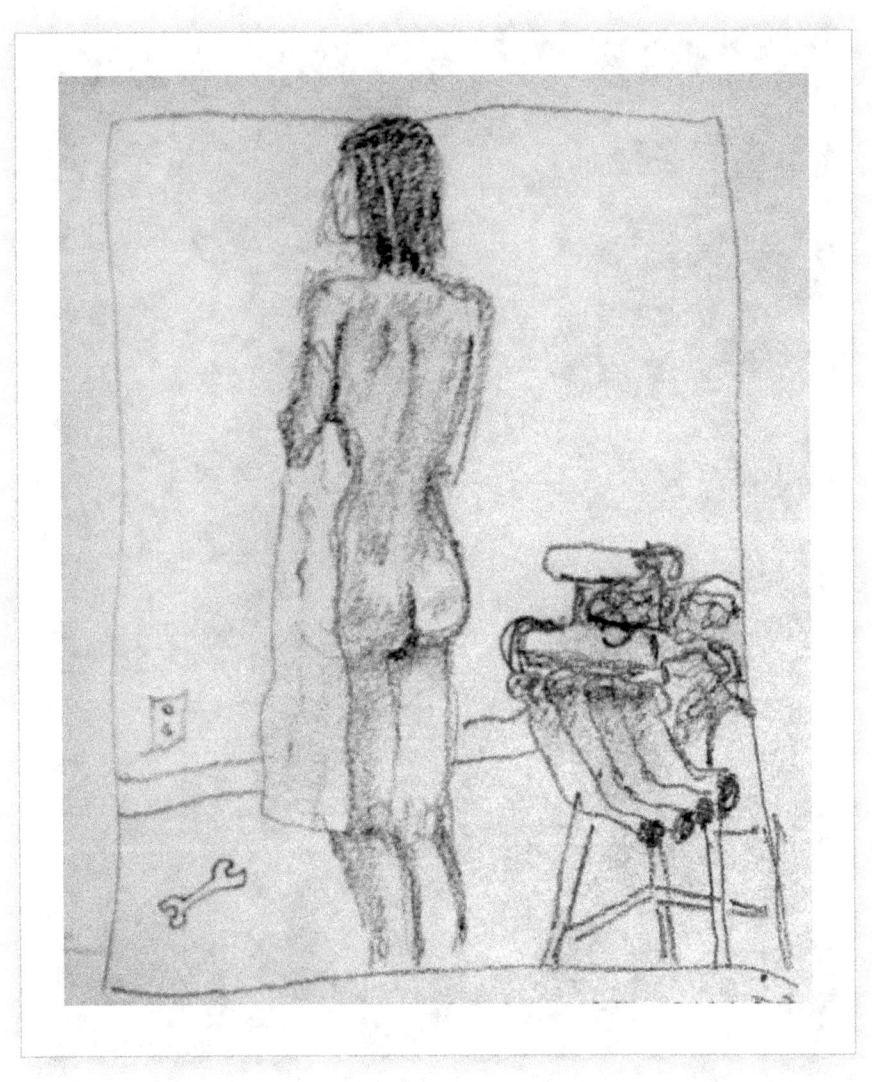

Nude with V8.

It was a small block Chevy.

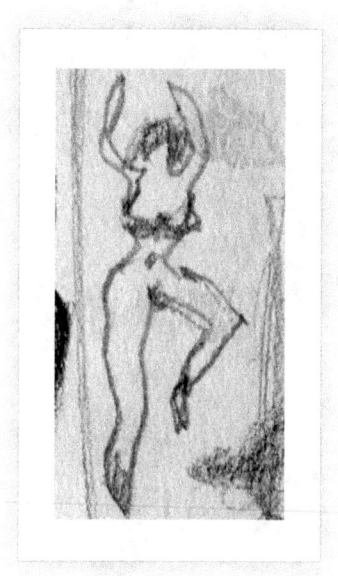

Micro dancer.

Small with big moves.

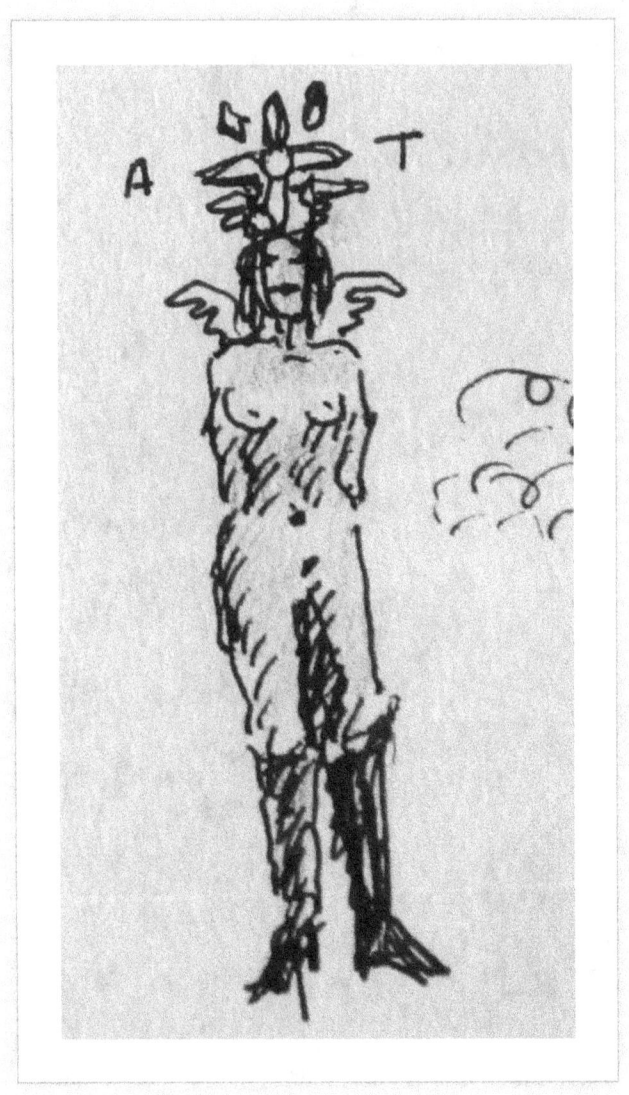

Angel.

Cannot for the life of me remember what the A and T stands for.

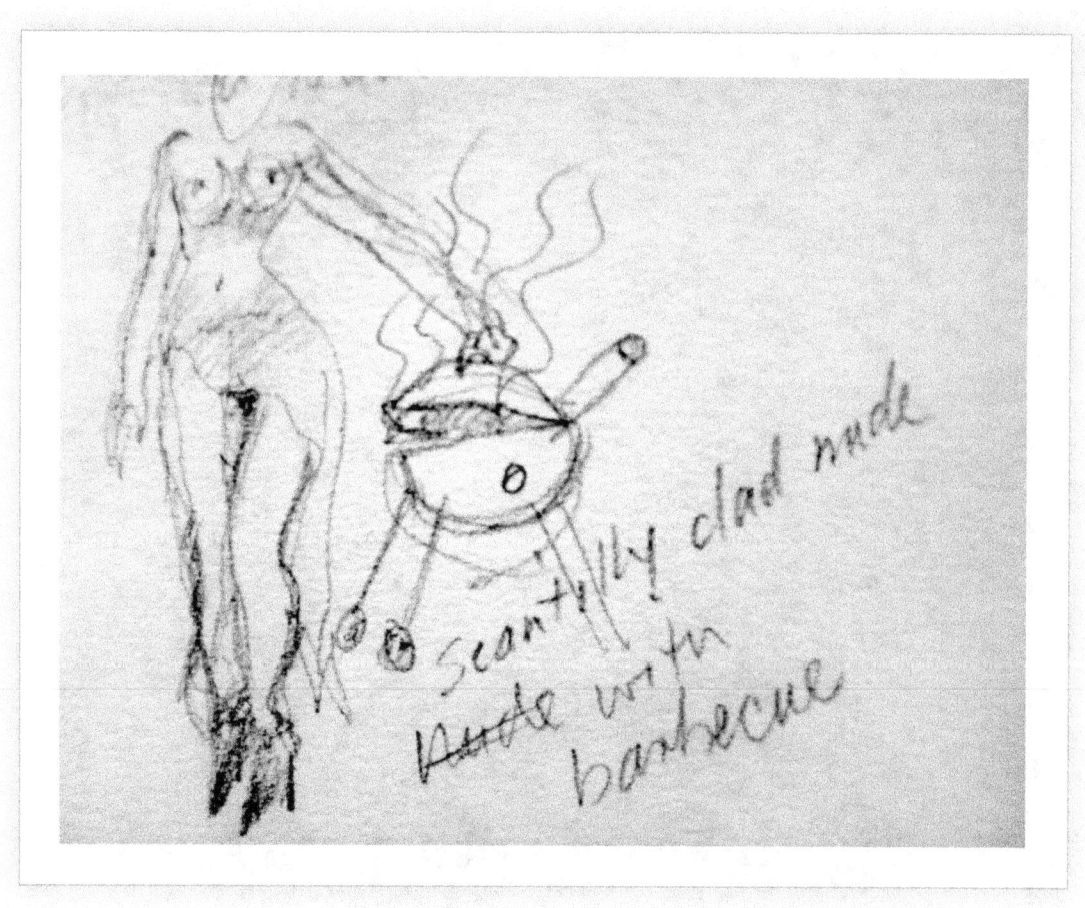

Scantily clad nude with barbecue.

Cooking up a storm.

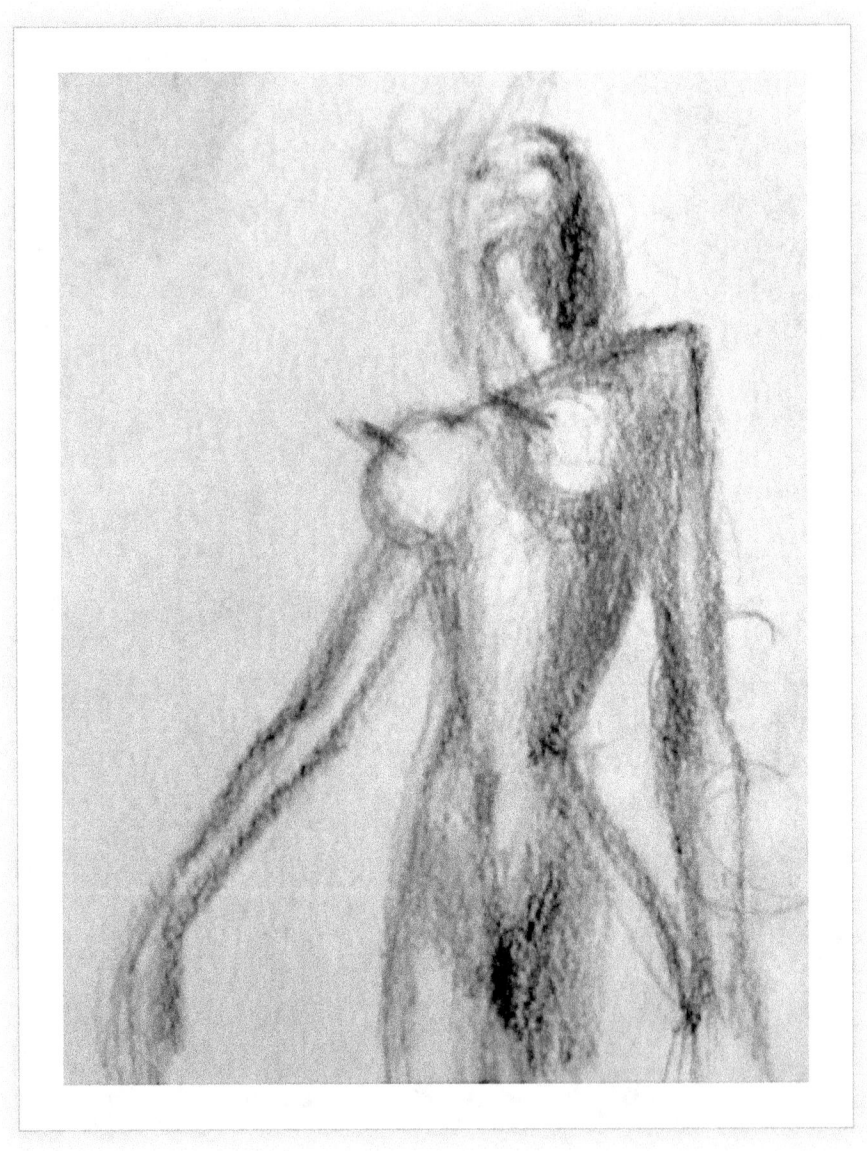

Tall nude.

Not to scale.

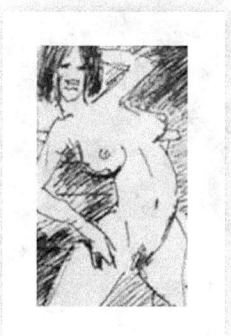

Tiny nude.

Not to scale but very popular.

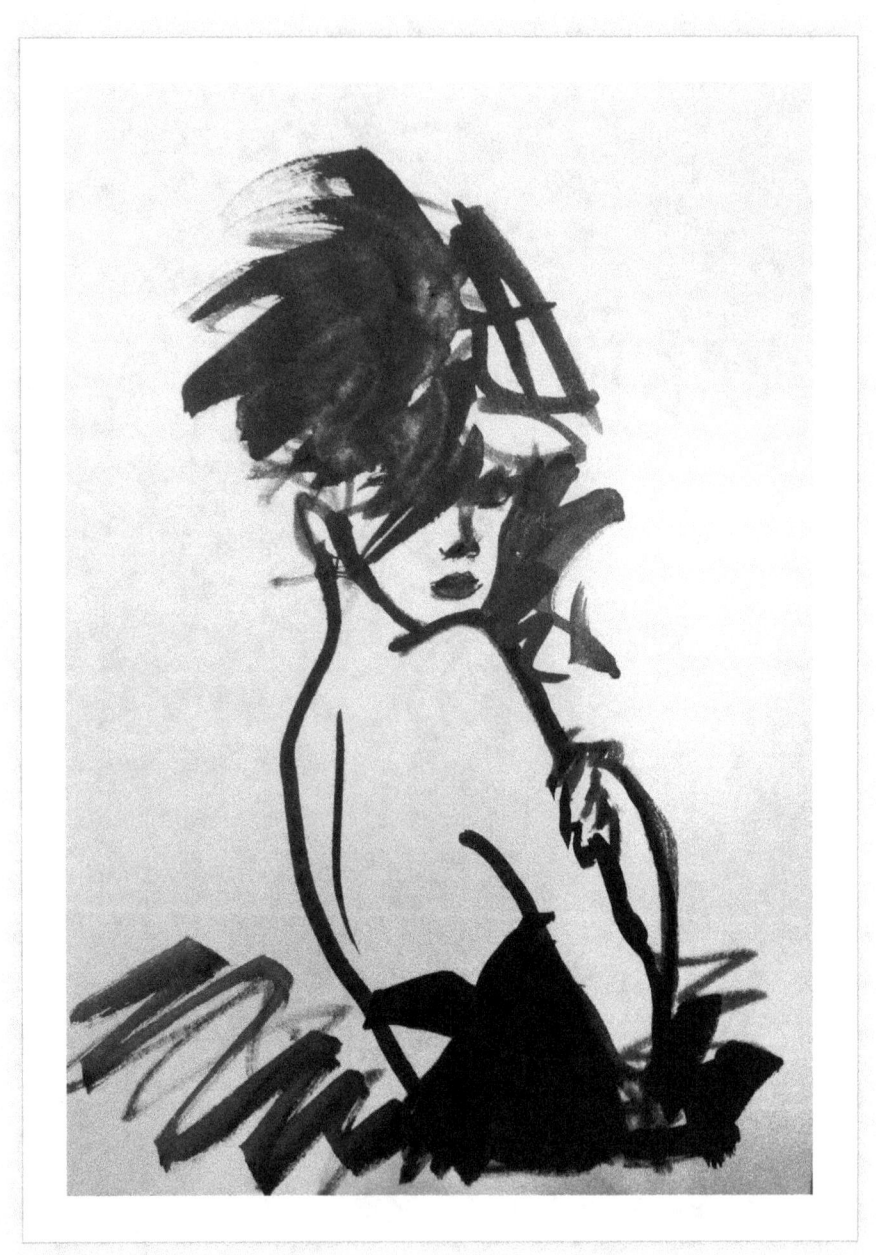

A cold shoulder.

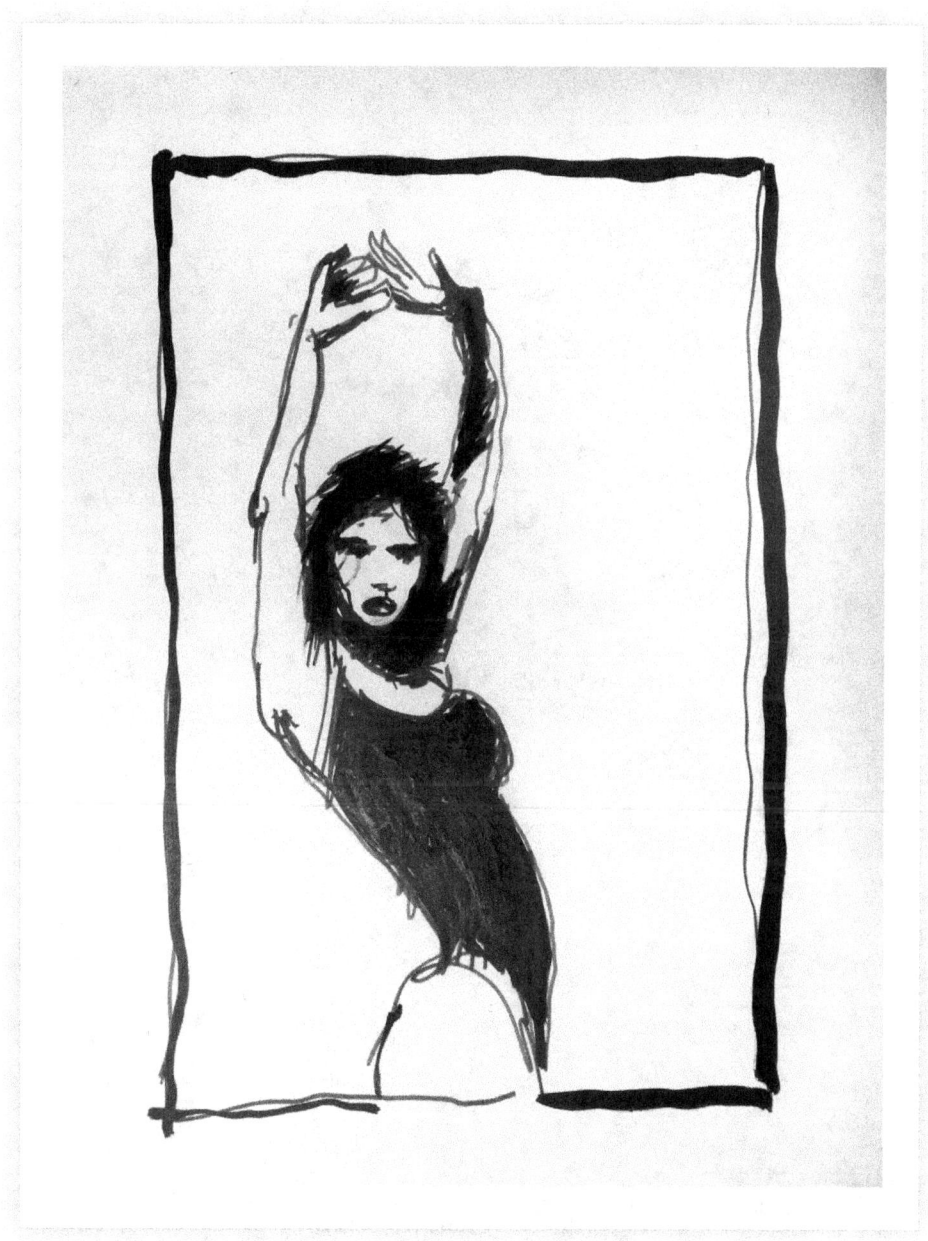

Stretched to the limit.

She could snap at any moment.

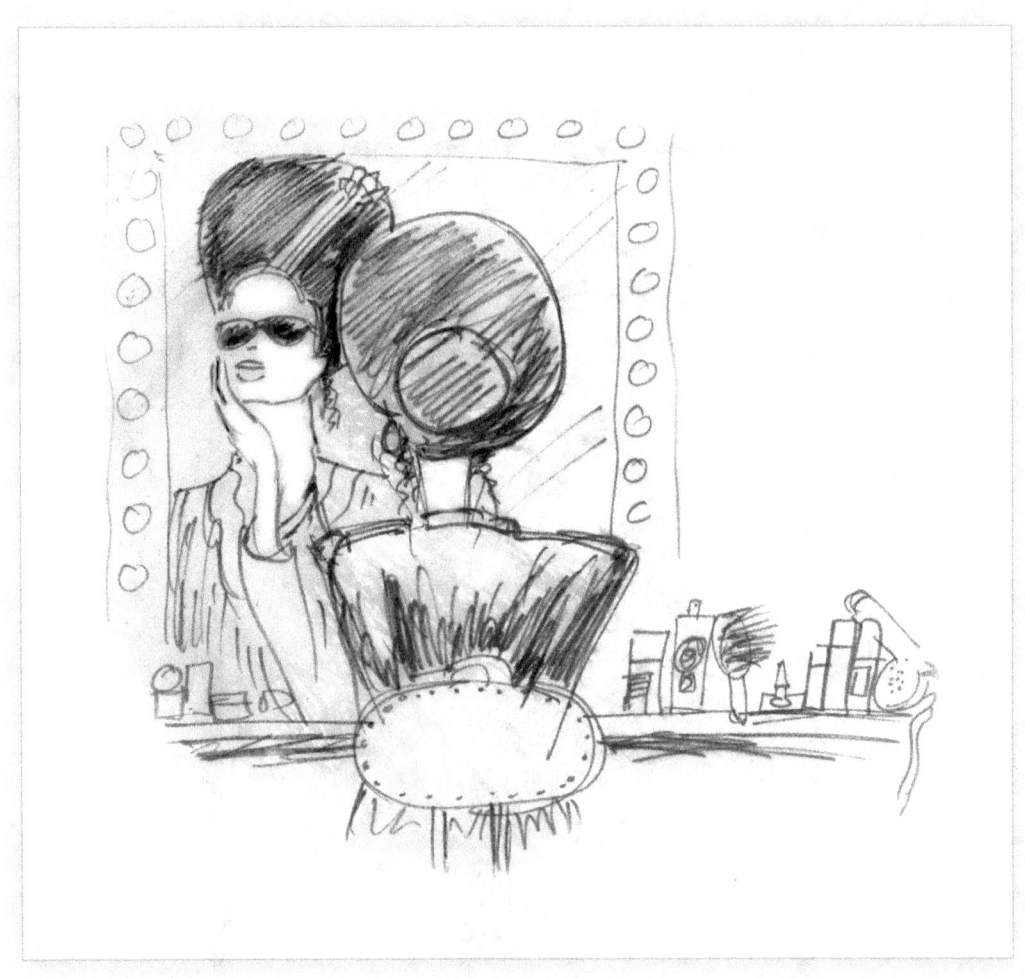

Working with what she's got.

Using all of the tools at her disposal.

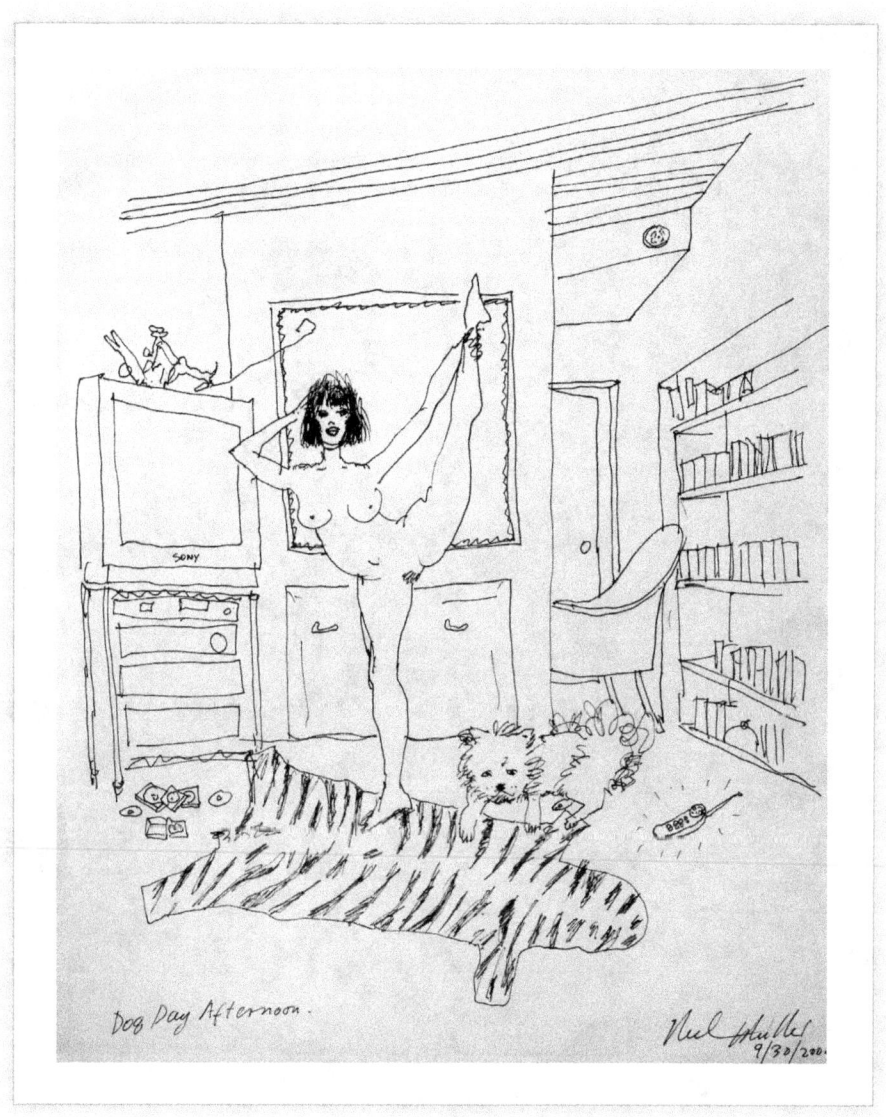

Dog Day Afternoon.

Dog day afternoon.

The universe was in perfect alignment.

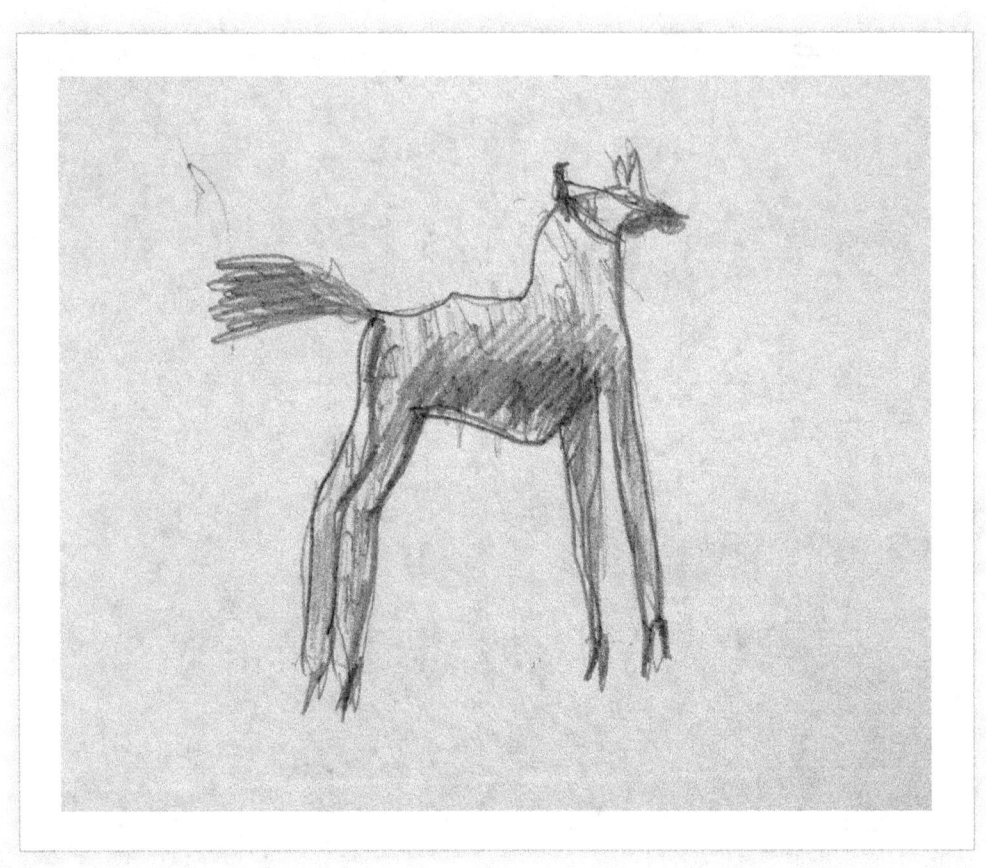

Sitting on her high horse.

Heaven knows when she'll get off.

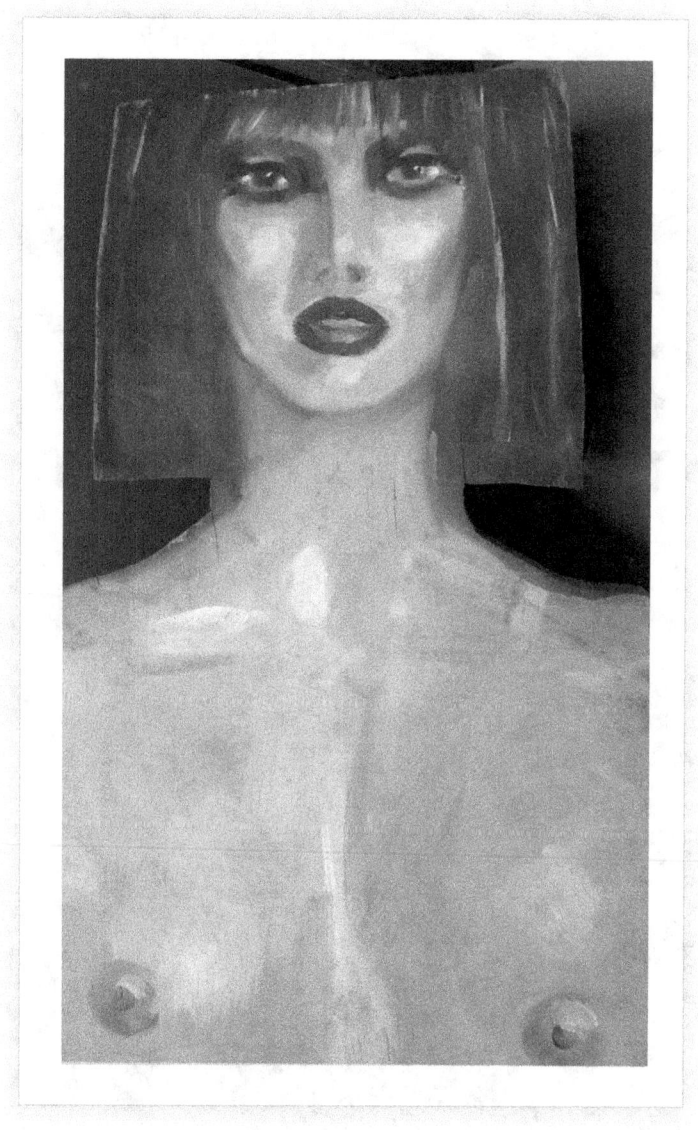

Woman in oil on a plank.

I had her out in the yard, but now she's in my shack.

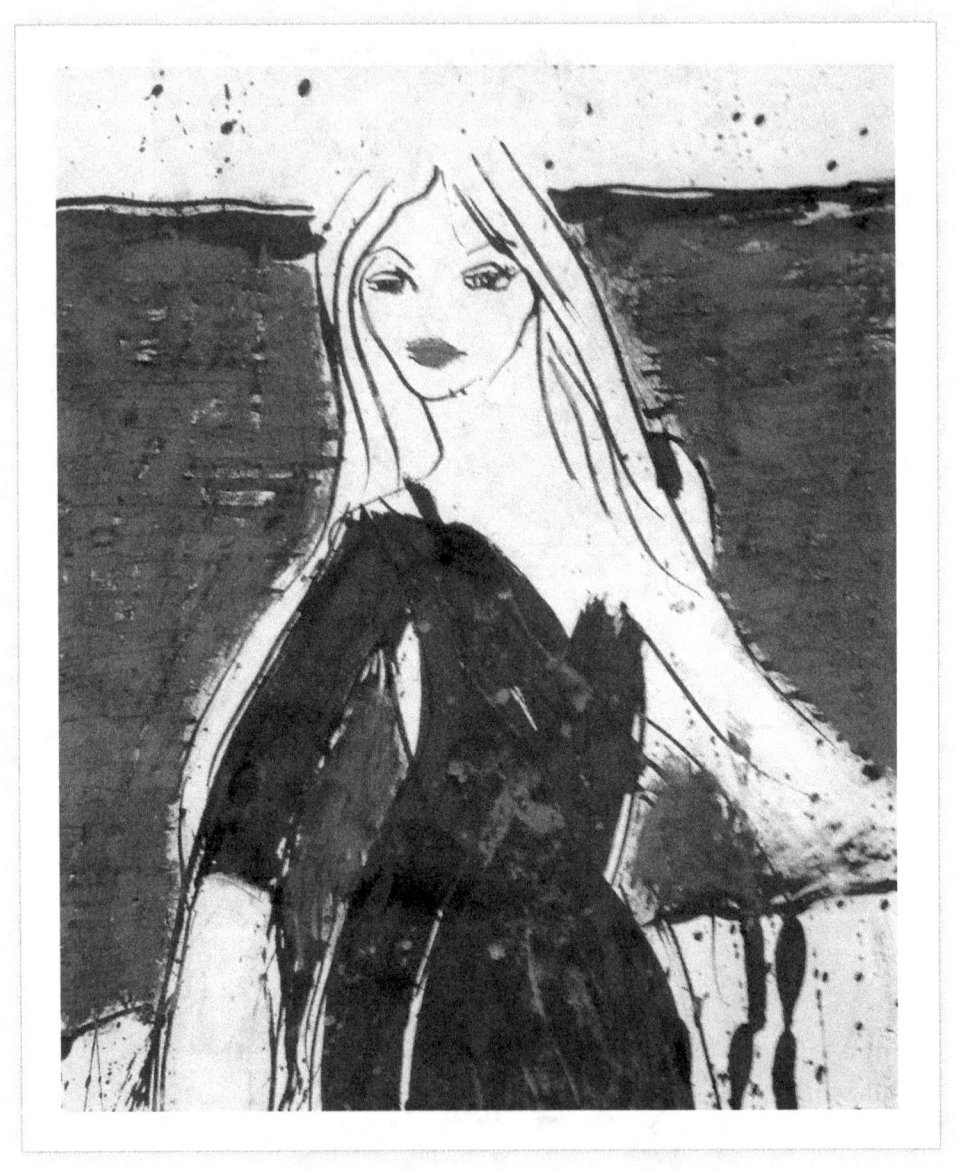

Not just a pretty face.

I was told she has a degree in molecular biology

and speaks five languages.

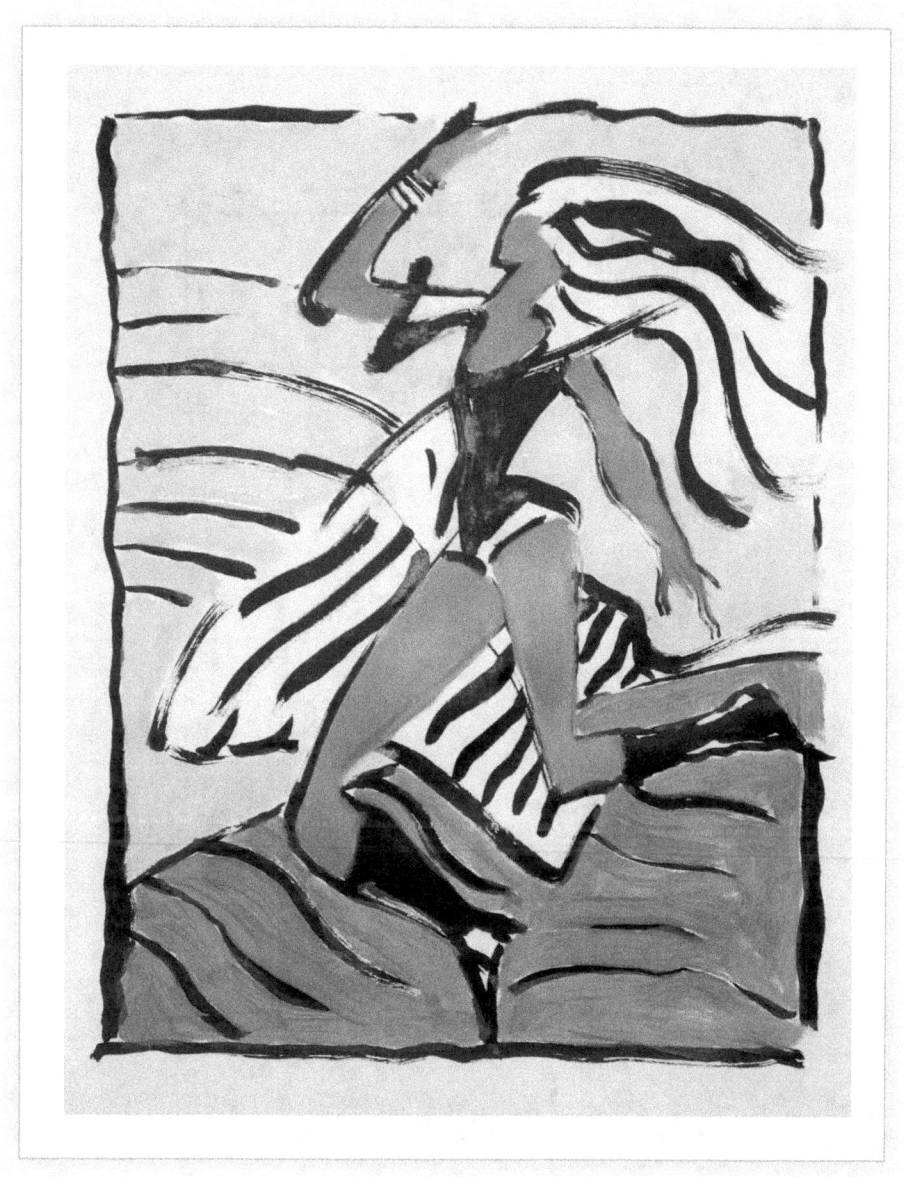

Fast woman.

She could outrun most men.

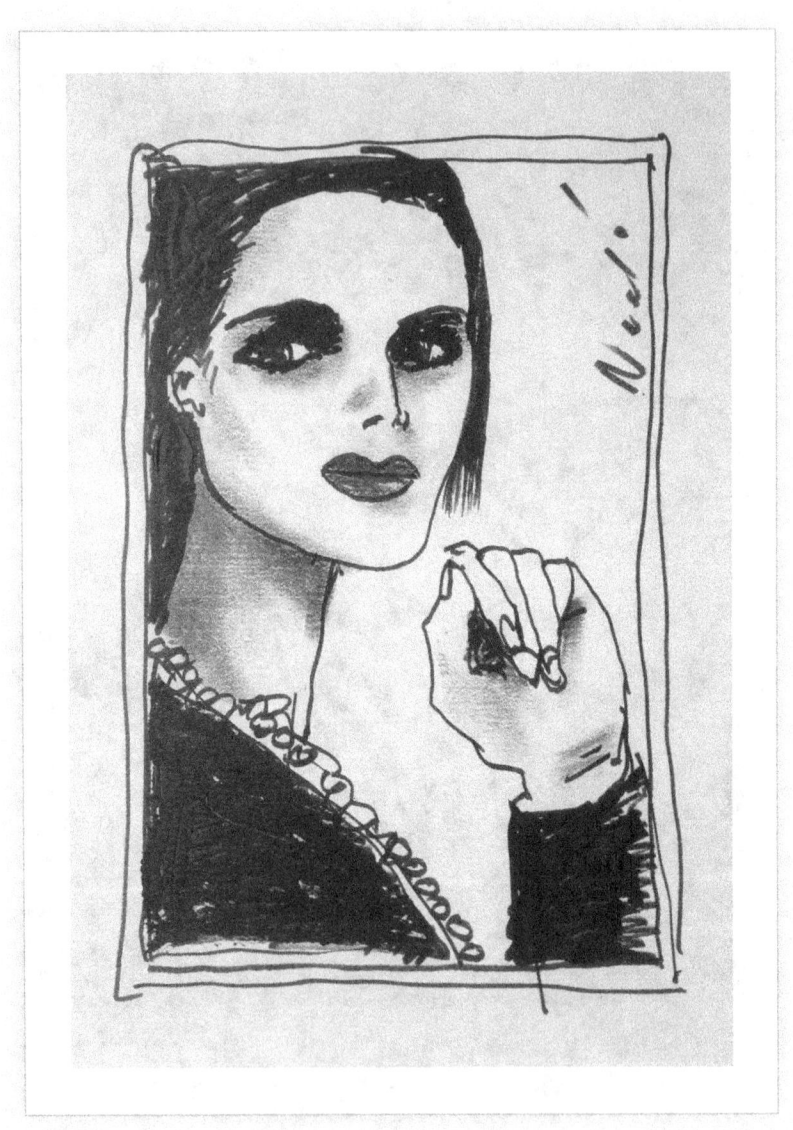

Unknown portrait.

I just don't know.

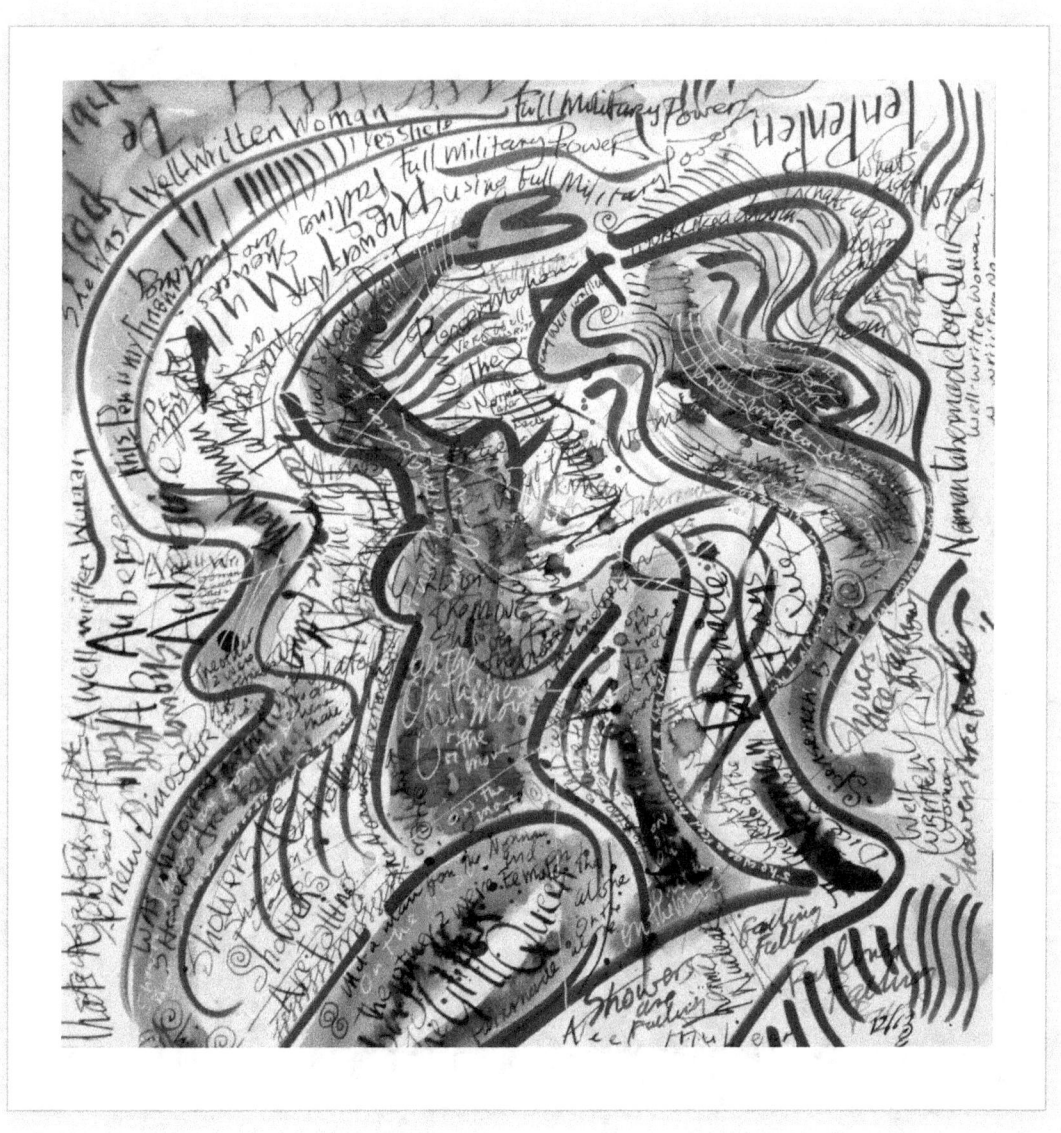

Well-written woman.

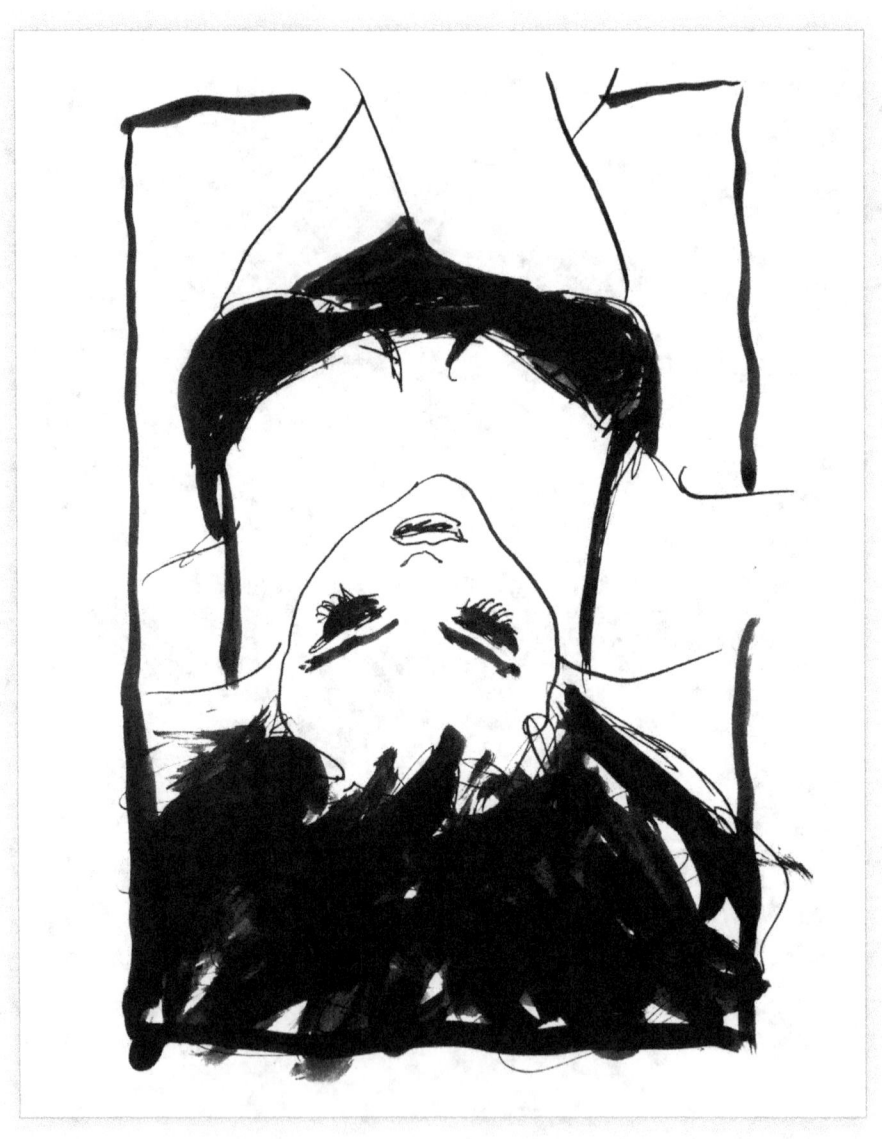

Her fall-back position.

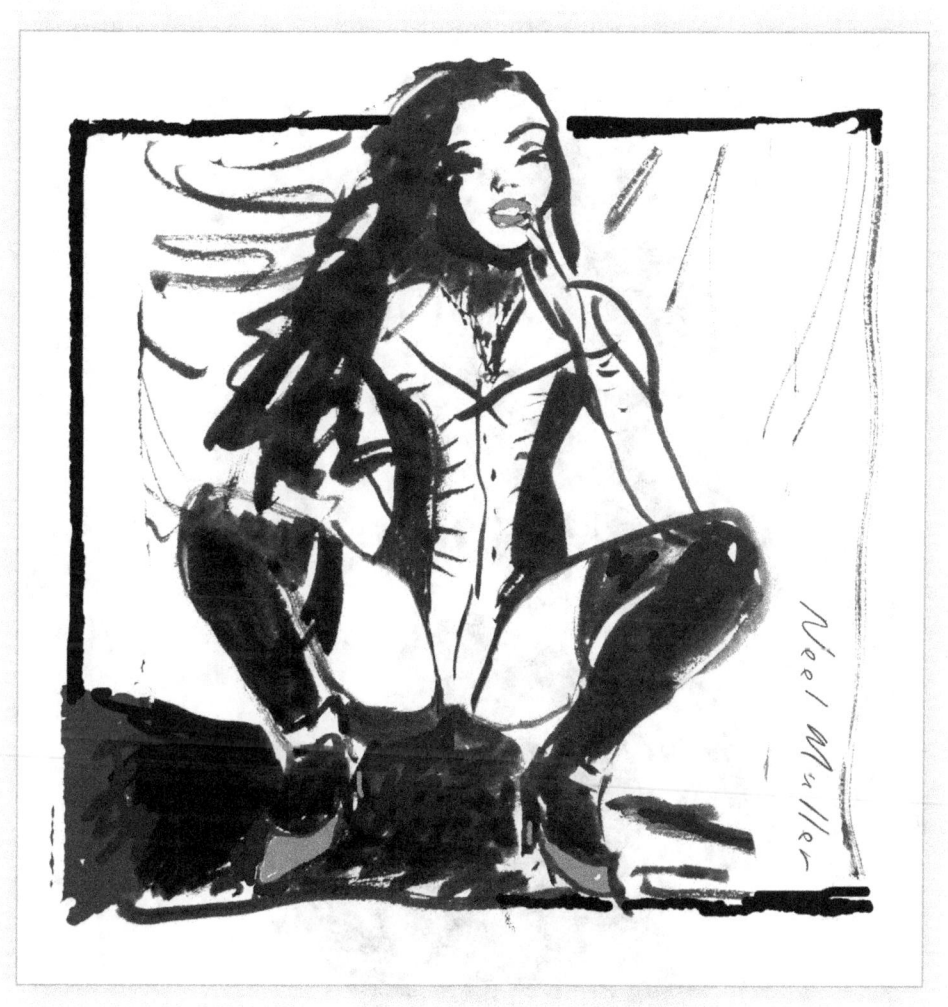

Chorus girl.

Seen here taking a short break.

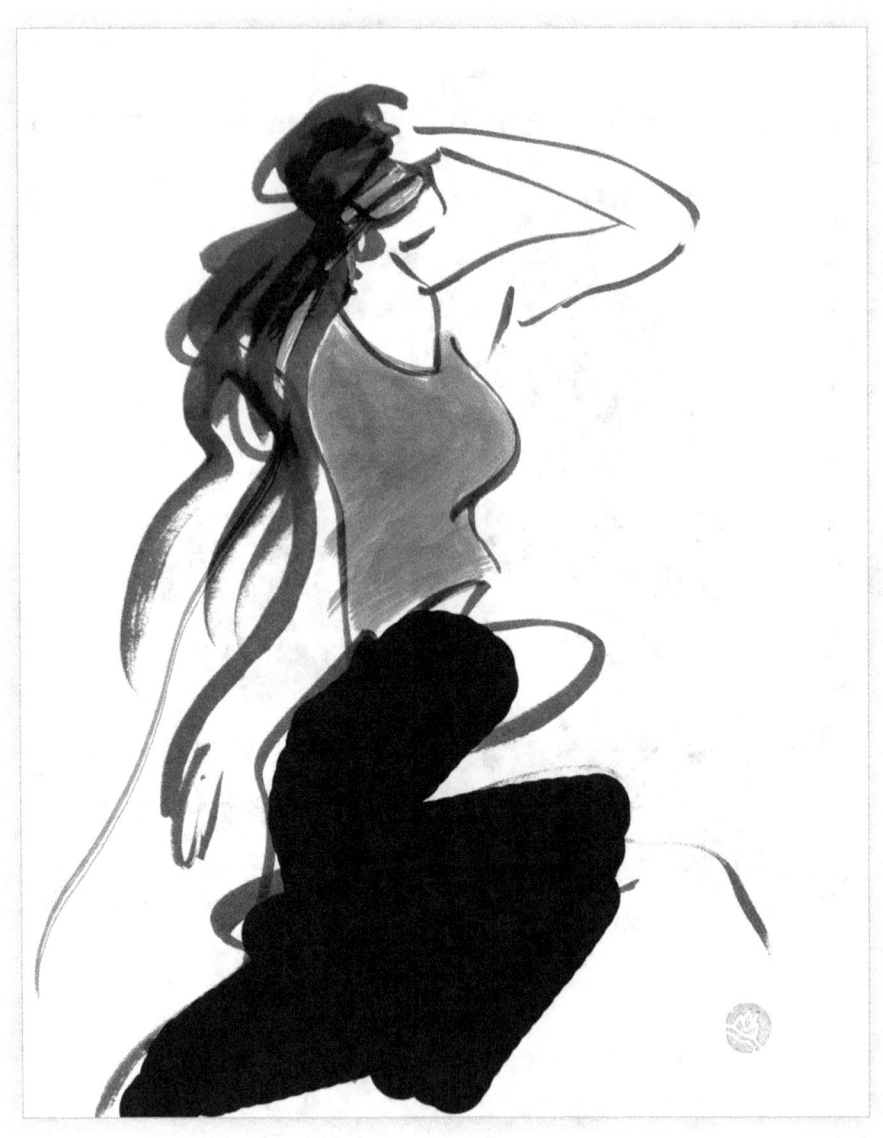

A damn good hair day.

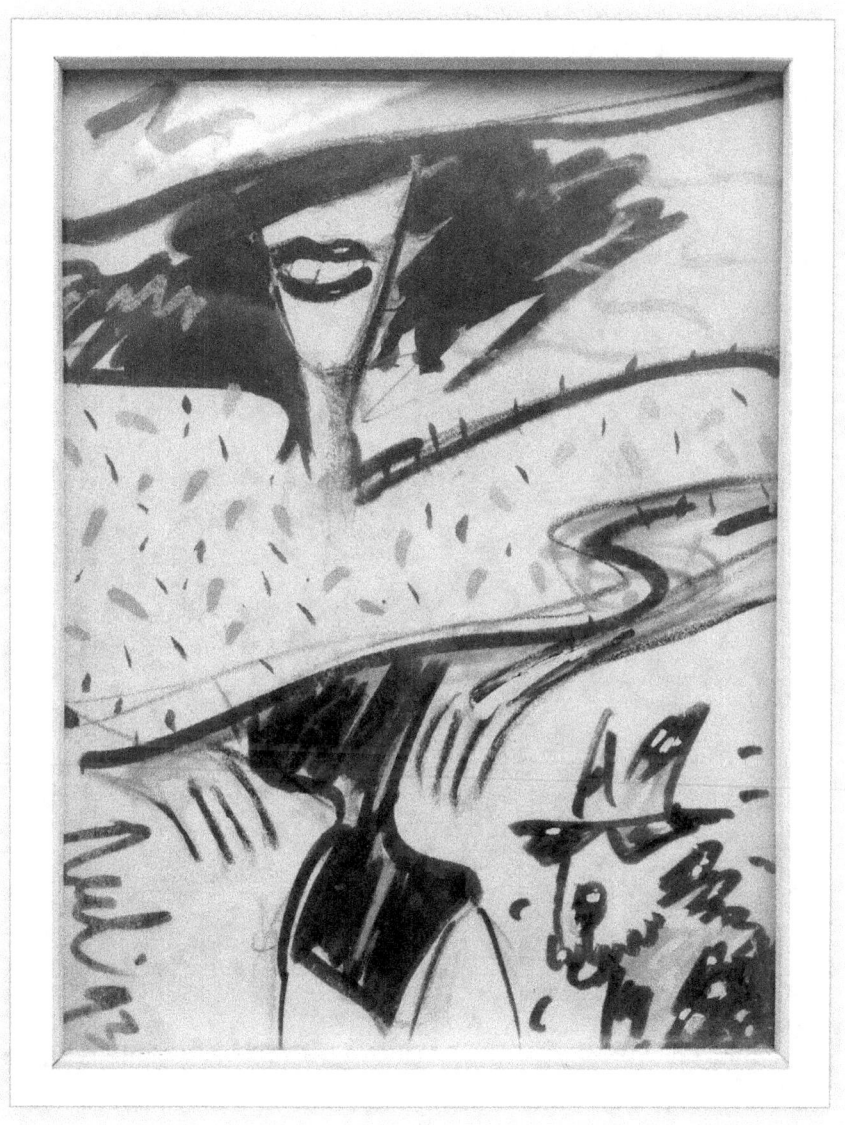

Fashion-conscious females.

Dressed to kill.

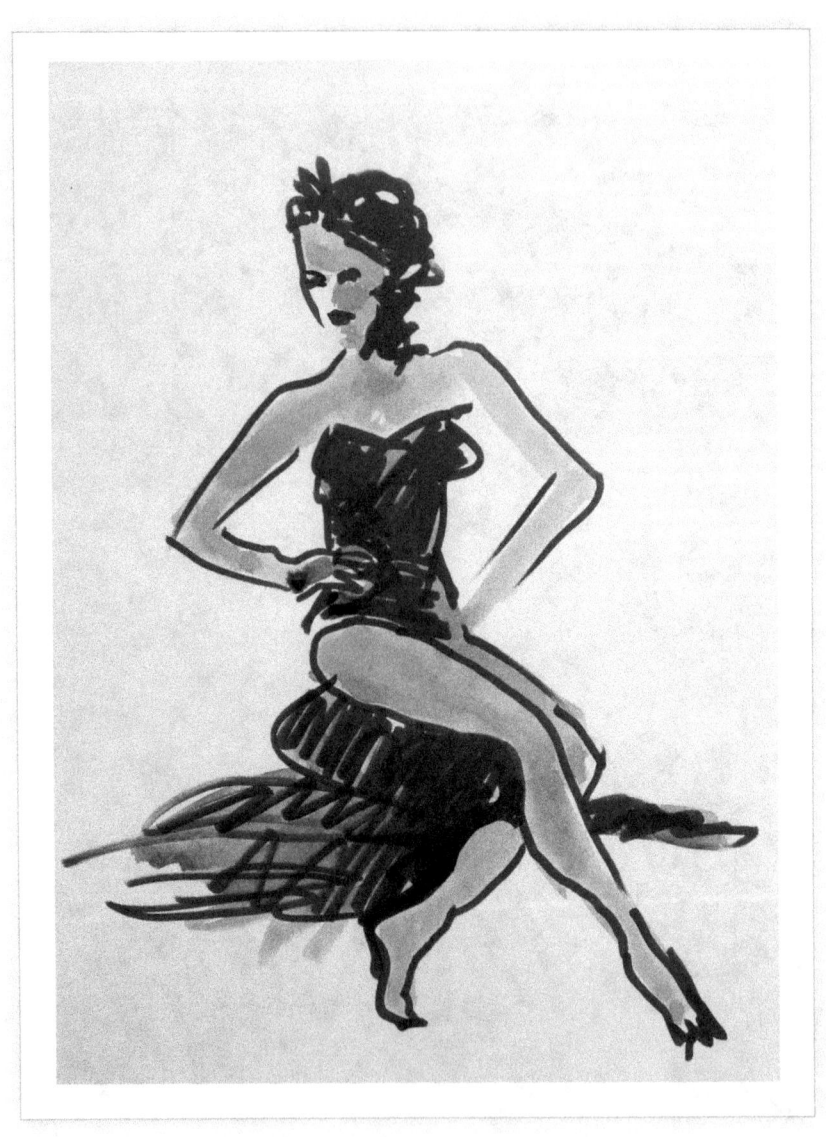

Poser.

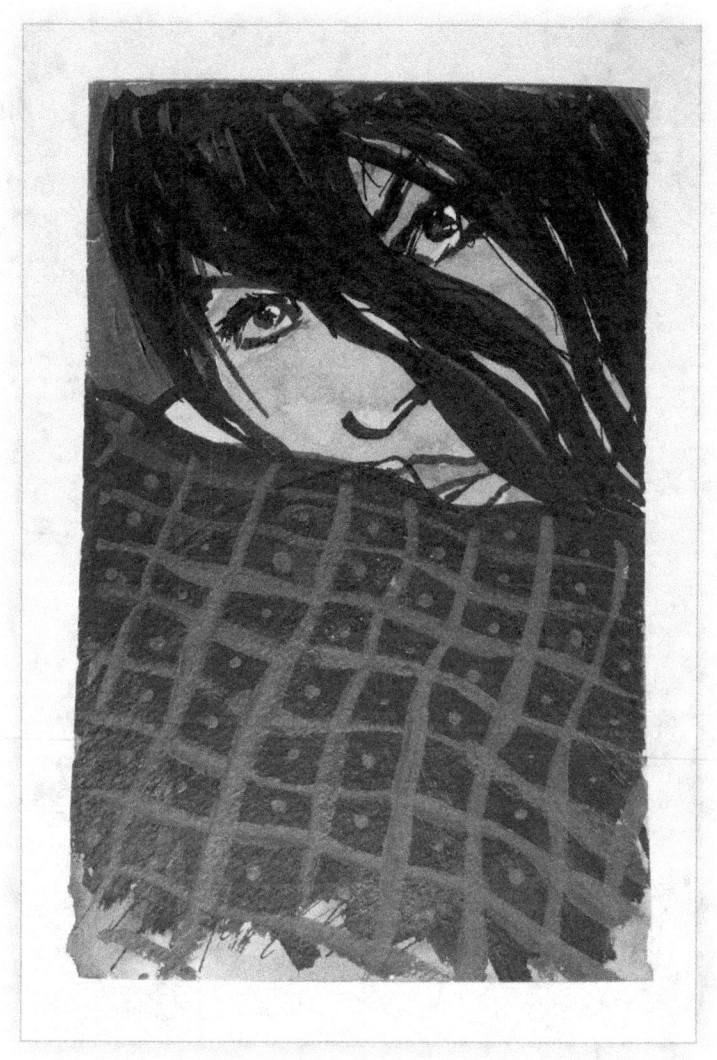

Woman of interest.

Interesting.

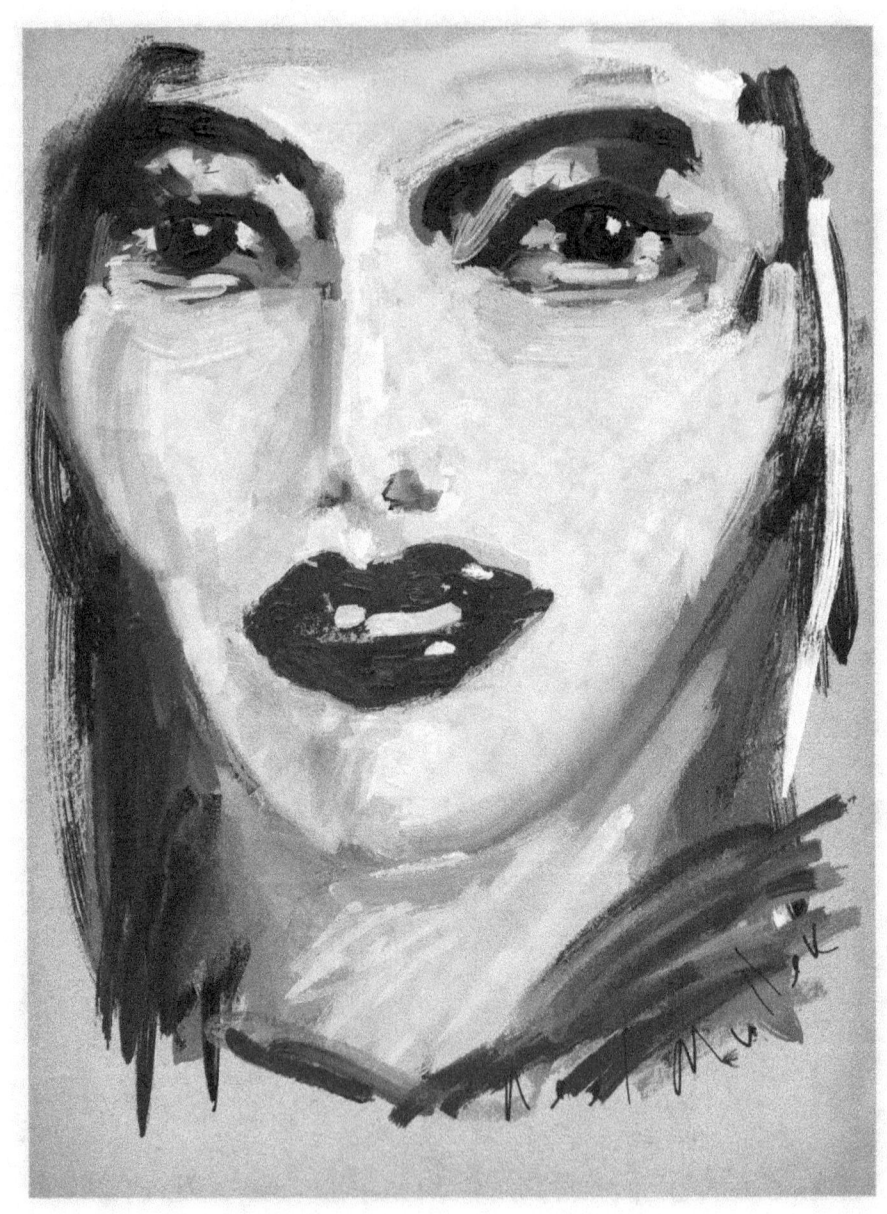

Woman done quick.

On my iPad in bed.

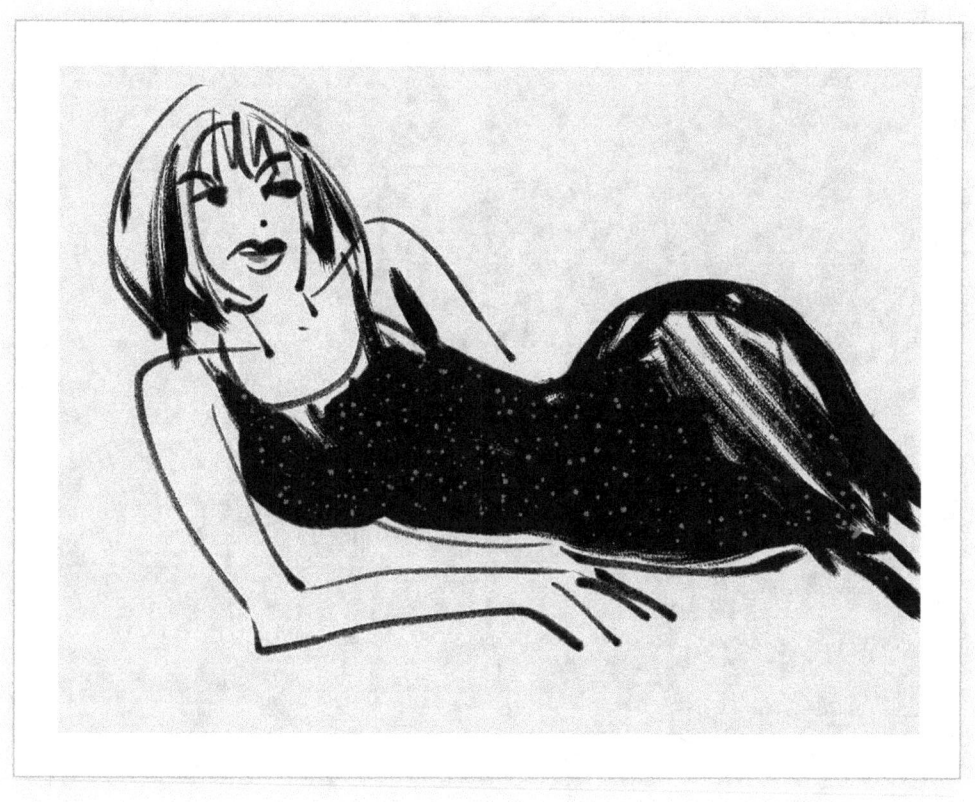

Maxed out relaxed.

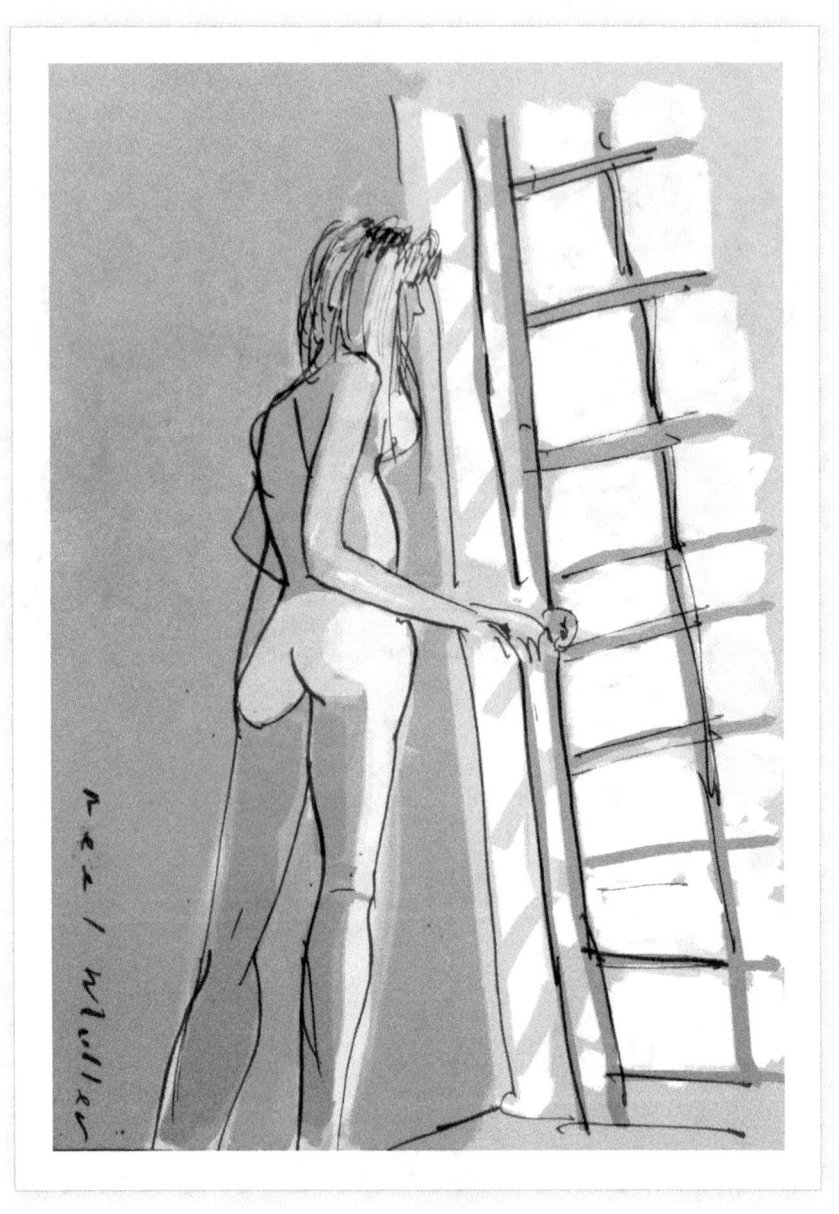

There's a nude at the door.

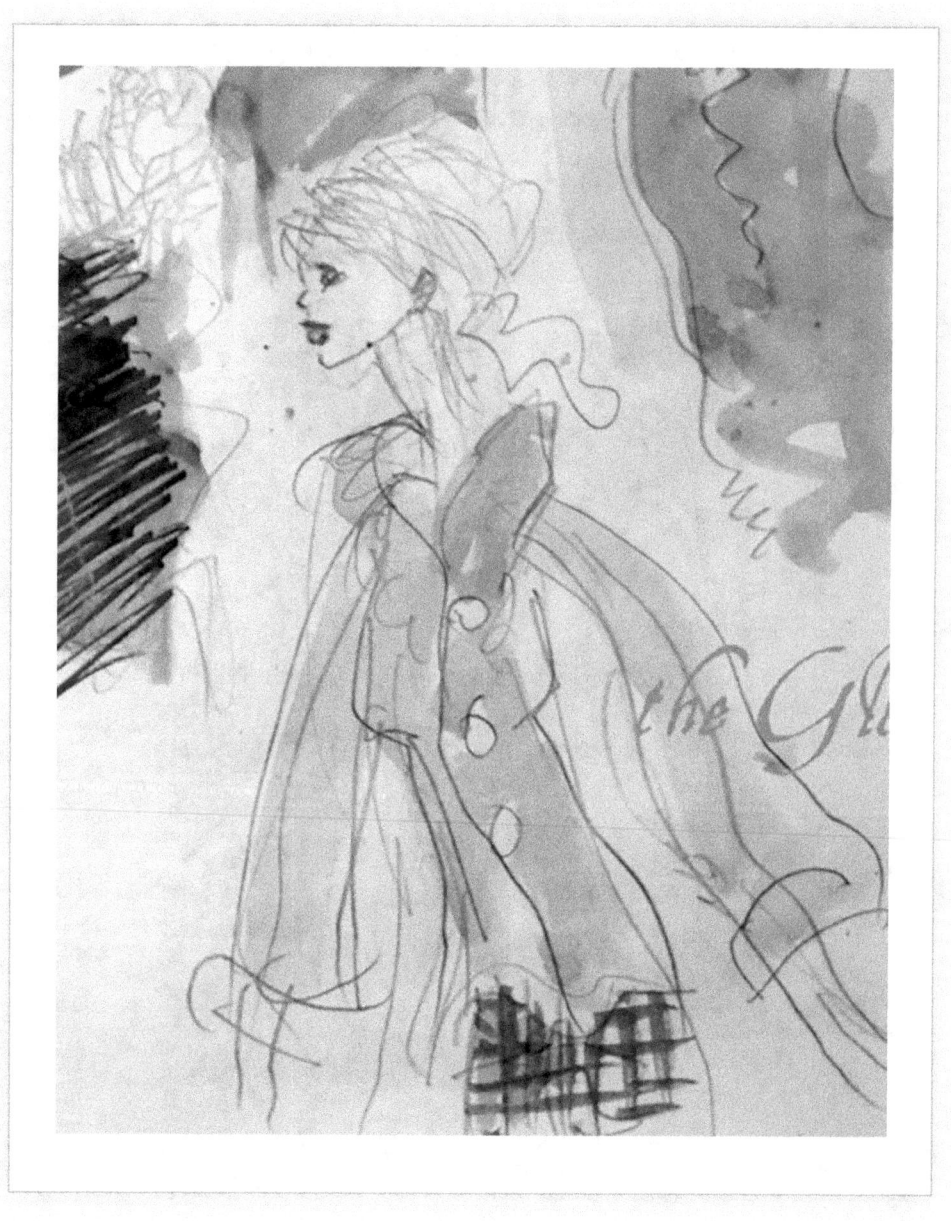

Dressed up and nowhere to go.

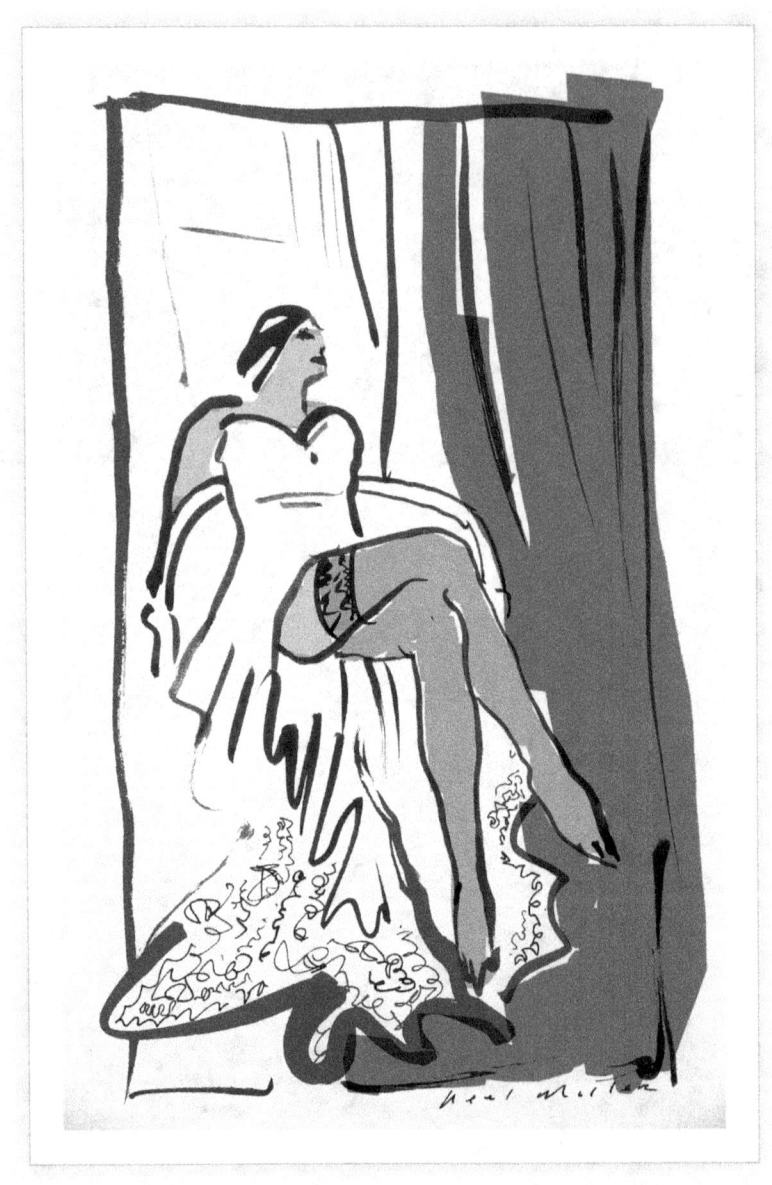

Working woman.

She does not keep regular office hours.

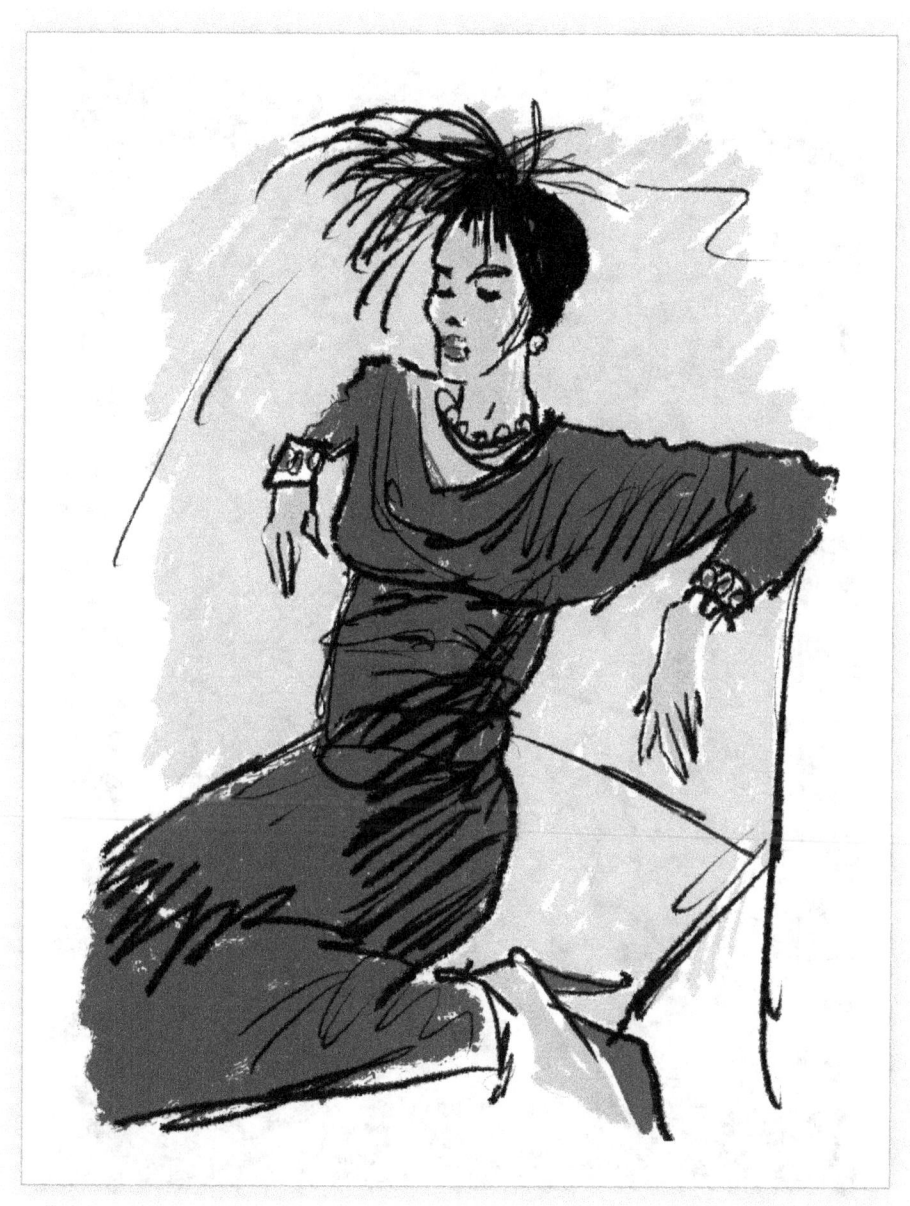

Sleepy woman.

I could tell it was well past her bedtime.

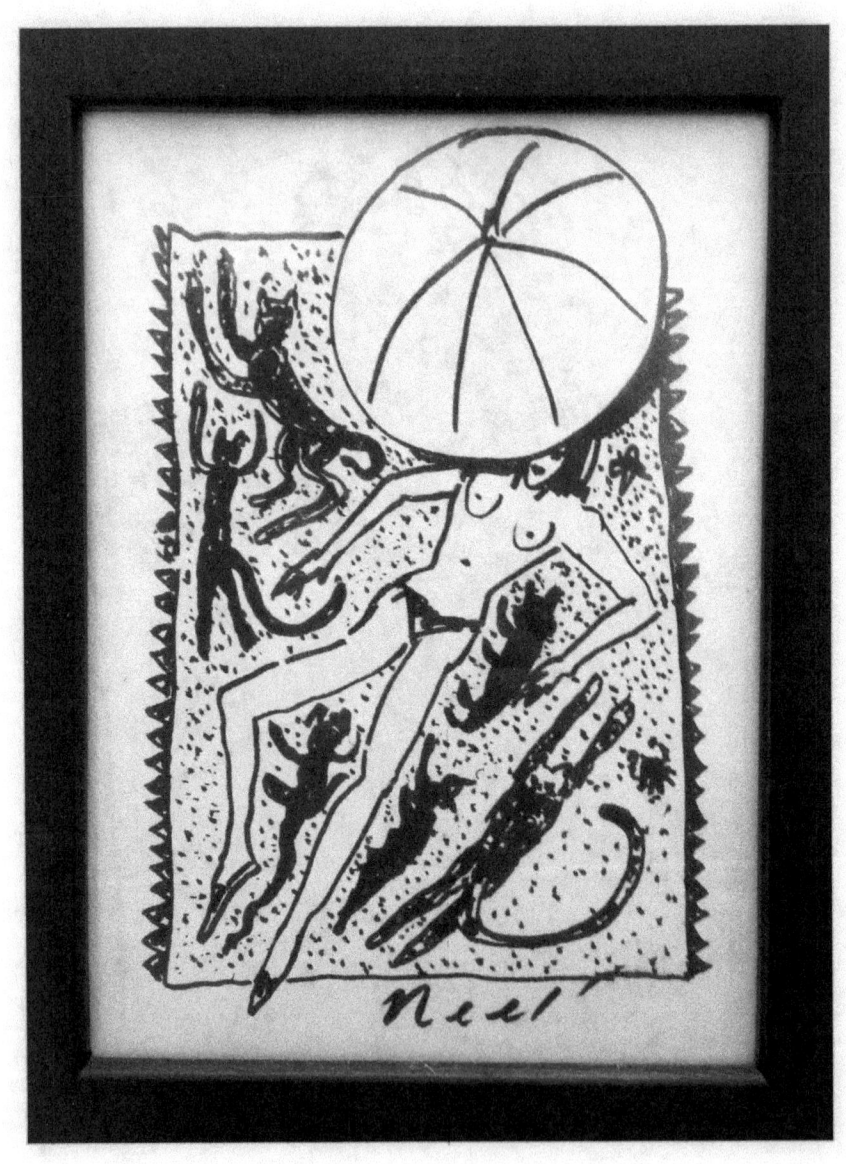

She found herself in good company.

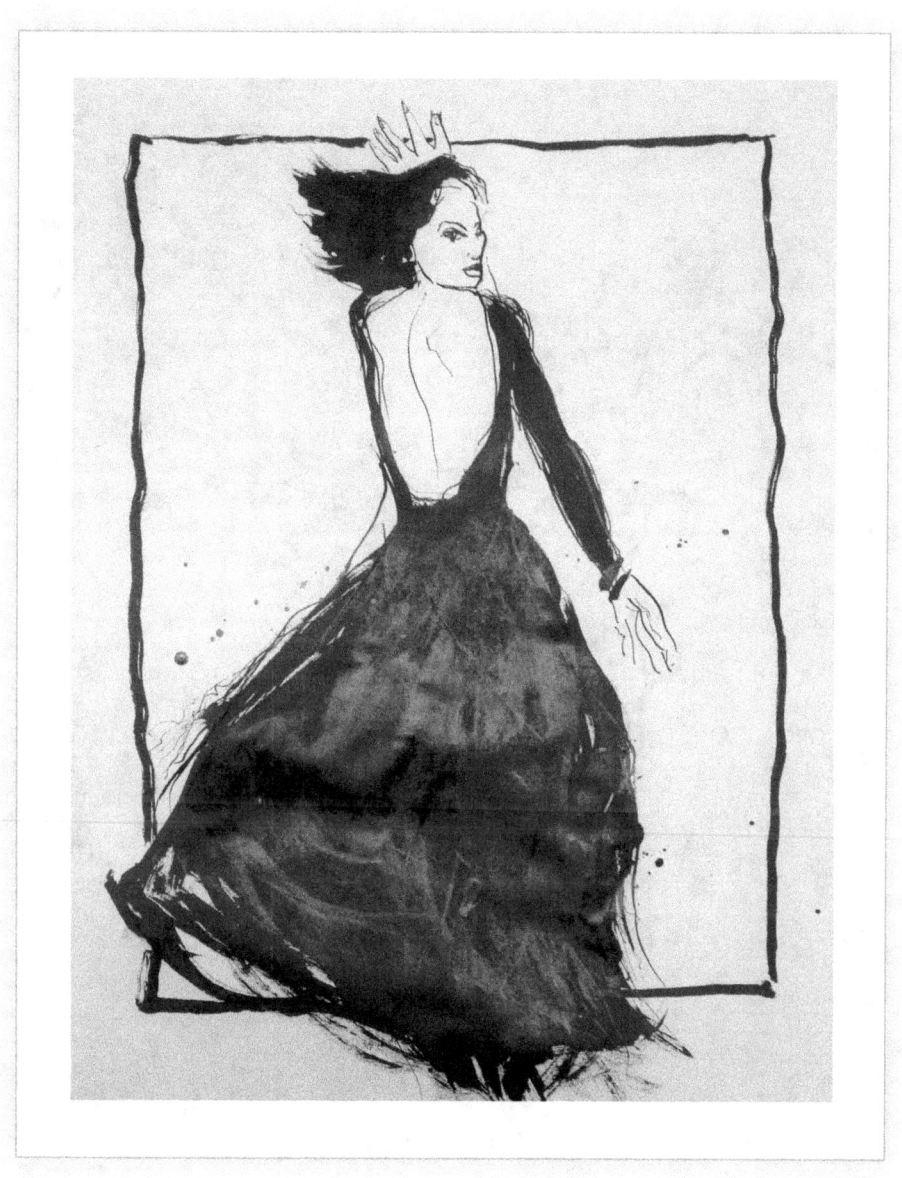

Waving goodbye for the very last time.

A real pity.

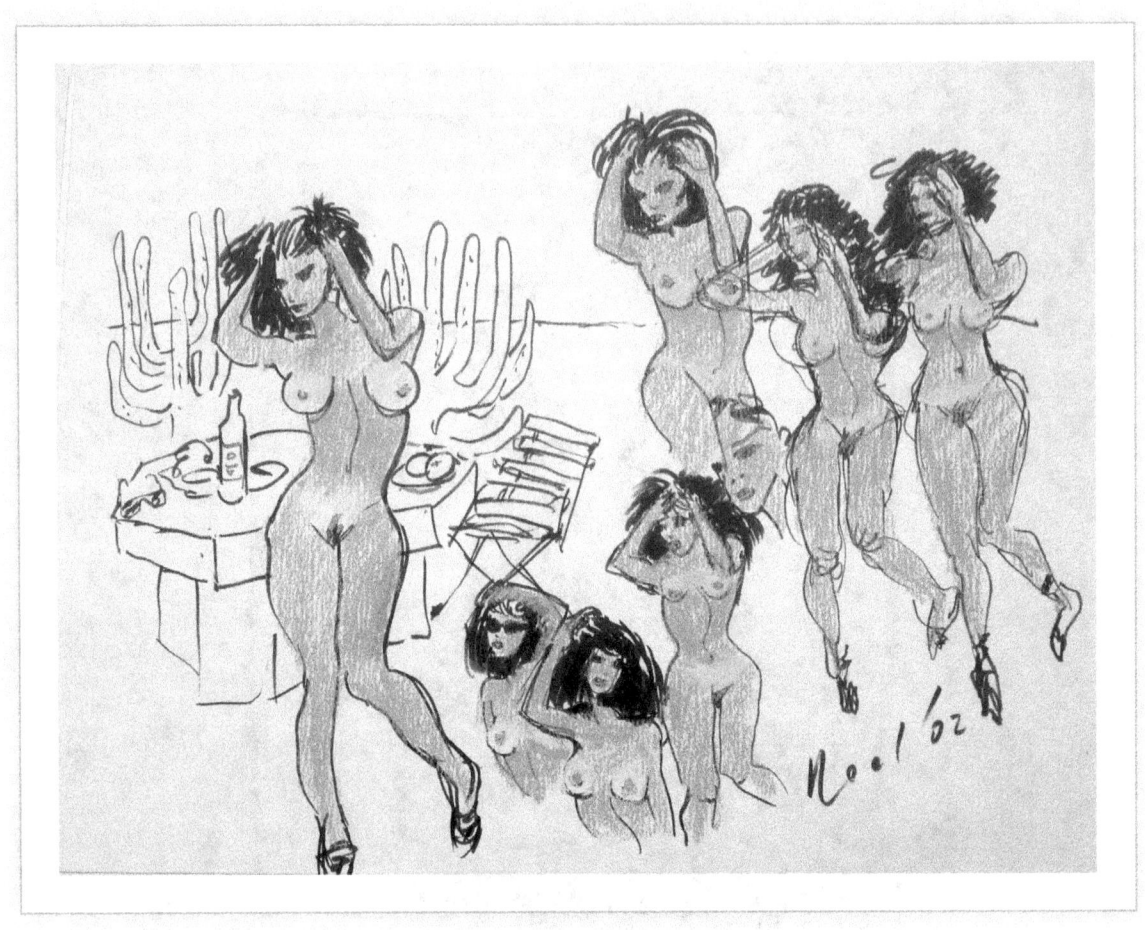

Multiple bombshells.

A total of 8. Count them if you like.

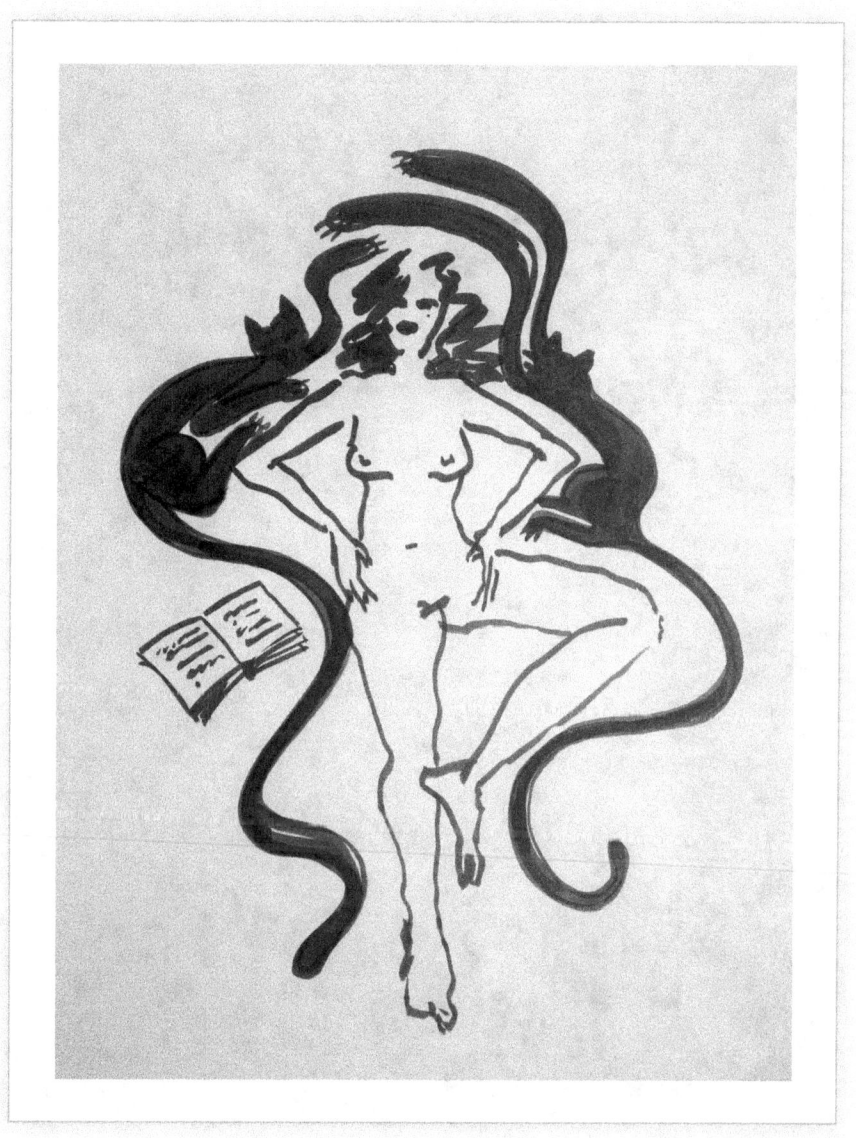

Well-read nude.

She had a tale and a tail to tell it with.

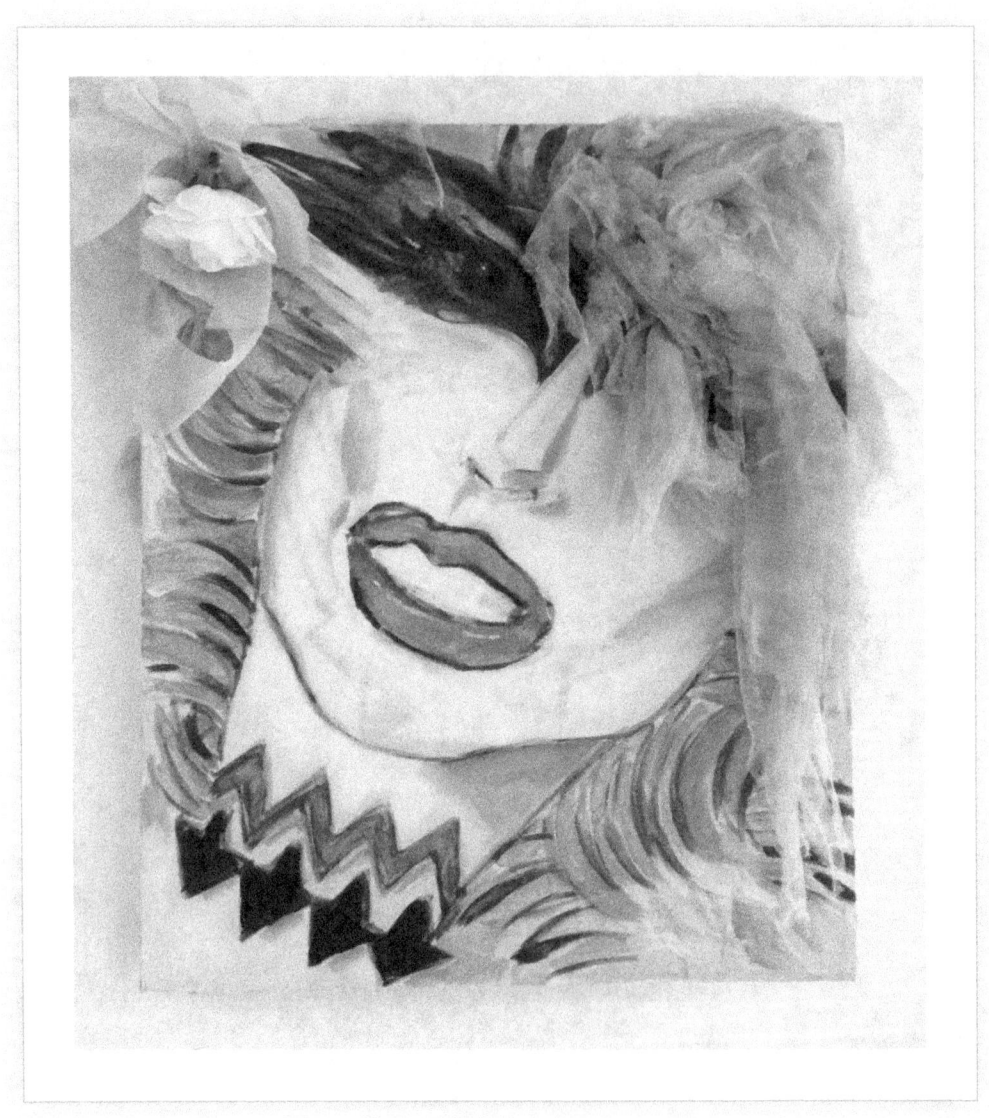

Mystery woman.

And that is how it shall remain.

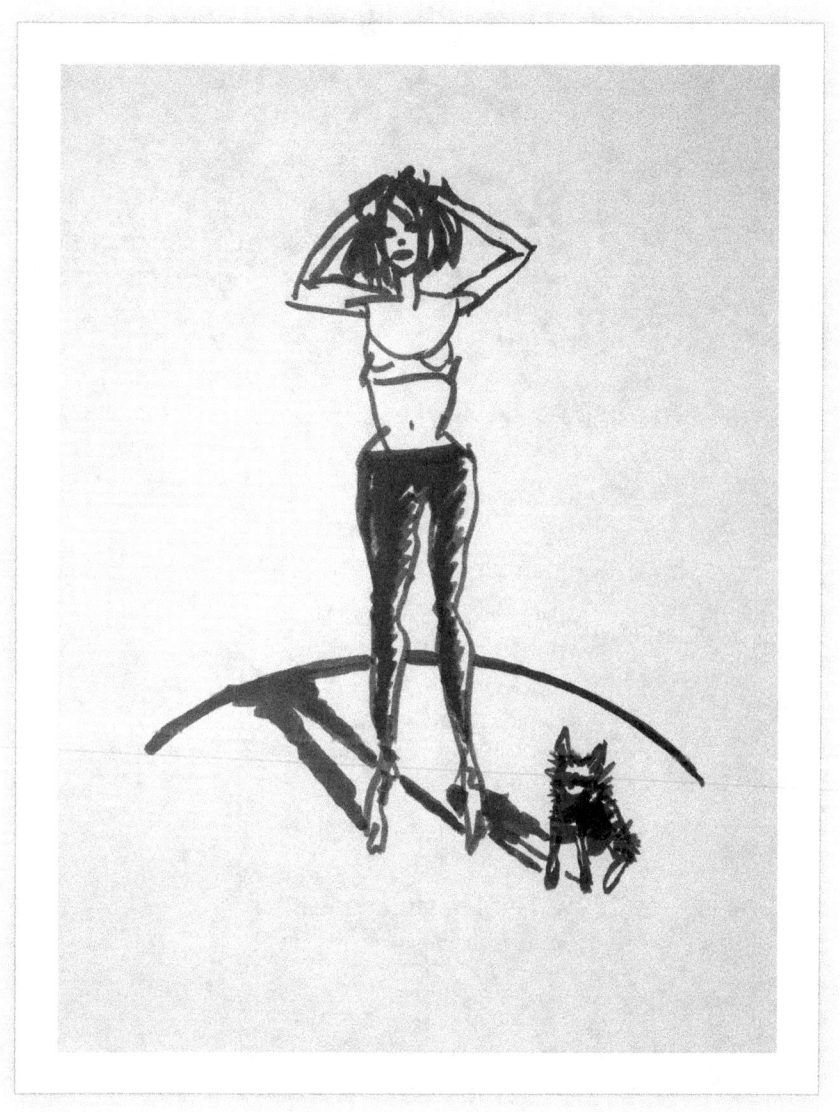

Thinkers.

Thinking about what to do next.

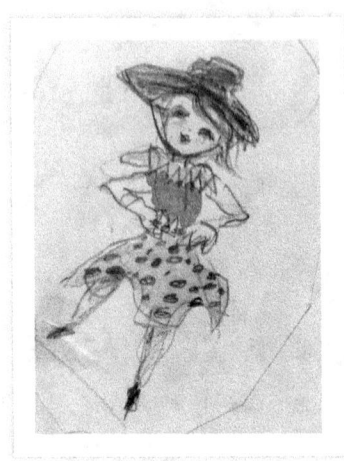

Maurice Chevalier - Thank Heaven For Little Girls

Each time I see a little girl
Of five or six or seven
I can't resist a joyous urge
To smile and say
Thank heaven for little girls
For little girls get
Bigger every day
Thank heaven for little girls
They grow up in
The most delightful way.
Those little eyes
So helpless and appealing
When they were flashing
Send you crashing
Through the ceiling
Thank heaven for little girls
Thank heaven for them all
No matter where,
No matter who
Without them
What would little boys do
Thank heaven
Thank heaven
Thank heaven for little girls.

www.ingramcontent.com/pod-product-compliance
Lightning Source LLC
Chambersburg PA
CBHW081723220526
45468CB00008B/1953